FRANK LLOYD WRIGHT

A VISUAL ENCYCLOPEDIA

IAIN THOMSON

THUNDER BAY
P·R·E·S·S

This edition published in 2000 by

Thunder Bay Press

An imprint of the Advantage Publishers Group

5880 Oberlin Drive

San Diego, CA 92121-4794

www.advantagebooksonline.com

Produced by

PRC Publishing Ltd,

Kiln House, 210 New Kings Road, London SW6 4NZ

Conceived by: Suneel Jaitly

Designed by: Sunita Gahir

Edited by: Martin Howard & Simon Forty

Picture Research: Louise Daubeny

Production: Alison Comonte

Photography: Simon Clay

© 1999 PRC Publishing Ltd

ISBN 1 57145 187 0

3 4 5 00 01 02 03

Printed in Hong Kong

CONTENTS

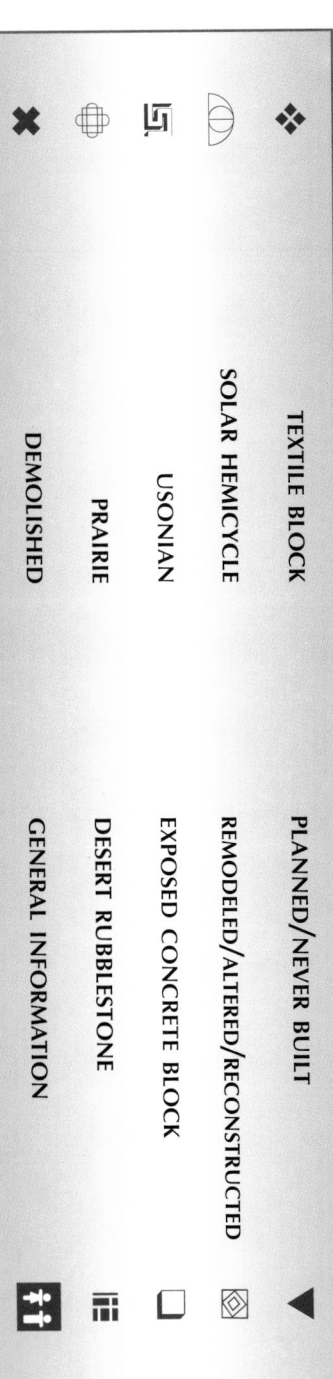

TEXTILE BLOCK

SOLAR HEMICYCLE

USONIAN

PRAIRIE

DEMOLISHED

PLANNED/NEVER BUILT

REMODELED/ALTERED/RECONSTRUCTED

EXPOSED CONCRETE BLOCK

DESERT RUBBLESTONE

GENERAL INFORMATION

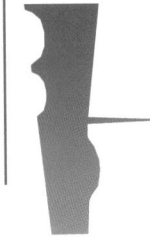

CIVIC BUILDING
FROM THE MARIN COUNTY CIVIC CENTER

COMMERCIAL BUILDING
FROM THE ANDERTON COURT SHOPS

PUBLIC BUILDING
FROM THE GUGGENHEIM MUSEUM

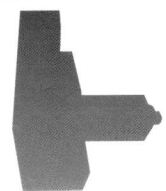

CORPORATE BUILDING
FROM THE JOHNSON WAX BUILDING

RELIGIOUS BUILDING
FROM THE FIRST CHRISTIAN CHURCH

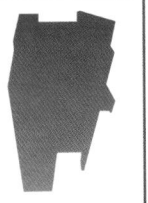

PRIVATE BUILDING
FROM THE PERRY HOUSE

KEY TO SYMBOLS

INTRODUCTION

INTRODUCTION

Frank Lloyd Wright is regarded as one of the greatest architects of the 20th century. With a life span that extended nearly 100 years, he was certainly one of the most long-lived! Over his lifetime he witnessed an age of great change as the world moved into the machine age — and a period in which a new architecture would emerge. Few architects would display a greater creativity nor contribute more to this development than Wright. His legacy to the field of architecture in general, and American architecture in particular, comes in many forms — his innovative use of materials; his rejection of rooms as defined boxes of walled-in space and his great commissions such as the Price Tower or Guggenheim Museum. Wright was one of the first American architects to provide an alternative to the ideas prevailing at the end of the 19th and the beginning of the 20th centuries — those of Art Nouveau, and styles such as Queen Anne or Tudor.

His ideas of "organic architecture," which were influenced greatly by his friend and *Lieber Meister* Louis Sullivan, evolved over his lifetime. His essay "In the Cause of Architecture" defined the following principles:

- **Simplicity** — Everything that was unnecessary, including interior walls, should be eliminated. There should be as few rooms as possible.

- **Multiple styles** — There should be less lip service paid to the styles of the times and more concern about the requirements of the individual.

Pages 8/9: The Ennis house which demonstrate how effective the textile-block technique is. Wright supervised the construction himself to ensure that the pattern of the blocks was correct. The architect used decomposed granite taken from the site of the construction to color these blocks and blend the house with its surroundings.

Above: Frank Lloyd Wright.

Right: Forest Avenue.

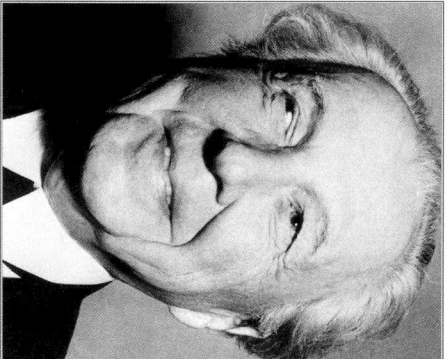

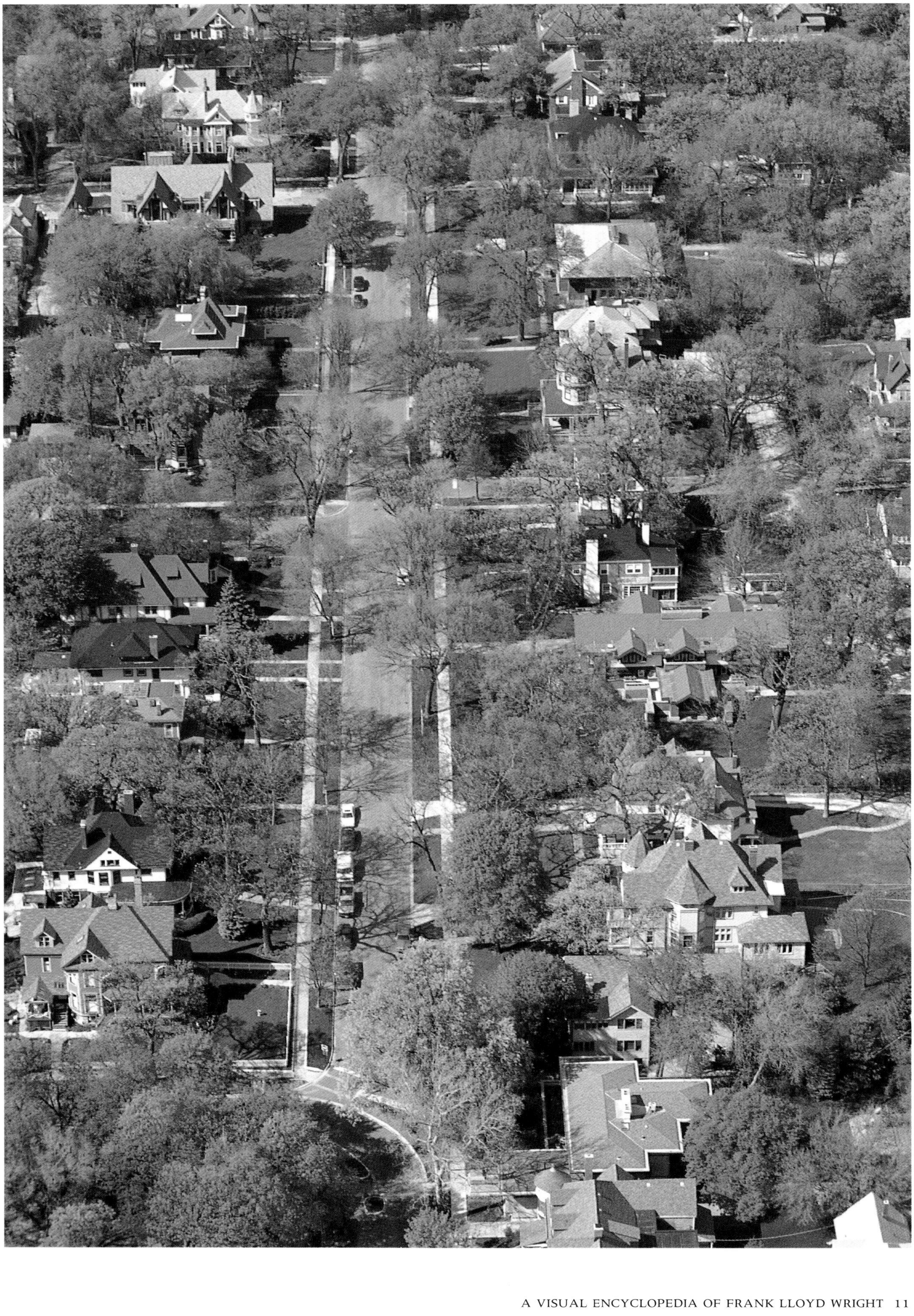

Above all, that architects should design for their clients' requirements.

- **Sympathy with the environment —** Site and architecture should be in harmony. Buildings should seem to "grow" from their environment. The colors should also be in sympathy with their surroundings. Building colors should be natural and local materials used to ensure that colors blended.

- **The "nature" of materials —** All building materials should show their natural characteristics and shouldn't be disguised. This concept carried through to the structural use of the materials so that the characteristics of load and support should be apparent through the use of the materials.

- **Buildings should bring people joy.**

These principles were similar to those of the Arts and Crafts Movement — but Wright was not as innately conservative or rooted in tradition as the members of that movement. He not only embraced new materials but used them joyfully to "break the box" and open up his buildings — steel beams allowed him to span space and create dramatic cantilevered roofs, and poured concrete, whether as used in Oak Park's Unity Temple or the textile block houses of California, enabled him to produce structures vastly different to anything that had gone before.

Organic architecture, however, meant that the architect was not only involved in the structure of the building, but the contents as well. In order to maintain consistency, Wright felt that it was quite impossible to consider the building as one thing, its furnishings another and its setting and environment still another. "The Spirit in which these buildings are conceived," he wrote "sees all of these together at work as one thing." The chairs and tables, and internal furnishings, therefore, were part of the building itself — so he would himself design furniture and fitments for many of his houses.

The Cheney house is better known for its occupants than its design. However, this house includes many interesting features including art glass in each of the 52 windows and an iron-spot Roman brick fireplace

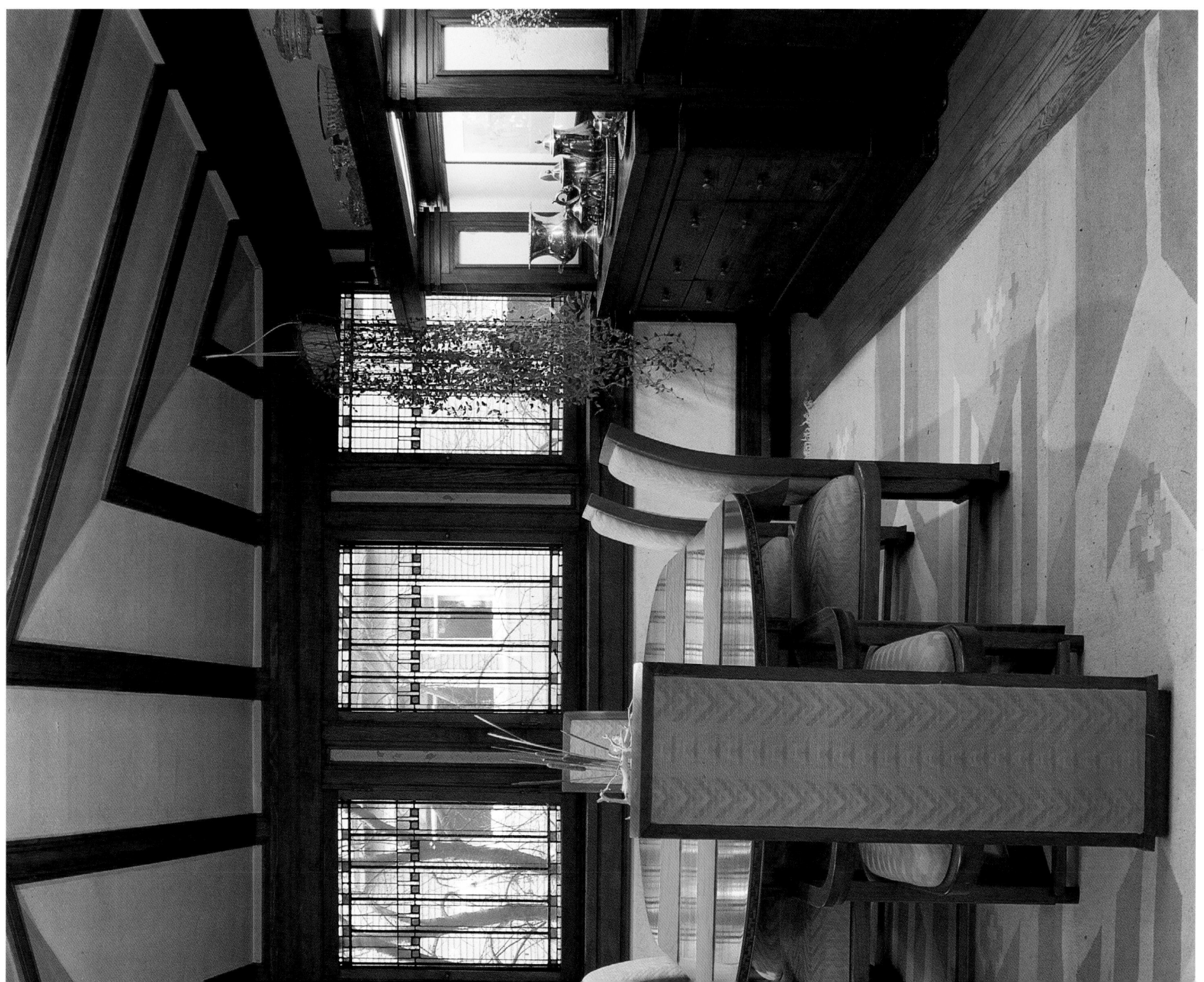

Frank Lloyd Wright's work can be divided into periods:

- **Early Period** — Derivative of the work of his contemporaries, the Queen Anne or shingle styles, for example, his early work at Adler & Sullivan was heavily influenced by Louis Sullivan. Even his freelance work, the "bootlegged houses," did not show what was to come.

- **The Prairie Period** — Beginning in 1901 and extended into the 1910s, this phase saw Wright produce a new house form which was characterized by strong horizontality and organic architectural principles — use of natural materials and harmony between the building and its site.

- **The Textile Block Period** — Having left Oak Park and his family following his involvement with Mamah Cheney, this phase saw Wright build his decorative, Mayan-inspired, cast concrete houses in California — La Miniatura, and the Ennis, Freeman, and Storer houses.

- **The Usonian period** — Identified as being dated around 1935-55, Usonian houses were lower-cost than Prairies, could be self-built by the client (Usonian "automatics") and could also be prefabricated — the Marshall Erdman buildings.

On top of these design periods, Wright also completed major public commissions throughout his career. Some are no longer extant (and Wright himself took pleasure from just how difficult they were to get rid of), such as the Larkin Building,

Midway Gardens, and Imperial Hotel, Tokyo. Others, such as the Johnson Wax company headquarters and research tower, the Guggenheim Museum in New York, the Beth Sholom Synagogue, the Florida Southern College, and the Marin County Civic Center, are testament to his ability to build both for the individual and on the grand scale.

His continued popularity is evidence of the strength of feeling for him — from the listing of his great works by the A.I.A., to the care with which his houses are restored and looked after by their inhabitants. Furthermore, designs for buildings he planned but which were not built have been completed since his death, for example the Hilary and Joe Feldman House built in 1974, and Monona Terrace in Madison, Wisconsin. But most of all, the strength of feeling for Frank Lloyd Wright is shown by the continued fascination that thousands of visitors bring to his home at Taliesin, and the sheer weight of publications about his work.

A *Visual Encyclopedia of Frank Lloyd Wright* provides a companion to the other titles on the market, providing a concise guide to his buildings, his life, and the people that populated it.

Below: The Nathan G. Moore Tudor house is an early testament to Wright's flexibility.

Right: "A home in a Prairie town" published in the *Ladies' Home Journal*.

A Home in a Prairie Town

By FRANK LLOYD WRIGHT

This is the Fifth Design in the Journal's New Series of Model Suburban Houses Which Can be Built at Moderate Cost

PERSPECTIVE OF QUADRUPLE BLOCK PLAN·

A CITY man going to the country puts too much in his house and too little in his ground. He drags after him the fifty-foot lot, soon the twenty-five-foot lot, finally the party wall; and the home-maker who fully appreciates the advantages which he came to the country to secure feels himself impelled to move on.

It seems a waste of energy to plan a house haphazard, to hit or miss an already distorted condition, so this partial solution of a city man's country home on the prairie begins at the beginning and assumes four houses to the block of four hundred feet square as the minimum of ground for the basis of his prairie community.

The block plan to the left, at the top of the page, shows an arrangement of the four houses that secures breadth and prospect to the community as a whole, and absolute privacy both as regards each to the community, and each to each of the four.

THE perspective view shows the handling of the group at the centre of the block, with its foil of simple lawn, omitting the foliage of curb parkways to better show the scheme, retaining the same house in the four locations merely to afford an idea of the unity of the various elevations. In practice the houses would differ distinctly, though based upon a similar plan.

The ground plan, which is intended to explain itself, is arranged to offer the least resistance to a simple mode of living, in keeping with a high ideal of the family life together. It is arranged, too, with a certain well-established order that enables free use without the sense of confusion felt in five out of seven houses which people really use.

The exterior recognizes the influence of the prairie, is firmly and broadly associated with the site, and makes a feature of its quiet level. The low terraces and broad eaves are designed to accentuate that quiet level and complete the h͟ ͟ious relationship. The curbs of the terraces an͟ ͟ and enclosures for extremely informal masses of ͟ ͟iage and bloom should be worked in cement with the walks and drives.

Cement on metal lath is suggested for the exterior covering throughout, because it is simple, and, as now understood, durable and cheap.

The cost of this house with interior as specified and cement construction would be seven thousand dollars:

Masonry, Cement and Plaster	$2850.00
Carpentry	3100.00
Plumbing	400.00
Painting and Glass	375.00
Heating — combination (hot water)	345.00
Total	**$6970.00**

IN A HOUSE of this character the upper reach and gallery of the central living-room is decidedly a luxury. Two bedrooms may take its place, as suggested by the second-floor plan. The gallery feature is, nevertheless, a temptation because of the happy sense of variety and depth it lends to the composition of the interior, and the sunlight it gains from above to relieve the shadow of the porch. The details are better grasped by a study of the drawings. The interior section in perspective shows the gallery as indicated by dotted lines on the floor plan of the living-room.

The second-floor plan disregards this feature and is arranged for a larger family. Where three bedrooms would suffice the gallery would be practicable, and two large and two small bedrooms with the gallery might be had by rearranging servants' rooms and baths.

The interior is plastered throughout with sand finish and trimmed all through with flat bands of Georgia pine smaller back bands following the base and casings. This Georgia pine should be selected from straight grain for stiles, rails and running members, and from figured grain for panels and wide surfaces.

All the wood should be shellacked once and waxed, and the plaster should be stained with thin, pure color in water and glue.

EDITOR'S NOTE.—As a guarantee that the plan of this house is practicable, and that the estimates for cost are conservative, the architect is ready to accept the commission of preparing the working plans and specifications for this house to cost Seven Thousand Dollars, providing that the building site selected is within reasonable distance of a base of supplies where material and labor may be had at the standard market rates.

GROUND FLOOR PLAN

CHAMBER
19'0"x15'0"

CHAMBER
20'0"x120"

HALL

HALL

HALL

BATH

CHAMBER

CHAMBER
19'0"x16'-0"

SECOND FLOOR PLAN

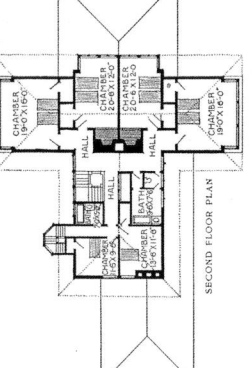

THE LIBRARY

HALL, LOOKING TOWARD ENTRANCE

LIVING-ROOM AND GALLERY

INTERIOR VIEW OF THE FIRST FLOOR OF THIS HOUSE

THE DINING-ROOM

Ablin, George, House (1958)
In this house there is a contrast between the large south-facing living room of glass and wood and the poolside main construction of salmon **exposed concrete block** — the latter perforated to provide windows.

Abraham Lincoln Center (1903)
Wright's son, **John Lloyd**, claims that the original design for this building was his father's first architectural work and should be dated 1888. Originally intended as a community center when commissioned by the Reverend Jenkin **Lloyd Jones**, it was finally built in a changed form in 1903 under the auspices of Dwight Heald **Perkins**.

Adams, Harry S., House (1913)
This is Wright's last work in **Oak Park**. It is built to a longitudinal plan which runs through the house from porte-cochère through the porch, living room, and hall to the dining room.

Adams, Jessie M., House (1900)
This house is untypical of Wright's designs with its

double-hung windows. Jessie Adams's husband William was contracter for the **Husser** and **Heller** houses.

Adams, Mary M.W., House (1905)
A plaster-surfaced, wood-framed **Prairie** style structure built near the shore of Lake Michigan.

Addams, Jane
Founder of an **Arts and Crafts** society at Hull House.

Adelman, Albert, House (1948)
Wright designed a laundry for Adelman in 1945 which was never constructed. However, this house and a house for Adelman's father in **Arizona** were built. It is an in-line I-plan dwelling, whose garage is offset to the north and accessed by a covered walkway.

Adelman, Benjamin, House (1951)
A two-story **Usonian automatic** house, the plans for which were conceived before the **Pieper House** in Paradise Valley though it was built later.

Pages 16/17, Above and Left: George Ablin house.

Right: An aeriel view of the Abraham Lincoln Center.

Below: Harry S. Adams house.

The Albert Adelman House. One of two homes built for the family, this is in Fox Point, WI.

Adler, Dankmar

Partner of the firm he formed in 1881 with Louis **Sullivan** and which Frank Lloyd Wright joined in 1887. Adler was very much the practical mind in the partnership, author of numerous articles on foundations, acoustics, and the nuts and bolts of the business.

Adler & Sullivan

The Chicago firm of architects where Frank Lloyd Wright became a designer in 1887 after leaving school. The Adler & Sullivan partnership was formed in 1881 and together they produced more than 100 buildings. **Adler** secured the clients and handled the engineering and acoustical problems, while **Sullivan** concerned himself with the architectural designs. This team of efficient visionary and engineer manager, two men with such expansive ideas, was an immediate success. One of their earliest and most distinguished joint enterprises was the ten-story Auditorium Building (1886-89) in Chicago. This famous showplace incorporated an hotel, an office building, and a theatre renowned for its superb acoustics. The Wainwright Building, also ten stories high, with a metal frame, was completed in 1891 in Saint Louis, MO. Wright left Adler & Sullivan in 1893 and, after peaking in the mid-1890s, the practice declined precipitously and ended in 1895.

Aesthetic Movement

In vogue in the post-Civil War years when Wright was growing up, this artistic movement had a major influence on him. It encouraged students to return to first principles and to understand "the organic and natural laws that created them."

Affleck, Gregor S., House (1940)

Today owned by the Lawrence Institute of Technology, who restored the house in the 1980s, the Affleck House is another example of Wright's ability to maximize the dramatic settings of his houses. One of Affleck's relatives was Wright's secretary at **Taliesin** and Affleck spent much time in his youth in **Spring Green**. It is unsurprising, therefore, that he chose Wright to build his home. The living room (the interior has been flawlessly restored) is built on piers, cantilevered over a basement and garden level, which has seats and a pool. It is open to the public for guided tours by appointment only.

Alabama

The only example of Wright's work in Alabama is the Stanley **Rosenbaum** house in Florence. It is a large **Usonian** private house built in 1939 and enlarged in 1948. The living area built-in furniture was specially designed by Wright and made from cypress wood.

Alabyan, Karo

A Soviet architect whom Wright met when he visited Russia.

Allen, Senator Henry J.

An influential friend of Wright, editor of the *Wichita Beacon* and the former governor of Kansas; he helped secure Olgivanna **Wright**'s safe refuge in the United States.

Allen, Henry J., House (1916)

This is Wright's only private house in **Kansas** — but is a superb example of his work. Built for presidential hopeful Henry Allen, governor of Kansas 1919-23, the exterior appearance of a brick **Prairie House** hides the enclosed garden, terrace, pool, and summer house. Bequeathed by the second owner to Wichita State University in the 1980s, it was subsequently sold to the Allen-Lambe House Association. It is now open to the public and guided tours are available by appointment.

Alpaugh, Amy, Studio (1947)

A single-story house with views over Lake Michigan, it is built, primarily, of brick, oak, and ash. Its most obvious asset is the southwest-facing studio/living room. The house has seen alterations — the porch has been enclosed to form an extra room, there is now a playroom where Amy Alpaugh used to keep goats, and the greenhouse has become a bedroom.

Alsop, Carroll, House (designed 1948; built 1951)

An L-plan single-story house with an angled main bedroom. Built of brick and cypress with a red shingled roof.

Amberg, J. H., House (1909)

This house's attribution has been questioned. It seems likely that Wright did the preliminary work before going to Europe in 1910, leaving the design and construction to be finished by **Van Holst** and Marion **Mahoney**.

American Institute of Architects (A.I.A.)

The A.I.A. designated 17 Wright buildings as examples of his contribution to American culture, although in his lifetime he steadfastly refused to join — he referred to it as the "Arbitrary Institute of Appearances." He maintained that the organization was founded to protect the members of the profession rather than to uphold the quality of architecture. On March 17, 1949, he was awarded the Gold Medal of the A.I.A. and on accepting the award said: "Honors have reached me from almost every great nation in the world. Honor has, however, been a long time coming from home. But here it is at last.

Above and Below: Wright's stylish interior for the Allen house in Kansas. This refined residence is almost square; the design effectively blocks outside noise from traffic and creates an environment of quiet serenity.

Left: The Stanley Rosenbaum house, the only example of Wright's work in Alabama.

Handsomely, indeed. Yes . . . I am extremely grateful."

The 17 buildings are: **Barnsdall Hollyhock House, Beth Sholom Synagogue, Guggenheim Museum, Hanna House, Johnson Administration Building, Johnson Research Tower, Kaufmann House, Morris Gift Shop, Price Company Tower, Robie House, Taliesin, Taliesin West, Unitarian Church, Unity Church, Willits House, Winslow House** and **Wright Home and Studio.**

Angster, Herbert, House (1911; since demolished)
Hidden in dense woodland in ideal natural fashion, this was a plaster-surfaced, wood-trimmed **Prairie House.**

Anderton Court Shops (1952)

Built on four levels in a desirable Beverly Hills location, the levels are accessed by an upward winding ramp. The key visual element is the striking mast around which the ramp is built. The building is still open to the public.

These photographs are of the Anderton Court Shops in fashionable Beverly Hills. The ramp is built to a diamond-shaped parallelogram pattern around the central mast.

Annunciation Greek Orthodox Church (1956)

The main level plan forms a Greek cross. The structure and roof form of this church is a concrete shell originally surfaced with blue ceramic mosaic tiles, although these were later replaced by synthetic plastic resin. The truss is held by four concrete piers at the ends of the inward curving walls of the Greek cross. The church may be visited and guided tours are available by appointment.

Anthony, Howard E., House (1949)
With views over the St. Joseph River, this single-story stone building is trimmed with cypress and has a roof of cedar shingles.

Ardmore, Pennsylvania
(see **Suntop Homes**)

Armstrong, Andrew F. H., House (1939)
Cleverly fitted to the contours of the site, this house has been restored following some years of neglect. Additions, including a garage, were made by John H. **Howe**.

Arnold, E. Clarke, House (1954)
This house was originally built to a plan of two wings set

Above, Right, and Below: Three stunning views of the Annunciation Greek Orthodox Church. This beautiful building combines form, structure, function, and symbolism to invest the church with an inherently religious and serene character.

Pages 28/29: Another aerial view of the same building a masterpiece of form and design.

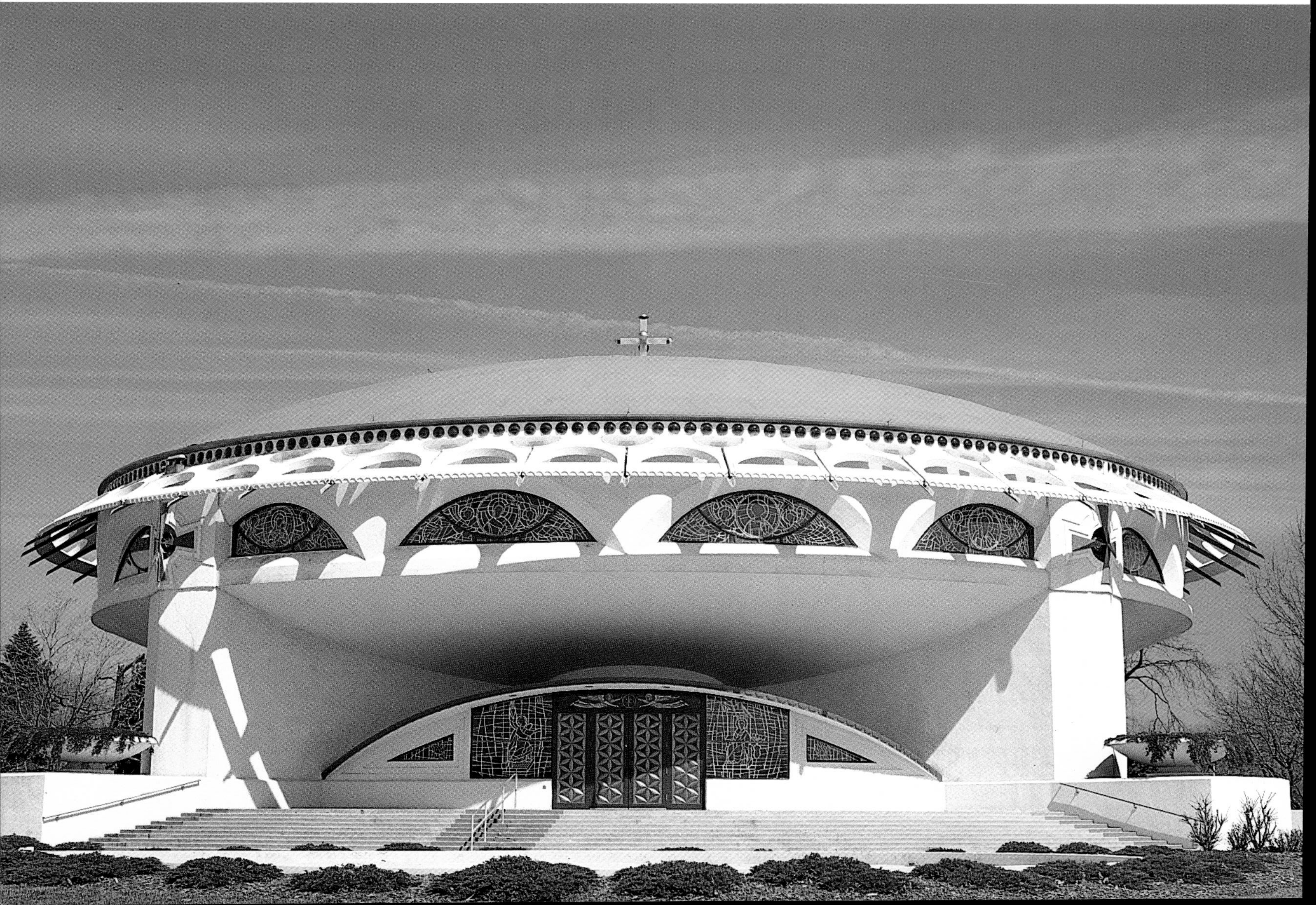

at a 120-degree angle on a diamond module and constructed from stone. The 1959 addition is by John H. **Howe**, of **Taliesin Associated Architects**, who converted the plan to a Y.

Arizona

There were 12 examples of Wright's work in Arizona, built between 1927 and 1973, but one has now been demolished. Arizona is home to **Taliesin West**, Wright's winter establishment: he died there in 1959. Taliesin West in **Scottsdale** offered a new challenge in building materials. The architect conceived the **desert rubblestone** wall to produce a more colorful and natural effect than pure concrete. Taliesin West houses the **Taliesin Fellowship** for much of the year. The state also has the first constructed example of an **Usonian automatic** house. Arthur **Pieper**, a Taliesin West student, built it himself, making his own blocks. This do-it-yourself approach is the essence of automatic construction.

A selection of views of Taliesin West, Wright's winter home and the establishment which still houses the Taliesin Fellowship (**left**). Wright's philosophy of taking inspiration from nature finds a perfect expression in this building.

Often associated with the **Arts and Crafts Movement** (the British know it as stained glass), Wright made extensive use of art glass in his buildings.

Arts and Crafts Movement

Evolving in Britain in the 1880s as a reaction against a century of mass production, the Arts and Crafts Movement tried to revive the concept of medieval guilds and hand-crafted objects of lasting beauty and utility. This credo greatly interested the young Frank Lloyd Wright and he set himself the daunting task of reflecting truth, beauty, and moral feeling in his own work.

Ashbee, C. R.

A British architect, who founded the Guild of Handicrafts (which had distinct similarities to Wright's later **Taliesin Fellowship**), Ashbee was a gifted designer and a devoted follower of William **Morris**. Ashbee's tireless willingness to travel and lecture made him a natural leader of the **Arts and Crafts Movement** when Morris died in 1896. Ashbee met Wright in the same year, while making his first trip to the United States. He was one of the first European enthusiasts for Wright's work.

Auldbrass Plantation (1938)

This includes the C. Leigh **Stevens** house, a brick and cypress construction linked to the other buildings in the complex by esplanades. Restoration of the main house and one of the cottages has been completed with many of the attributes not finished in the original construction corrected from Wright's plans.

Austin,

Gabrielle and Charlcey, House (1951). Built into a hillside, this single-story house used **desert rubblestone** and, internally, quantities of cypress. A wooden terrace was added in the 1980s off the south-facing dining area.

Auvergne Press

Two clients of Wright, Chauncey **Williams** and William **Winslow**, joined forces in 1895 to found this small publishing firm. Winslow was an amateur and, presumably, chief financial backer while Williams was a publisher by profession. Wright joined the firm as chief designer.

Right: The motifs in the magnificent art-glass windows of the Dana-Thomas house are based on butterflies and the sumac, a native tree of North America.

Inset: One of more than 200 lighting fixtures designed by Wright for the Dana-Thomas house.

B

Bach, Emil, House (1915)
A cantilever design is employed here to enable the second story to overhang the first. Apart from the fact that the wood and plaster has been painted, the house is unaltered and retains its original brickwork.

Bagley, Joseph J., Summer House (1916)
This two-story summer house overlooks Lake Michigan and spreads into single-story wings. It has been much altered from the original Wright design.

Bagley, Frederick, House (1894)
This house, like many of Wright's early works, records the tastes of the client rather than Wright. It is built with stained wood shingles (now painted) and a stone veranda. The library is built to an octagonal plan.

Baird, Theodore, House (1940)
A typical **Usonian** brick house with horizontal cypress board and sunk batten, it has an back-to-back double fire arrangement in the living room and a specially built indentation in the living room wall to fit an upright piano.

Baker, Frank J., House (1909)
The plan for the ground floor of this house is cruciform with a second-story L-plan. The building is a **Prairie** style wooden house with plaster surfaces, and features the characteristic two-story high living room. As with many of Wright's houses, the once open porches are now enclosed.

Balch, Oscar B., House (1911)
A plaster-surfaced, wood-trimmed **Prairie House**. The original dark brown wood trim on white plaster (Wright's preferred color scheme) has been modified to an orange-tinted wood trim on gray plaster.

Baldwin, Hiram, House (1905)
This **Prairie** style house has had extensive interior remodeling.

Bancroft, Levi H.
Wright's attorney when an acrimonious hearing took place in February, 1926, to discuss the impending divorce of Frank and his then wife — Miriam Noel **Wright**. It

Above: Oscar B. Balch house.

Left: Emil Bach house.

Below, Right, and Pages 38/39: Baldwin house.

Pages 34/35: The Beth Sholom Synagogue.

Baxter, Catherine Wright

The eldest daughter of Frank and his first wife, Catherine, born in 1894, was headstrong like her father. She was the mother of Anne Baxter, the late film star and actress.

Bazett, Sidney, House (1938-40)

Wright's second house in San Francisco is of brick and redwood batten, designed in hexagons, with a **Usonian** workspace.

Left and Below: Interior of the Bazett house. A playroom was added by Wright to the original house to provide more room in this compact home.

Beachy, Peter A., House (1906)
This **Prairie House** incorporates an earlier Gothic style cottage into its structure.

Berger, Robert, House (1950)
A **Usonian** house of one story, constructed from rubblestone and wood. Set into the steep slopes of the hillside, it was built by Berger himself.

Berlage, Dr. Hendrick P.
He was the most important pioneer of modern architecture in the Netherlands and was instrumental in introducing Wright's work into that country.

Besinger, Curtis
A **Taliesin Fellowship** member, later professor of architecture at the University of **Kansas**. In 1941 he was sent to a camp for conscientious objectors for following the pacifist beliefs of his mentor Frank Lloyd Wright.

Above and Below: Aerial views of the Beachy house in Oak Park. Constructed of brick and plaster with a wood trim, an earlier house constitutes part of the structure.

Right, above and below: Interior and exterior of the Berger house, so well set into the slope that it is difficult to spot from the road.

Beth Sholom Synagogue (1954)

One of Wright's most original buildings, the synagogue in Elkins Park PA was dedicated in September 1959 and is one of 17 of his buildings protected by the A.I.A. The main feature — the roof space — is produced by suspending the main sanctuary from a tripod frame so that a full upper floor, directly above the chapel, is completely free of any internal supports. The synagogue is constructed from concrete, steel, aluminum, glass, fiberglass, and oiled walnut. Guided tours are available by appointment only. There is a booklet explaining the symbolism of the architecture, of which there is much.

The inspired Beth Sholom Synangogue. The 1,030-seat great hall of the synagogue is completely free of internal support. To achieve this the sanctuary is suspended from a steel tripod which weighs 160 tons. Incredible lighting effects are provided by the double layer of translucent panels which filter soft daylight into the hall during the day and make the building glow with artificial light at night.

Biltmore Hotel, Arizona (1927)

The hotel was probably the largest of Wright's **textile block** designs, although there is some debate about how much of the design was his. He was called in during the work to act as a consultant by the job architect, Albert **McArthur**. However, much of the detail work bears his hallmarks, particularly the patterned **exposed concrete blocks**, the lobby (which is reminiscent of the **Imperial Hotel**, Wright's demolished Japanese venture), the adjoining single and two-story cottages, and the fabulous multi-colored glass mural adapted from a design in *Liberty* magazine. Guided tours by appointment.

Bitter Root Inn (designed 1908; demolished by fire 1924)

The inn was originally intended to be part of the Bitter Root Irrigation District. Houses in the area show **Prairie school** influences, although none of them have been specifically attributed to any of the major Chicago architects of the time.

Blair, Quintin, House (1952)

A stone and wood house with an upward tilting living room ceiling, built on the Wyoming plains east of the Yellowstone National Park. As with many of Wright's houses, the porch has now been enclosed. This is the only example of his work in **Wyoming**.

Left, Below left, Far left, and Pages 50/51: Views of the Biltmore Hotel. Wright labored for five months in the desert heat to produce the drawings which lend the building his characteristic flavor.

Below: The Blair house. Panoramic views of the eastern horizon can be seen from the living room which features a rising ceiling.

Blossom, George, House (1892)
This house — one of Wright's **"bootleg"** designs — with its clapboard siding, is a classic example of Colonial Revival architecture. It is built on a symmetrical plan and contrasts sharply with the **Prairie** style garage built at a later date on the back.

Blossom, George, Garage (1907)
This **Prairie** style building of Roman brick with wood trim is built on the back of the **Blossom** house.

Blum, Jerome
The painter Jerome Blum was Wright's friend and confidante who introduced him to Olgivanna Lazovich.

Exterior and interior of the Blossom house. This house demonstrates that Wright was a master of different styles and is a fine example of academic Colonial Revival. Another of the "bootlegged" houses, Wright designed it while working for Adler & Sullivan.

Bock, Richard

A sculptor with whom Wright worked on several of his commissions. For John D. **Larkin** they developed the motif of a globe of the world (held up by angelic figures), on which the name LARKIN was superimposed, to act as the chief ornament for the building's exterior. Bock was also responsible for the work *Flower in the Crannied Wall*, a sculpted nude named for the famous poem by Alfred, Lord Tennyson, which took pride of place at **Taliesin.** The sculpture had originally been designed for the house Wright built for Susan L. **Dana** in Springfield, IL, some years before.

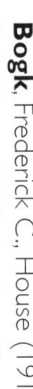

Bogk, Frederick C., House (1916)

Based on a 1907 plan from the *Ladies' Home Journal* this four-square house has a terracotta frieze under the eaves.

Boomer, Jorgine, (1953)

This is a two-story mountain cottage constructed from **desert rubblestone.**

Above and Below: The square plan Bogk residence with its highly ornamental facade of Roman brick.

Right: Richard Bock sculpture from the Dana-Thomas house.

Booth, Sherman M.

Wright's lawyer, who commissioned the **Ravine Bluffs Development.**

Booth, Sherman M., House (1915)

Located in the **Ravine Bluffs Development.** The landscaping was by Jens Jensen. Wright extensively remodeled an earlier structure.

"bootlegged" houses

Term given to the houses Wright designed for private customers while still in **Adler & Sullivan's** employ. They include the **Blossom** and **Emmond** houses.

Boswell, William P., House (1957)

A single-story L-plan brick structure, whose wings (west — bedrooms; north — services and playroom) join into the substantial living room.

Bott, Frank, House (1956)

Built from **desert rubblestone** and trimmed with mahogany, the house is seen at its best from the ravine at the south. From here the jutting terrace, a cantilevered living room, and balcony can be seen to good effect. Construction finished in 1962, under supervision from the **Taliesin Associated Architects.**

Boulter, Cedric G., House (1954)

Built of **exposed concrete block** and **Taliesin** red-stained wood, this two-story house had the 1958 addition of a guest room. The second-story bedrooms jut both inwards — forming a gallery over the living room — and outwards, making an exterior balcony to the northwest.

Boynton, E. E., House (1908)

An elongated T-plan **Prairie House,** the building is surfaced with plaster with a wood trim. Porches at the top of the T emphasize the elongation of the plan.

Bradley, B. Harley, House (1900)

This house, built to a cruciform plan, is of plaster with wood trim and has leaded-glass windows. Wright also designed a stable. At one time converted into a restaurant, it was renovated for use as offices in 1990.

Left: Three aerial views of the Ravine Bluffs Development, commissioned by Sherman Booth. In addition to the houses there are poured concrete sculptures and a bridge which marks the northeastern entrance to the development.

Right: The Boulter residence. The striking Taliesin red conforms with the house's woodland surroundings to create a building which, in true Wright fashion, is an extension of its environment.

Brandes, Ray, House (1952)
A single-story house with a central living space. Its retaining wall is not by Wright.

Brauner, Erling P., House (1948)
Close to the Edwards House is this single-story adaptation of the **Usonian** concept with **textile blocks** replacing brick.

"break the box"

Wright was concerned to "break the box" of the conventional room plan and achieve spatial continuity. He did this by treating wall surfaces simply and in as unbroken a manner as was feasible. Doors and other openings were conceived as part of the integral structure.

Breen, Nellie
The housekeeper Wright unwisely put in charge of **Taliesin** in 1915. Miriam Noel's arrival at Taliesin offended her highly developed sense of propriety and she protested because Wright's children were also in the house. After being dismissed by Wright, Nellie Breen accused him of violating the **Mann Act** and demanded that Miriam Noel be deported as she was not an American citizen. Wright's lawyer brought counter

Above, Below, and Right: The Brauner house, an adaptation of the Usonian concept.

charges that Miriam had been threatened with bodily harm, the deportation orders were dropped and no formal charges were brought against Wright under the Mann Act.

Brickbuilder, The, Magazine

Wright published his design for a monolithic bank building in concrete in this magazine in 1901. In his vision of the bank, Wright let the cast concrete become the aesthetic of the building much as he would do, more eloquently, in the **Unity Temple** three years later.

Brigham, E. D., House (1915)

The only house in Glencoe that Wright designed in 1915 independent of **Booth**'s development, the Brigham house design dates back to 1908. The house was restored in the 1980s although the garage, built at the same time, was demolished in 1968.

Broadacre City

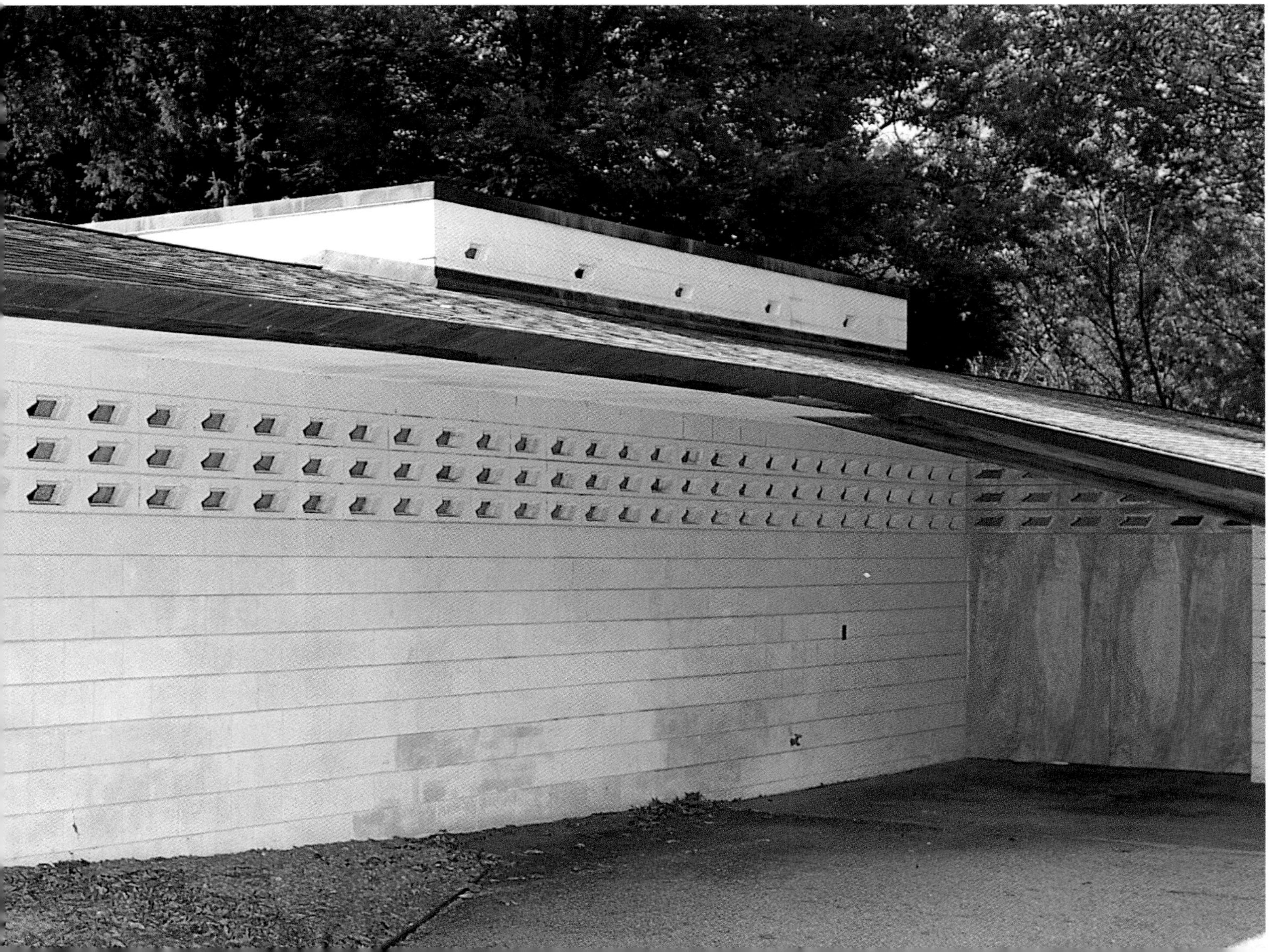

The dream project of an utopian development that Wright worked on for the latter part of his life. He envisioned whole communities where each family would live on an acre of land, hence the name; it was to be a development that considered social needs as well as personal ones. Broadacre City was not a model of buildings but rather a scheme for buildings, themselves represented by blocks, set into the countryside. The model, after initially being exhibited at the Rockefeller Center, traveled to Pittsburgh, PA, **Washington, D.C., Madison** and Iowa County, WI, and Marquette, MI, before returning to **Taliesin**. The theme of his utopian city would return throughout Wright's life from the time the model was first built in 1934 to his death in 1959.

Brodelle, Emil
Architectural draftsman who was at **Taliesin** when the murders happened. An earlier dispute between Brodelle and Julian **Carlton** might have been partly to blame for Carlton going berserk. Brodelle was one of Carlton's victims, killed in the ensuing massacre.

Brown, Charles E., House (1905)
With a rectangular plan and an open front porch, this house is built with horizontal board and batten, and plaster under the eaves and between the top-story windows. The double-hung windows are a rarity in Wright designs.

Brown, Eric V., House (1949)
One of four houses built at **Parkwyn Village**, although several more were designed in the original master plan. A single-story house overlooking Lorenz Lake, it was built with **textile blocks** and mahogany. The living room has a terrace attached.

Browne's Bookstore (1908; since demolished)
This was the first of three units Wright designed in the Chicago Fine Arts Building.

Brunker, Thomas
Foreman of the work crew at **Taliesin** when the murders occurred. Brunker was killed by **Carlton**.

Buckingham, Clarence
An avid and established collector of Japanese prints. He lived in Chicago and it is likely, through connections with the Art Institute, that Wright was known to him.

Buehler, Maynard P., House (1948)
An L-plan **exposed concrete block** and wood house. The sleeping quarters are in the long leg of the L with the work space in the short leg.

Buffalo Exposition Pavilion (designed 1901, since demolished)
This was a pavilion designed for the Universal Portland

Cement Company's exhibit at the Pan-American Exposition held in Buffalo. Wright designed another in 1910 for the New York City Exhibition held in Madison Square Garden.

Bulbulian, A. H., House (1947)
A one-story house built on the brow of a hill and constructed from cement, brick, and cypress.

Burnham, Daniel H.
Partner in the firm of **Burnham & Root**, a rival architectural firm to **Adler & Sullivan** in Chicago. He was the chief organizer of the great Chicago World's Fair of 1893 and new president of the **A.I.A.** when Wright met him in the spring of that year. Frank courageously turned down a very generous offer made to him by Burnham which his instincts correctly told him would lead him in the wrong direction to a possible dead end.

Burnham & Root
The Chicago firm of architects which was given the honor of co-ordinating the plans for the great Chicago World's Fair.

Byrne, Barry
A young novice who quickly gained expertise in Wright's employ during the architect's first year of independence. Byrne went on to become one of the number of architects, part of the **New School of the Midwest**, who Wright believed were "throwing up sordid little imitations of his work all over the Midwest."

Above right and Pages 62/63: Charles E. Brown house. This house has many interesting features, including the cantilever over the veranda which extends over nine feet, and the beautiful Roman brick fireplace in the living room (see page 62). Inside, an early example of mechanical air conditioning has been fitted.

Below and Right: Eric V. Brown house. So eager were the Browns to begin building their home, that they arrived at Taliesin West with their children and announced that they would wait for the drawings. They stayed for five days.

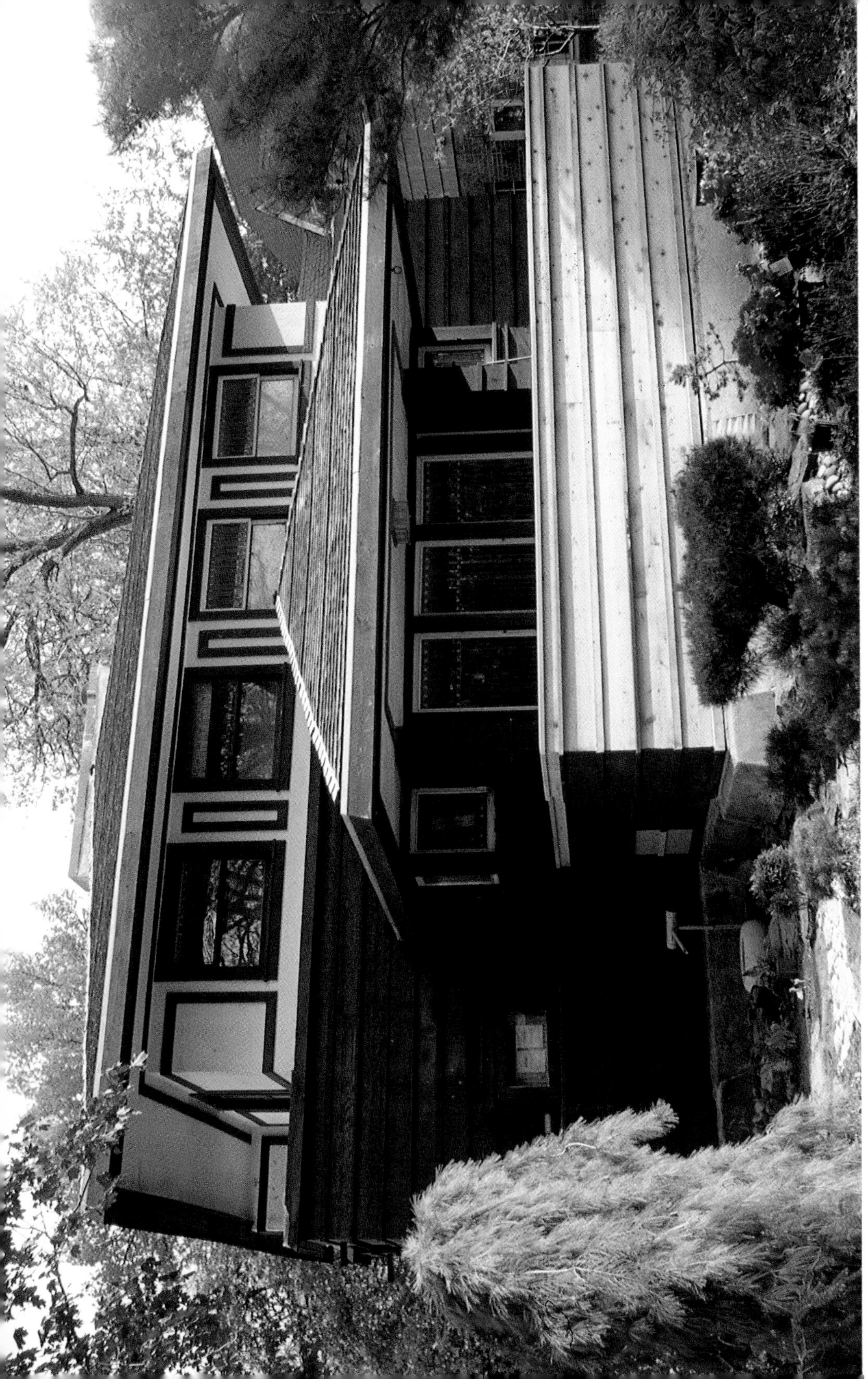

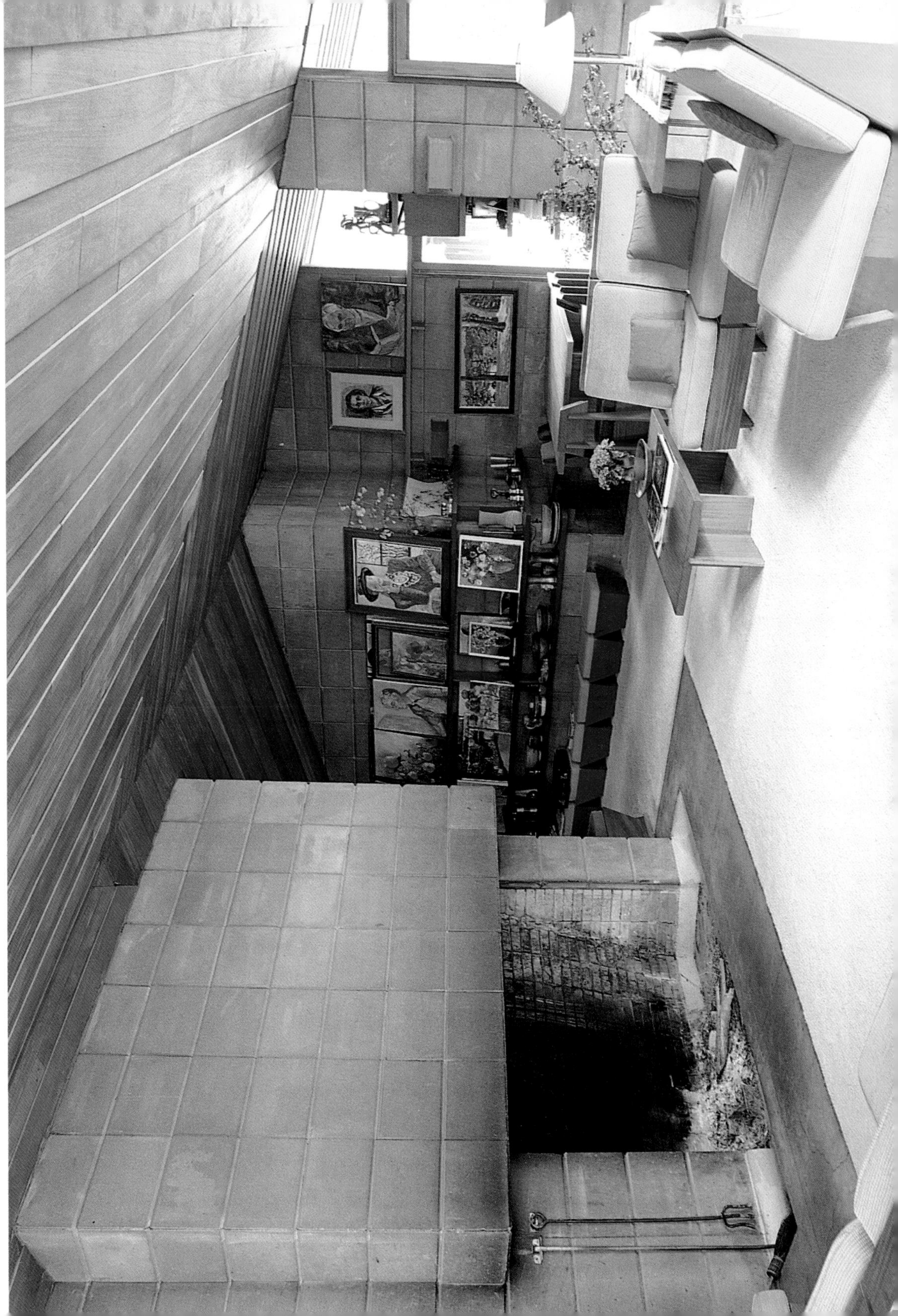

California

Buildings from Wright's designs in California span almost 90 years from the first in Montecito, the **Stewart House** of 1909, to **Eaglefeather** in Malibu, set high in the Santa Monica Mountains. Aline **Barnsdall's Hollyhock House** in **Los Angeles** is undoubtedly one of his great masterpieces, intended to be part of a larger complex of buildings only two of which were subsequently built. It has been a public park since 1927 when Aline Barnsdall gave it to the City of **Los Angeles.** Wright maintained an office in Los Angeles and it is therefore not surprising that, apart from the states on the shores of the Great Lakes, there are more examples of Wright's works in California than anywhere else in the country.

California Deco style

Wright's early work had the refined geometrical formalism found in much later Art Deco. The **Hollyhock House,** in particular, was almost the prototype for the Californian Deco style — more than a decade before the East Coast discovered the style.

cantilevered roofs

A feature of many of Wright's designs, his roofs became ever longer and wider until, in the **Robie** House of 1906, he built a cantilevered roof that extended 20 feet beyond the last masonry support.

Carlson, Raymond, House (1950)
This is a three-story building built of wood and cement for the editor of *Arizona Highway* magazine. It had additions in the 1970s and was restored in the 1980s.

Carlton, Julian
Julian Carlton and his wife Gertrude, originally from Barbados, were recommended to Wright by a Chicago restaurateur. Julian unaccountably went berserk, setting fire to **Taliesin** and slaughtering Mamah **Cheney,** her children, and four others on Saturday, August 15, 1914.

Carr, John O., House (1950)
This salmon-colored **exposed concrete block** house is built to a T-plan. The living room has a patterned concrete block divider from the kitchen.

Pages 64/65: Corbin Educational Center at the Wichita State University.

Above and Right: The Sturges house is in Brentwood Heights, CA, a state rich in examples of Wright's work over nine decades.

Left: The Marin County Civic Center, San Rafael, California. See also page 220

Carr, W. S., Summer House (1916)
Four-bedroom vacation house on Lake Michigan.

Cass, William, House (1956)
The first of two prefabricated house designs by Wright to be constructed for the Marshall Erdman Company. This is a Marshall Erdman Company Prefab No. I, an L-plan brick building with a masonry core and painted horizontal board and batten siding on the bedroom wing. The living room is below the entrance at the intersection of the L, and the kitchen and dining facilities, with attached carport, are in the short leg.

Chahroudi, A. K., House (1951)
Triangular modules are used in this single-story building. Its walls are of **desert rubblestone** with horizontal wood sheathing.

Chandler, Dr. Alexander
The owner of a large hotel, Wright met him while staying in **Arizona** in 1928. Chandler was the founder and owner of much of the town of Chandler and he wanted to build a large, elegant, hotel-cum-resort in the desert outside the town where the rich could escape the rigors of winter. The project was called **San Marcos-in-the-Desert**.

Charnley, James, House (1891)
The style of this house was ahead of its time. It was originally built symmetrically about an east-west axis. Later additions squared off the dining room bay window. Tours are available on Tuesdays and Thursdays.

Charnley, James, Summer House and Guest house (1890)
The main residence is built to a T-plan, featuring bay windows of octagonal geometry. The house was restored in the 1930s and alterations included replacing the front wooden steps with brick. As with a lot of Wright's work, the porches have been enclosed. The guest house was built to a large octagonal plan and was divided by a single wall into two rooms.

The Charnley house, Chicago. As Sullivan became more involved with larger, commercial buildings, Wright was given the opportunity to work on the domestic side of the business. This residence clearly shows Wright's early promise and is an elegantly structured and confident work.

Cheney, Edwin H.

Mamah **Cheney**'s husband and a client of Wright's, Cheney was an electrical engineer who shared the architect's enthusiasm for those new mechanical marvels, automobiles.

Cheney, Edwin H., House (1903)

A single-story brick and wood-trim house with a terrace enclosed by a brick wall. Here Wright met Mamah **Cheney**, a meeting that would change his life and career. The Cheney house has over 50 examples of **art-glass**. In 1997 it was being used as a bed and breakfast establishment.

Cheney, Mamah Borthwick

The wife of Edwin H. **Cheney**, one of Wright's neighborhood clients in **Oak Park**, she left her husband and two children to join Wright in Europe. The break-up of Wright's marriage and his association with Mrs. Cheney became a public scandal which seriously inhibited the architect's career. Mrs. Cheney and her two children were subsequently murdered on August 15, 1914, by house servant Julian **Carlton**, who also deliberately set

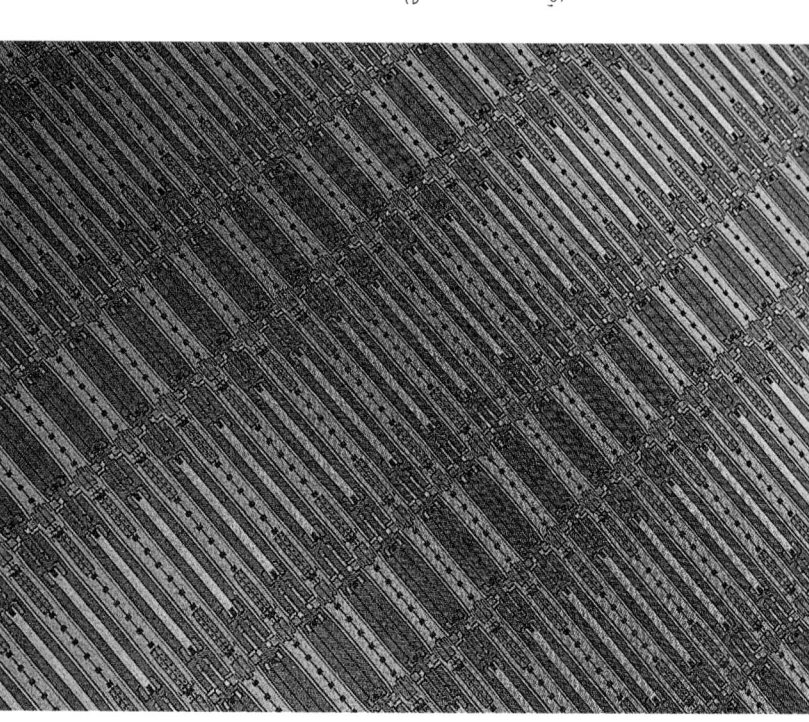

The Cheney house is better known for its occupants than its design. However, this house includes many interesting features including beautiful art glass and an iron-spot Roman brick fireplace (**above right**). The detail (**above**) is of a patterned sofa.

fire to Wright's house, **Taliesin**, in **Wisconsin**. As well as Mamah and her children, three apprentices, and a workman were slain by the axe-wielding Carlton.

Christian, John E., House (1954)
A four-foot-square module structure. This single-story house with a clerestory is built from brick and wood. The clerestory has a copper fascia.

Christie, James B., House (1940)
A single-story house built to an L-plan. The living space occupies the end of one of the legs.

City National Bank and Hotel (1909)
Designed by Wright for J. E. E. Markley, whom he had met at his aunt's **Hillside Home School**, construction was finished under the guidance of William **Drummond** while Wright was in Europe. Both the bank and the Park Inn Hotel behind it have been substantially altered over the years — particularly by the insertion of shop windows in the bank's side. It is open to the public during normal working hours.

Clark, W. Irving, House (1893)
For many years attributed to E. Hill Turnock — even, surprisingly, by Wright himself — plans found at Taliesin in the 1960s show it to have been designed by Wright around the same time as his "bootlegged" houses for George **Blossom** and Robert **Emmond**.

Below and Right: The Clark house, LaGrange, IL.

Above: City National Bank and Hotel (see page 72). Sadly, much alteration has done little for the elegance of the building.

Codman, Henry Sargent
The famous landscape architect who, along with Frederick Law **Olmsted**, drafted the preliminary plan for the 1893 Chicago World's Fair.

Como Orchard Summer Colony (designed 1908; since demolished)
Today mostly demolished, the Como Orchard Summer Colony at one time had 14 buildings from Wright's designs including clubhouse, manager's office, and various cottages. A small land office and one altered cottage are all that remain from this project.

Connecticut
There are only two examples of Wright's work in Connecticut, both private residences built in the 1950s. The **Rayward** House in New Canaan is the more interesting of the two (the other being the **Sander** House in Stamford). The **Rayward** House is called "Tirranna," an Australian aboriginal word for "running water"; it is built in the hills beside a pond of the Noroton River. The pond has been dammed to create a waterfall and a series of fish-steps was built to facilitate the passage of fish through the grounds, which contain an extraordinary variety of flora and also a tree house designed by William Wesley **Peters, Taliesin Architects'** chief architect. The house is a delight with a solar hemicycle for the living area, a swimming pool off the terrace, and an observatory above. The free-standing furniture in the house is of Wright's original design.

Conover, Allan D.
Wright failed to graduate high school and in 1885 became apprenticed to the only builder in **Madison,** Allan D. Conover. As luck would have it, Conover was also dean of engineering at the **University of Wisconsin** and he allowed his young apprentice to attend classes in the department of engineering where Wright displayed his adroitness as a draftsman.

conscientious objectors
Wright adopted an anti-war stance to the Second World War and was personally affected by the drafting of some of his **Taliesin** apprentices. Instinctively hating conscription, Wright also showed solidarity with those who refused it and were imprisoned.

"As for conscription, I think it has deprived every young man in America of the honor and privilege of dedicating himself as a free man to the service of his country … Were I born 40 years later than 1869, I too should be a conscientious objector."

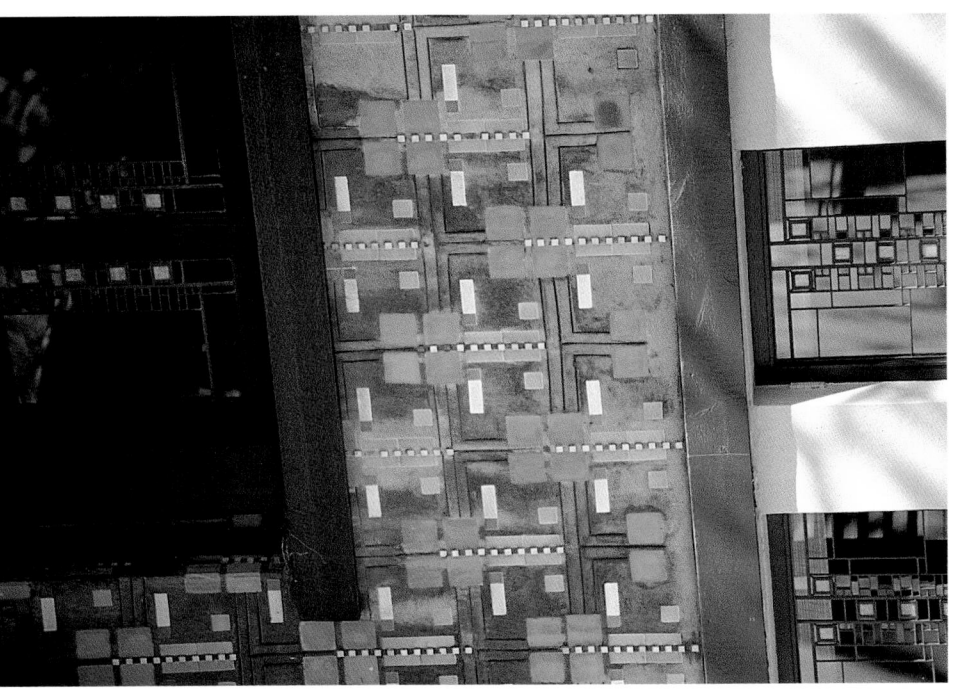

Cooke, Andrew B., House (1953)

A substantial hemicycle contains the living rooms and master bedroom. The main building materials are baked brick, made from imported clay from West Virginia, to blend in with the Crystal Lake environment. It is topped with a cantilevered copper roof.

Coonley, Mrs. Avery

One of the seven of Wright's friends and clients who contributed, between them, some $57,000 to defend him and get him back to work at **Taliesin** in the 1920s.

Coonley, Avery, House (1907)

The house is Wright's first work using the zoned plan. Inlaid tiles are used to form a geometrical pattern on the plaster-surfaced, wood-trimmed house. It has raised living quarters in the **Prairie** style with a pavilion linking the various spaces. The gardener's cottage was built in 1911, and the coach house, originally a stable, the same year. Both of these buildings were featured in the original published plans but were constructed later. The residence has now been converted into three separate apartments.

Right and Below: The Avery Coonley house. Coonley was a wealthy Chicago industrialist and the estate was an opulent home for himself and his wife, Queene Ferry. Their move to Illinois was due to their commitment to the Christian Science religion.

Above, Below, and Left: Views of the Avery Coonley house.

Coonley, Avery, Private Playhouse (1912)
Built to a symmetrical plan, this post-**Prairie** design is now significantly altered from the original. The clerestory windows, designed by Wright in multi-colored geometrical designs, are no longer fully intact.

Copeland, Dr. William H., House (1909)
Wright extensively altered an existing residence, inside and outside, and built a garage in the **Prairie** style.

Corbin Educational Center (1957)
Harry Corbin, president of the University of Wichita, pushed Wright's credentials to build the **Juvenile Cultural Study Center** and a laboratory. In the end, only the former was constructed.

Corbusier, Le
The great French architect Charles-Edouard Jeanneret, better known as Le Corbusier, was an exponent of the **International Style**.

Corwin, Cecil
A draftsman at the office of Joseph L. **Silsbee**, Wright became good friends with Corwin. In 1893, to protect himself while "bootlegging" on six houses when he was still working for **Adler & Sullivan**, Wright took the precaution of persuading Corwin to admit publicly that he was their architect. The ruse was discovered, and Wright and Corwin set up an office together.

Cram, Ralph Adams
A prolific architect and writer, and the most prominent of the Gothic Revival architects in the United States — as such he often came into conflict with Wright.

Cranbrook Academy
The academy, founded by the millionaire publisher George **Booth** in the 1920s, was conceived as a school, atelier, and art colony with the **Arts and Crafts** goal of producing tasteful designs to replace the shoddy commodities in American homes. It became famous in the 1950s for elegant, mass-produced objectsbased upon its original designs. Wright certainly knew of Cranbrook when he was planning his **Fellowship** at **Taliesin**.

Crista, Heloise
The sculptress of a bust of Wright which he much admired and is now on exhibit at **Taliesin**. The architect admired the sculpture because it depicted him "at the moment of inspiration" — Crista's piece shows her subject with his eyes raised, his habitually raised eyebrow having the effect of widening his eyes even further.

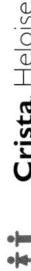

The Coonley house. This is perhaps the most lavish example of Wright's Prairie architecture. For many years it was divided up between five owners.

Cummings, E.W. Office (designed 1905; since demolished)

This real estate office was a **Prairie** structure of wood and plaster with broad overhanging eaves, partially hidden by a large curtain wall.

Cuppley, Frances Wright

The youngest daughter of Frank and his first wife Catherine, she was born in 1898. When Catherine **Wright**'s marriage to Ben **Page** failed she went to live with her daughter Frances in West Virginia.

Curtis, Charles

A 79-year-old Cornish mason from Mineral Point who, with his wife, stayed with Wright for the duration of the building of **Taliesin West.**

Curtis Publishing Company

The publishers of the **Ladies' Home Journal,** the Curtis Company commissioned Wright four times to design custom houses for the magazine — twice in 1901, again in 1907 and in 1945.

D

Dallas Theater Center (Kalita Humphreys Theater) (1955)

The design employs modules with 60° and 120° angles as well as circles. It is a concrete cantilever construction. The circular stage drum contains a 40-foot circular stage which itself contains a 32-foot turntable. The foyer has subsequently been extended, and the terrace above it enclosed. Tours by appointment only.

Dana, Susan Lawrence

One of Wright's clients who, in 1902, gave the "Aunts" the little Art and Science building next to the **Hillside School** building. She also loaned them $27,000 more to help complete the main school building.

Dana-Thomas House (Susan Lawrence Dana House, 1902, and Lawrence Memorial Library, 1905)

The house is of cruciform plan and it incorporates an earlier house into its brick structure. It is a **Prairie** style house and is the first example of Wright's work to feature what would become a trademark — a two-story high living room. The house is connected to the library

by means of a covered passage that doubled as a conservatory. As befitted an art collector, there is much art-glass and sculptures by Richard **Bock**. It was bought and restored by Mr. and Mrs. Charles C. Thomas (and subsequently is known as the Dana-Thomas house) in 1944. Both house and library are open to the public and tours are available.

Darrow, Clarence

A lawyer whose friendship proved invaluable to Wright, Darrow was the skilled defence lawyer who presented evidence to counter the allegations that Wright's house-keeper, Nellie **Breen,** had brought against Miriam **Noel.**

Pages 80/81: The Dana-Thomas house, a beautiful Wright interior much of which remains intact.

Above and Right: The Dallas Theater Center, named the Kalita Humphreys Theater. The theater has eleven rows, seating 404 people.

Pages 84/85: The Dana residence and Lawrence Memorial Library. The two are joined by a raised walkway.

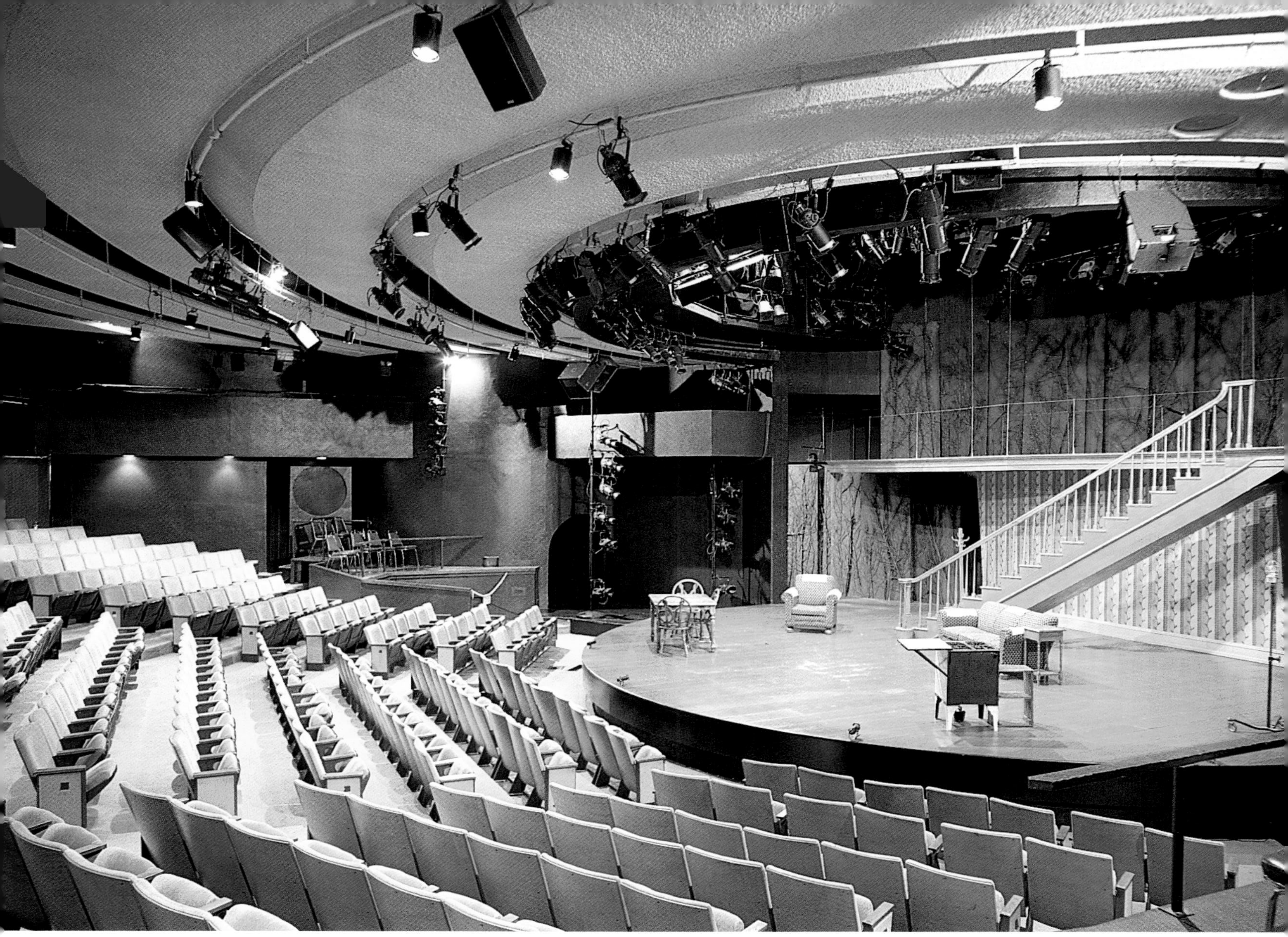

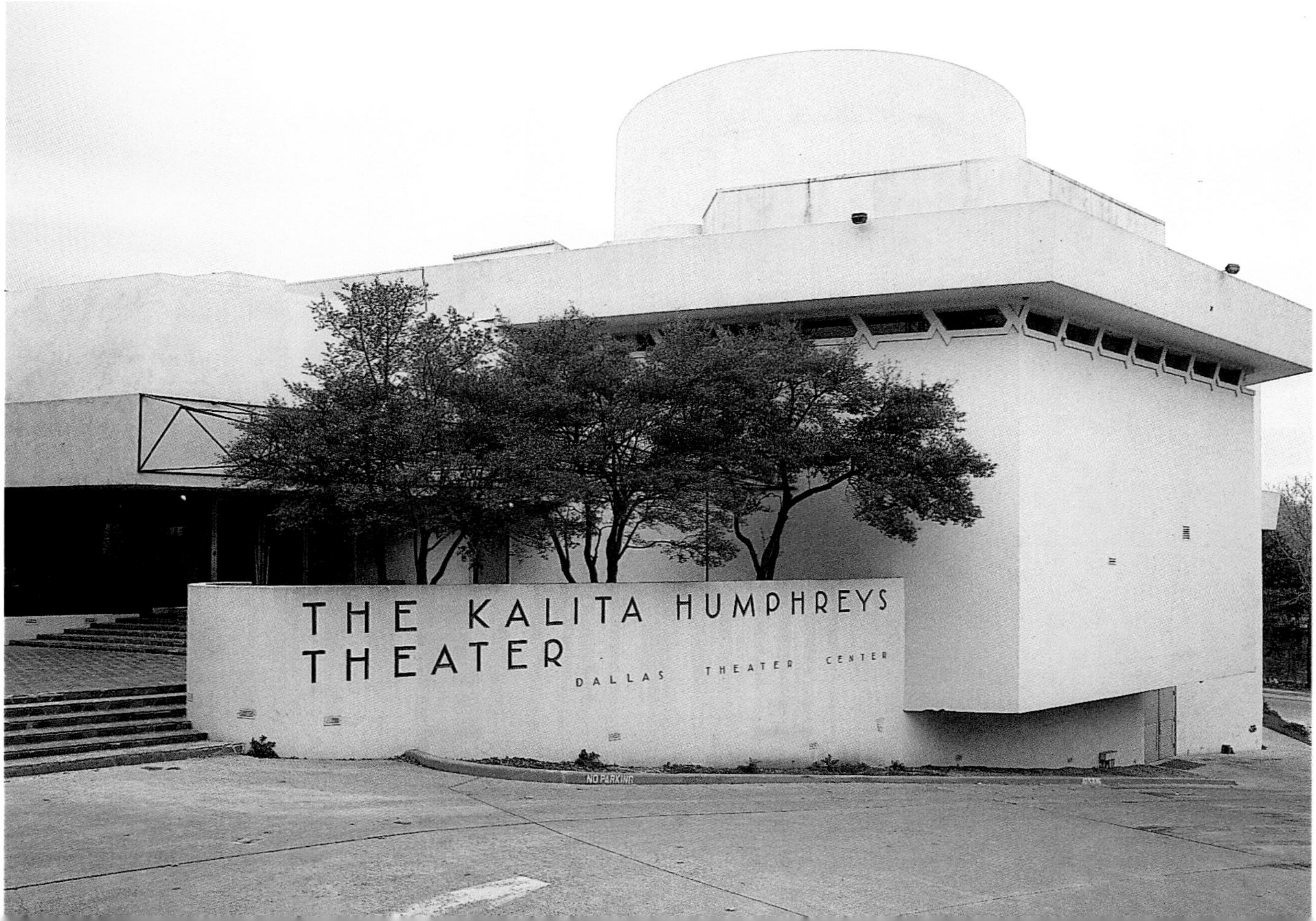
THE KALITA HUMPHREYS
THEATER
DALLAS THEATER CENTER
NO PARKING

Davenport, E. Arthur, House (1901)
This two-story house was a Webster **Tomlinson** collaboration. It is a stained wood board and batten structure with plaster under the eaves of a gable roof. Its original front terrace has been removed. The house was executed using Wright's second design for the **Ladies' Home Journal.**

E. Arthur Davenport house. A front terrace has been removed since construction.

Davidson, Alexander, House (1908)

This is built to a cruciform plan with its two-story living room facing south. It is a typical **Prairie House.**

Davies, Joe

The American Ambassador in Moscow whom Wright met on his visit there — he was a Madison University man.

Davis, Richard, House (1950)

This remarkable design is constructed from painted concrete block and is cedar-shingled with redwood trim. It works like an octagonal "teepee" and the living room rises to the full height of some 38 feet.

Davison, Davy and Kay

Davy Davison was a **Taliesin** apprentice who, with his wife Kay, bought some property on the Taliesin estate which had once belonged to Wright's Aunt Mary and Uncle James Philip. Davy, a young idealist, was party to Taliesin's inner circle by virtue of his wife's close friendship with the Wrights. When Frank Lloyd Wright spoke against America's involvement in the Second World War it was no accident that Davy Kay declared himself a **conscientious objector** and subsequently suffered a prison term.

Deknatel, William

He was one of the earliest apprentices at **Taliesin.** Deknatel later opened his own firm in Chicago which operated from 1936 to 1971; active in urban renewal and social welfare, he served as president of **Hull House** from 1953 to 1962.

Delavan Lake Group

A group of five summer residences on the shores of the lake in **Wisconsin.** They were the **Spencer** House (1902), the Henry **Wallis** Summer House (1900), the **Johnson**, A. P., House (1905), the **Ross** House (1902) and the **Jones** House (1902) "Penwern." The Jones house, including gate lodge, a barn with stables, and a boathouse, is the most extensive of the Lake Delavan Projects.

Delaware

The Dudley **Spencer** House in Wilmington, built in 1956, is the only example of Wright's work in the State of Delaware.

DeRhodes, K. C., House (1906)

The side entrances of this building turn a simple rectangle into a cruciform plan: it is a **Prairie** style house.

Above and Right: The Charles Ross residence — one of the Delavan Lake Group.

typically wood-trimmed and plaster-surfaced. A substantial living room occupies the full height of the building. It was a club for some years but has now been restored.

desert rubblestone (or desert concrete)

This involved placing large stones at random into forms and then pouring concrete around them, leaving most of the face next to the form exposed. The stone was then washed with acid to bring out its coloring. In the construction of **Taliesin West,** the slanting walls were topped off with superstructures of redwood and canvas. Wright wanted massive walls, in those days before air-conditioning, to keep the rooms cool in the daytime and warmer at night — "a dreamlike oasis in the desert."

Devane, Andrew

One of Wright's **Taliesin West** apprentices, Devane arrived from Dublin, Eire, penniless having spent his last dollar on a one-way bus ticket. It was Devane who accompanied Wes **Peters** when they drove to the

hospital with his fatally injured wife, Svetlana **Peters**, and their son Daniel, after a car accident in **Spring Green**.

Dobkins, John J., House (1953)
This house is rectangular in plan and surface. It is made from brick with wood trim and a copper roof.

Doyle, Isabelle
She had a full time job at the State Bank of **Spring Green** but, in 1929, started working evenings at **Taliesin II** as a secretary.

del Drago, Prince Giovanni
A member of the **Taliesin Fellowship** in 1946, he was from an old Italian aristocratic family. However, the prince did his duty in the kitchen along with everybody else.

Drake, Blaine
A young apprentice at **Taliesin** who worked on the dam below the complex during the first year of the **Fellowship**. During the work Drake helped haul dirt back to the fields in a dump truck. Along with Herbert **Fritz** on the cello, Svetlana **Peters** on the violin, and Jim **Thompson** on the recorder, he played the viola in what Wright called the **"Farmer-Labor Quartet."** They entertained the Wrights and their guests after dinner at the Fellowship at Taliesin.

Drummond, William
A valuable assistant to Wright during his first year of independence in Chicago.

Duell, Sloan and Pearce
Publishers of three important books on Wright. *In the Nature of Materials*, *Frank Lloyd Wright on Architecture*, and a new edition of *An Autobiography*.

Dunbar, Jack
He became a **Taliesin** apprentice in 1946 on the G.I. Bill and would later enjoy a reputation as a well-known **New York** designer. He was witness to an incident that demonstrated Wright's view that admiration for any other architecture other than his own was heresy or at least disloyalty; he discovered one of Wright's hired hands burning books on architecture, including Giedion's *Space, Time and Architecture*.

Duncan, Elizabeth and Don, House (1957)
This house is an **Erdman Prefab** No. 1 built in Lisle, Illinois. For illustration see pages 100/101.

Right: An excellent example of Wright's desert rubblestone at Taliesin West.

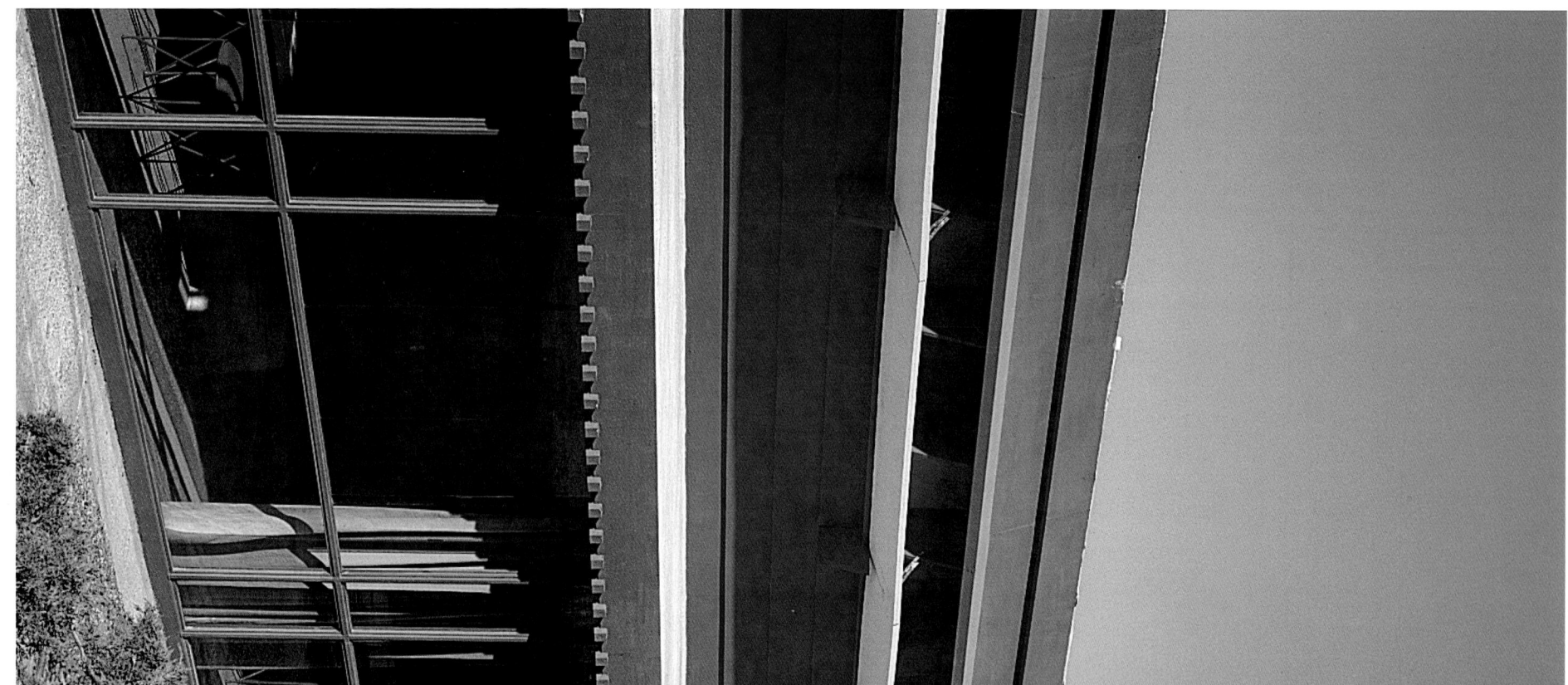

École des Beaux Arts, Paris
Louis **Sullivan** had studied at the École but rejected the French academic tradition considering it basically flawed. Wright's instincts told him to reject an offer made by Daniel **Burnham** for him to study, all expenses paid, at the École.

Eddleston, Babette
A young architect who became a watercolorist, print maker, and sculptor. Having been inspired by a former apprentice from **Taliesin** in **Wisconsin**, Eddleston once drove 1,000 miles and arrived uninvited at **Taliesin West**. On meeting Wright she was brusquely told, "We are not interested in visitors." She explained that she knew their mutual friend Eleanore **Petterson** and, in a typically dazzling *volte-face*, Wright indicated that she was welcome to stay as long as she liked.

Edelmann, John
Edelmann met Louis **Sullivan** in William Le Baron **Jenny**'s office and took him along when he joined Dankmar **Adler** in 1880.

Edwards, James, House (1949)
Edwards wrote to Wright in 1948 after seeing an article in the House Beautiful. He consequently received a pleasant red brick and cypress design with a glazed west-facing living room and a terrace along the length of the west wall. Additions were made by the **Taliesin Associated Architects** in 1968.

Elam, S. P., House (1950)
This two-story house is one of the largest late **Usonian** houses and is built of stone and cypress. It has an additional garage and rear terrace which are not part of Wright's original design.

Pages 92/93, Above, and Below right: Charles Ennis house (see page 96). This ornate building is the last of four textile block houses constructed in Los Angeles.

Above right: The Robert G. Emmond residence (see page 96), a "bootleg" house built while Wright was an employee of Adler & Sullivan.

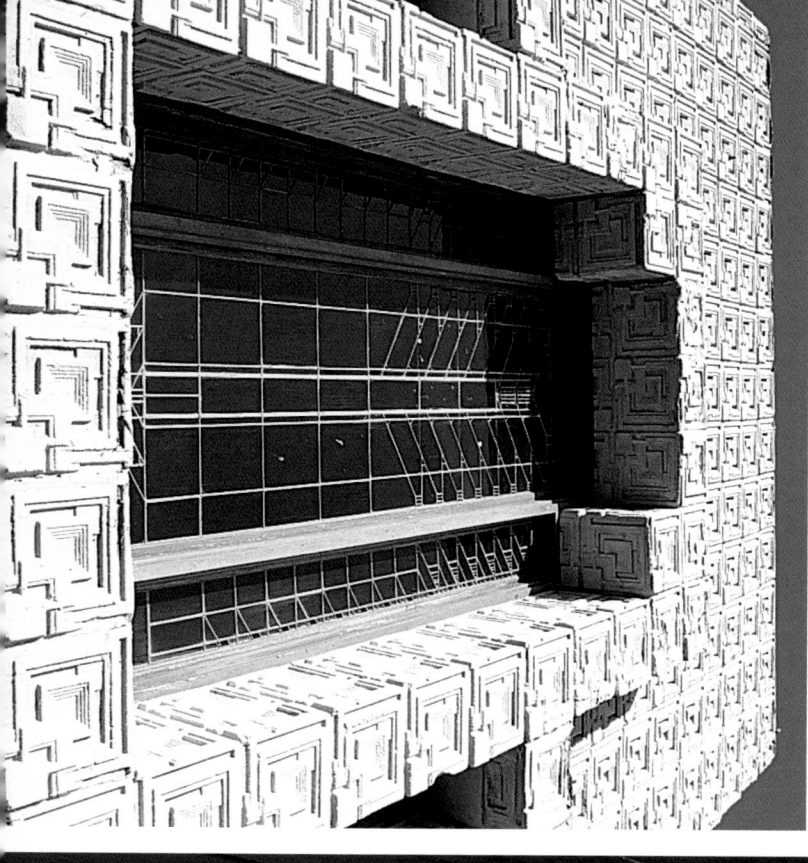

Elmslie, George Grant

A distinguished draftsman and friend of Wright who succeeded him as chief designer at **Adler & Sullivan** when Wright left to establish his own practice. **Sullivan** was forced to dismiss Elmslie in 1909 when the building boom in Chicago ended. He went on to become one of a number of new architects who formed the **New School of the Midwest.**

Emmond, Robert G. House (1892)

A **"bootlegged"** T-plan house set sideways to the street. Originally a clapboard structure, it has been resurfaced with brick on its lower story. The building has been changed considerably since it was designed and its terraces are now enclosed.

Endo, Arato

The Japanese architect who supervised the work on the **Imperial Hotel.** He was almost a collaborator on the project and was indispensable as liaison since Wright spoke no Japanese. He supervised the hotel's completion after Wright's return to the United States in 1922.

Ennis, Charles, House (1923)

The third and largest of the four **Los Angeles textile block** houses is even more massively Mayan than the others. It has a pyramidic feel to it. Lloyd Wright supervised the construction of this house himself. Guided tours available.

Details of the Ennis house. Like Aline Barnsdall's Hollyhock House, there is a resemblance to Mayan architecture. The building has recently been renamed the Ennis-Brown house in recognition of the restoration work done by Mr. and Mrs. August Brown.

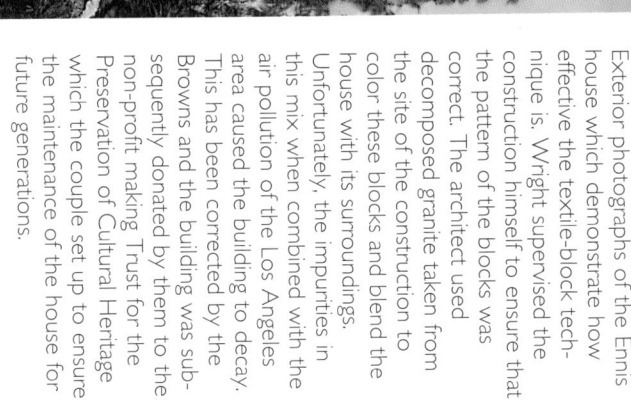

Exterior photographs of the Ennis house which demonstrate how effective the textile-block technique is. Wright supervised the construction himself to ensure that the pattern of the blocks was correct. The architect used decomposed granite taken from the site of the construction to color these blocks and blend the house with its surroundings. Unfortunately, the impurities in this mix when combined with the air pollution of the Los Angeles area caused the building to decay. This has been corrected by the Browns and the building was subsequently donated by them to the non-profit making Trust for the Preservation of Cultural Heritage which the couple set up to ensure the maintenance of the house for future generations.

Eppstein, Samuel, House (1948)
One of the **Galesberg Country Homes**, the Eppstein House is dug deeply into the hillside with the living room opening out into a large north-facing terrace.

Erdman Prefab
Wright designed three prefabricated houses for the Marshall Erdman company, but only two of the designs were realized. An example of the first — the No. 1 — is the **Duncan** residence of 1957. The No. 2 is exemplified by the **Rudin** residence.

Euchtman, Joseph, House (1939)
A **Usonian** I-plan building, the main feature of this two-bedroom house is the living room which opens onto both a southwest-facing terrace shaded by the extended roof, and also onto a southeast-facing deck inserted after construction had been completed.

European Modernism
The tremendous upheaval in the worlds of art and architecture that was ushered in with World War I had been sensed by Wright almost as it was being formed. Such developments in art as Futurism, Fauvism, Constructivism, Abstract, Expressionism, and Dadaism were giving rise to

a simultaneous revolution in architecture, led by men such as **Le Corbusier** and **Gropius**.

Evans, Robert, House (1908)
A **Prairie** structure built from a basic square extended into a cruciform plan. The house exists in its original form apart from the addition of a stone veneer.

Evjue, William T.
Editor and publisher of *The Capital Times*, a **Wisconsin** newspaper. A good friend to Wright, Evjue published editorials and articles by Wright in his newspaper.

exposed concrete block
The exposed concrete block constructions preceded the development of the **textile block** system. The **Hollyhock House** in **Los Angeles** is an interesting example of this technique on a very large scale.

E-Z Polish Factory and Offices (1905)
Commissioned by the brothers Darwin D. and W. E. **Martin**, the upper floors of this building were rebuilt after a fire in 1913. Most of the windows have now been bricked in although a painted mural still survives on the main office floor.

Top: The E-Z Polish Factory. Due to a fire in 1913 the upper floors were rebuilt and many of the windows have been bricked in. However, a Wright mural still exists on the office floor.

Above and Left: An example of the No. 1 Erdman prefab house — both photographs show the Duncan house.

F

Fabyan, Col. George, House (1907)
Wright's remodeling work to this house on Colonel Fabyan's game preserve was chiefly to the living room, some of the second story, and various exterior details. Now a museum, it is open during the summer months.

Fallingwater
(See **Kaufmann** House).

"Farmer-Labor Quartet"
Svetlana **Peters** on the violin, Jim **Thompson** on the recorder, Blaine **Drake** on the viola, and Herbert **Fritz** on the cello formed what Wright called the "Farmer-Labor Quartet." They entertained the Wrights and their guests after dinner at the **Fellowship** at **Taliesin**.

Farries, Jack
He found Mamah **Cheney** at **Taliesin** with her clothing almost burned off her body after the murders.

(Herman T.) Fasbender Medical Clinic (1957)
This one-story building is constructed from brick with a copper roof. It is currently used as office premises and is open during working hours.

Fawcett, Randall, House (1955)
This two-winged house is constructed from **exposed concrete blocks**. The wings make 60-degree angles to the main living space which contains a walk-in fireplace.

Feiman, Ellis A., House (1954)
The interior space of this house is based on an L-plan, with a south-facing living room opening onto a terrace.

Feldman, Hilary & Joe, House (Designed 1939; built 1974)
Built long after Wright's death, this **Usonian** house required 30,000 bricks. **California** clearheart redwood is used in the trim and for the board and batten walls.

Above: The Fabyan house, a Wright remodeling.

Right, above and below: The Fasbender Medical Clinic. The terne metal roof lends the building a unique character.

Pages 102/103: Florida Southern College (see page 108).

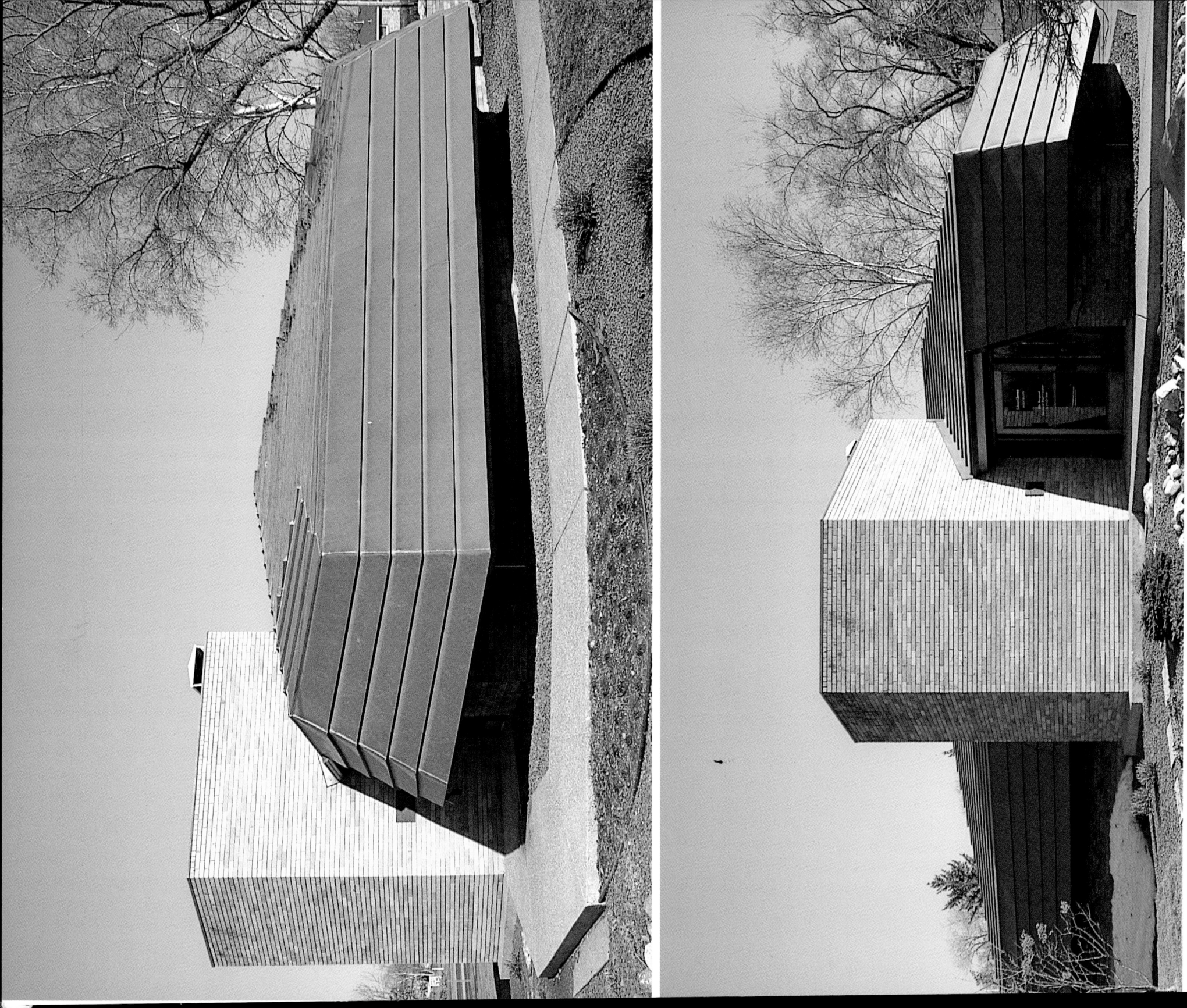

The original design was for the Lewis N. **Bell** House, intended for a west **Los Angeles** placement.

Fiesole, Italy

A town in **Italy** where Wright spent some time before the First World War and the site of the **Villa Medici**, much admired by the architect. Surviving sketches show that a house Wright was designing for himself and Mamah **Cheney** in Tuscany, while having the overall feeling of a **Prairie** style, was strongly influenced by classical dictates in imitation of the Villa Medici.

"A Fireproof House for $5,000"

Here Wright proposed the use of poured concrete for residential design, its particular advantage was to render the building fireproof. The **Curtis Publishing Company** commissioned the design for the *Ladies' Home Journal* in April, 1907.

First Christian Church (designed 1950)

Designed by Wright and built after his death, this was the last project to be completed in **Arizona**. Wright first produced plans of a university campus for the Southwest Christian Seminary in 1951. When the university failed to proceed, the First Christian Church decided to go ahead with the chapel, starting work on it in 1971, 12 years

Interior and exterior of the First Christian Church. The blue urethane roofing was used as an alternative to copper.

Various buildings of the Florida Southern College. **Above:** The Annie Pfeiffer Chapel. **Below:** The interior of the auditorium. **Above right:** The library. **Below right:** The Industrial Arts building.

after Wright's death in Phoenix. The chapel features a stained glass window by a member of the **Taliesin Fellowship**. Guided tours by appointment. Wright's designs are still being built today by the **Taliesin Associated Architects** (T.A.A.).

"floating foundation"

The Chicago "floating foundation" methods were developed as a result of the underlying soils of Chicago being unsuited to the new building style of **skyscrapers**. Buildings were either supported by enormous pilings, caissons of concrete and steel, or by "pads" of the same materials, resting or "floating" on the clay, sustaining and distributing the weight of the building above. Wright used these principles in the construction of the **Imperial Hotel** in Tokyo. He built concrete "posts" or "fingers," under the center of each section: the floors were cantilevered from these pivots so that each unit was supported as it "floated" on its unstable base.

Florida

Florida does not boast a large quantity of Frank Lloyd Wright buildings, but what this state does have is the campus of the **Florida Southern College**, Lakeland. It is a good example of how Wright planned and executed buildings on a grand scale — although not so grand a scale as the projected **Broadacre City**. Offered the job by president of the college, Dr. Ludd **Spivey**, Wright's plan for the campus was conceived in 1938, with the buildings being completed 1938-53. The most remarkable and certainly the tallest (the plan kept a uniformly low height on the other structures), was the Annie Pfeiffer **Chapel**, the decorative steel tower of which is visible from everywhere on the campus. This was designed as a means of lighting the interior of the chapel and is extremely effective. Wright's only other work in Florida is the **Lewis House** in Tallahassee.

Florida Southern College (1938–53)

Wright's buildings at the university are the **Pfeiffer Chapel** (1938), three Seminar Buildings (1940), the Library (1941), the Industrial Arts Building (1942), the Administration Building (1945), the Science and Cosmography Building (1953), and the Minor Chapel (1954) Esplanades — necessary to shelter students from tropical downpours and a fierce summer sun — were built in 1946 to link all of Wright's buildings on the campus; those buildings not linked were built by other architects. In the case of the Industrial Arts and the Science and Cosmography buildings, the esplanades form an extension of their outer walls; elsewhere they run between the other structures. The buildings were made

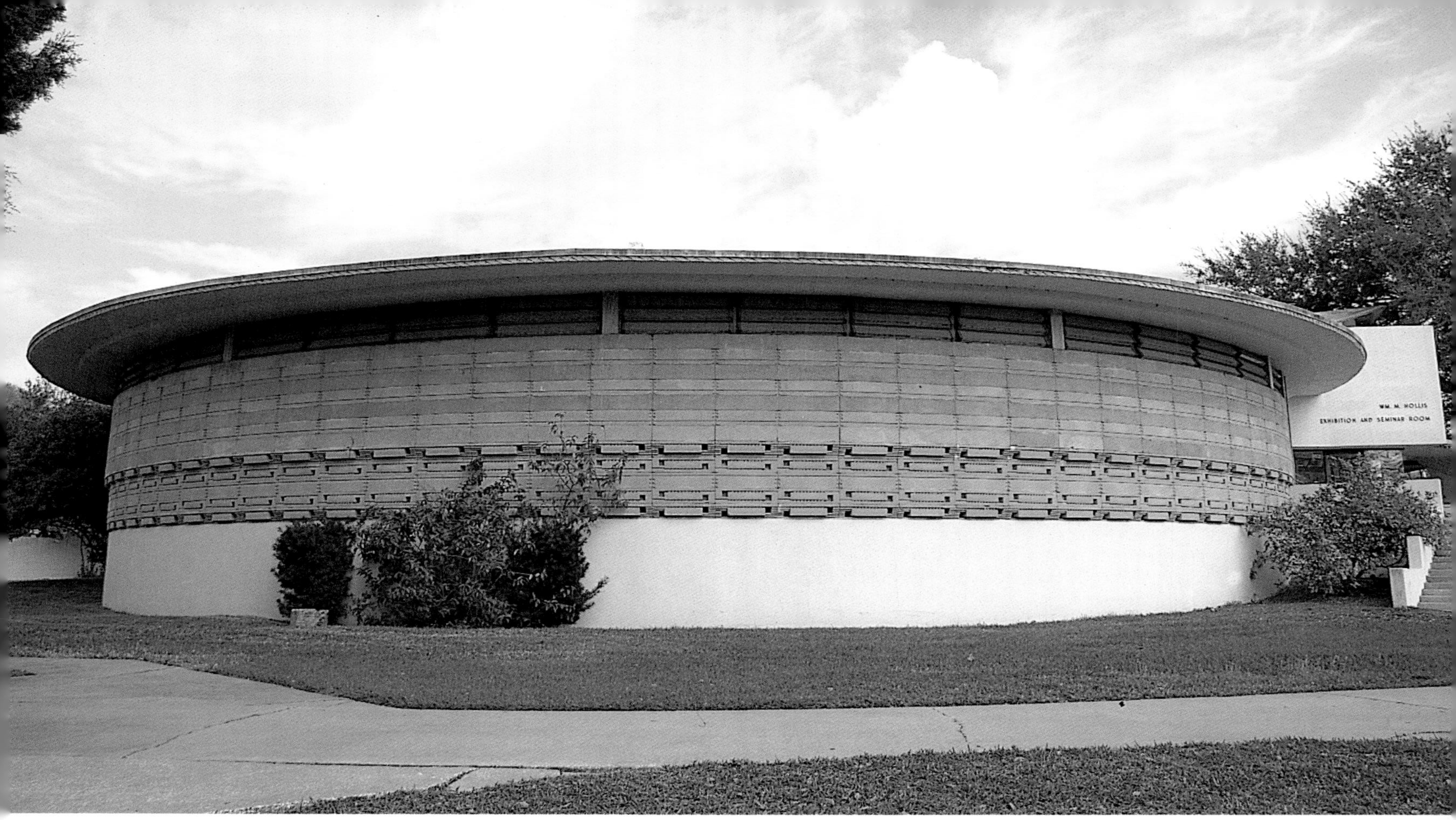
WM. M. HOLLIS
EXHIBITION AND SEMINAR ROOM

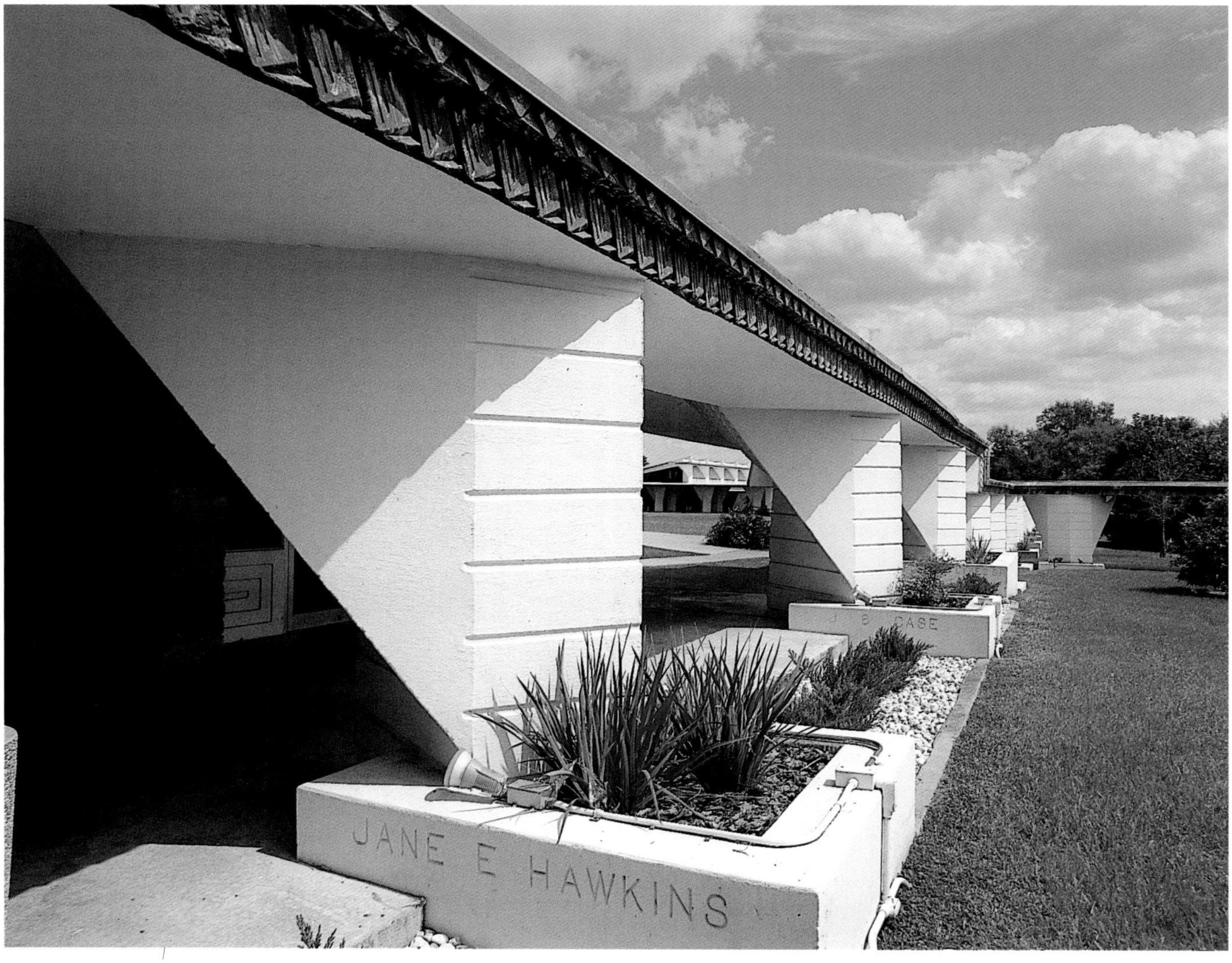
JANE E HAWKINS

Top: Smooth and textured surfaces combine to ornament the college in typical Wright fashion.

Above: Planetarium and Science and Cosmology Building.

Above right: The Minor Chapel.

Far right: The Annie Pfeiffer Chapel is the tallest building on the campus.

Center right: The E. T. Roux Library has been converted to administrative uses.

Right: Covered esplanades link the various facilities and administration buildings on campus.

from **textile blocks** of textured concrete — often inset with colored glass — brick and steel. Much of the hard construction work, the pouring of the concrete for the textured blocks and floor slabs, was done by the college students and set against their college costs. The site is open to the public.

Forest Avenue

One of the main thoroughfares of **Oak Park**, Forest Avenue features a number of fine examples of Wright's early work, including the "Harem" — the Frank Wright **Thomas** house — the **Heurtley** residence, and the building he called the forerunner of **Fallingwater**, the Mrs. Thomas H. **Gale** house.

Foster, S.A., House (1900)

An Oriental influence is evident in the curved, upward rising roof lines of this building, although Wright had not yet visited **Japan**. Private residence and stable.

Fox River Country Club (designed 1907; destroyed by fire 1910)

The existing country club belonging to Colonel George Fabyan on his private land was remodeled by Wright to bring it up to contemporary standards. It was a reworking of an existing structure.

Francis Apartments (designed 1895; demolished 1971)

Built for the Terre Haute Trust Company, the ground floor of this four-story building was surfaced in the style of **Sullivan** with a geometrical pattern. The north wing on the ground floor contained four shops.

Francisco Terrace, Apartments (designed 1895; demolished 1974)

This was a two-story brick complex intended as good quality but cheap housing. It was one of the two sets of apartments built for Edward C. **Waller**, a neighbor of Wright's friend William H. **Winslow**. General neglect led to vandalism and eventual demolition although the entry archway was reconstructed at Euclid Place, Oak Park, in 1977.

"Frank Lloyd Wright in the Realm of Ideas"

A retrospective exhibition of Wright's work **"Sixty Years of Living Architecture"** which was an immediate success when it opened in Florence, **Italy**, in May 1951.

Frank Lloyd Wright Field Office (1951)

Rebuilt in the Heinz Architectural Center, this is the office that Wright shared with Aaron **Green** in San Francisco.

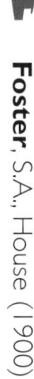

Above: Wright's Field Office as rebuilt in the Heinz Architectural Center.

Right: Forest Avenue.

Below: Francisco Terrace Apartments' entrance archway.

Francke, Kuno
Professor of the History of German Culture at Harvard who went to **Oak Park** to see Wright's work at first hand in 1908. He suggested that Wright should visit **Germany** and the architect did so the next year.

Frederick, Louis B., House (1954)
This three-bedroom house is built from buckskin range brick and Philippine mahogany.

Freeman, Samuel, House (1923)
The last and smallest of the **textile block** houses built in the foothills of the Santa Monica Mountains. Supervision of the construction and landscaping were by Lloyd Wright. Open to the public, tours are available.

Fricke, William G., House (1901)
A three-story house designed with Webster **Tomlinson.** Six years after its construction many alterations were made and a garage, in the style of the house, was added.

Friedman, Allen, House (1956)
A Y-plan house, the intersection of the Y houses the kitchen and entry area; the wings containing sleeping quarters, living room, and carport.

Friedman, Arnold, Summer house (1945) Fir Tree
Wright's only house in New Mexico is constructed of **desert rubblestone** walls with trim and roof of rough cedar shakes.

Friedman, Sol, House (1948)
The design for this **Usonian** house has two interlocking cylinders with a mushroom-shaped carport. Solidly constructed from stone and concrete.

Fritz, Eloise
Eloise and her husband Herb of **Spring Green** were close friends of Wright. They bought some property on the **Taliesin** estate which had once belonged to Wright's Aunt Mary and Uncle James Philip. Wright

The three-story Fricke residence. The current owners have preserved the house and made only minor modernizations.

complimented them on how nice the property was looking and suggested they donate it to the **Fellowship**. The Fritzes politely declined.

Fritz, Herbert
Herb was a former student at the **Taliesin Fellowship** whose father had survived the infamous **Taliesin murders**. Herbert Fritz grew up at Taliesin just as the Fellowship was being organized and shared quarters with the pioneers. Later he played the cello in what Wright called the **"Farmer-Labor Quartet."**

Froebel, Friedrich Wilhelm August
A pioneer in the field of early child development and inventor of the kindergarten. Wright's mother introduced her son to the ideas of Froebel at an early age and claimed that a great deal of Frank's genius was due to Froebel's enlightened teachings and the educational toys — Froebel's Gifts — with which he played as a child.

Fukuhara, Arinobu, House (designed in 1918; destroyed in 1923)
This house in Gora, Japan was a victim of the Kanto earthquake.

Above and Right: The George Furbeck house is now quite different from the original structure.

Below: The Rollin Furbeck house. This and his brother's house are thought to have been wedding presents from their father.

Fuller, Grace, House (designed 1906; since demolished)
A small house, this was the second and much more modest of the two **Prairie Houses** designed by Wright in Glencoe.

Fuller, Welbie L., House (designed 1951; demolished 1969 by Hurricane Camille)
With its **exposed concrete blocks** and rough-sawn pine colored red, this house was different to most of Wright's later works. However, it was not sturdy enough to survive the tidal wave caused by Hurricane Camille which struck Mississippi in 1969.

Furbeck, George W., House (1897)
Only the brown brick and wood trim remain from the original house. The porch has been enlarged and enclosed greatly altering the proportions of Wright's design.

Furbeck, Rollin, House (1897)
This three-storied house was built by Wright at the behest of Warren Furbeck for his son. It has a light tan brick, colored wood trim facade, and upper story windows which hug the broad overhanging eaves of the hipped roof in a band of stucco.

Gale, Thomas H., House (1892)
This two-story T-plan Queen Anne house of clapboard, set sideways to the street, was designed while Wright was with **Adler & Sullivan**.

Gale, Thomas H., Summer House (1897)
Thomas Gale and George **Gerts** had married two sisters and bought up adjoining lots of White Lake land for summer cottages with easy access to Lake Michigan and, therefore, Chicago. This was the first to be built and is much altered.

Gale, Mrs. Thomas H., House (designed 1904; built 1909)
Laura Gale's **Prairie House** was originally to have been built of concrete. It is completed roughly to a square-plan and is often said to be the inspiration for **Fallingwater**.

Gale, Walter H., House (1893)
The third of the clapboard houses on Chicago Avenue to have been built to an identical T-plan (see Thomas **Gale** and **Parker** Houses).

Gale, Zona
A **Wisconsin** author with whom Wright had a brief affair in 1925 after he had split up with Miriam Noel **Wright**. She was a member of a large family for whom Wright had designed some entirely conventional, Queen Anne style houses in **Oak Park** before he left **Adler & Sullivan**. She achieved great success when her satiric novel, *Miss Lulu Bett*, won a Pulitzer Prize in 1921 after the author turned it into a play.

Galesburg Country Homes, Michigan
A housing development conceived by a group of chemists working together at a company in Kalamazoo.

Gammage Memorial Auditorium (1959)
Wright's last non-residential design to be built was the

Above and Above right: The Walter M. Gale residence in Oak Park.

Pages 118/119 and Right: The Grady Gammage Memorial Auditorium seats 3,000 people and is the last non-residential building to be constructed by Wright.

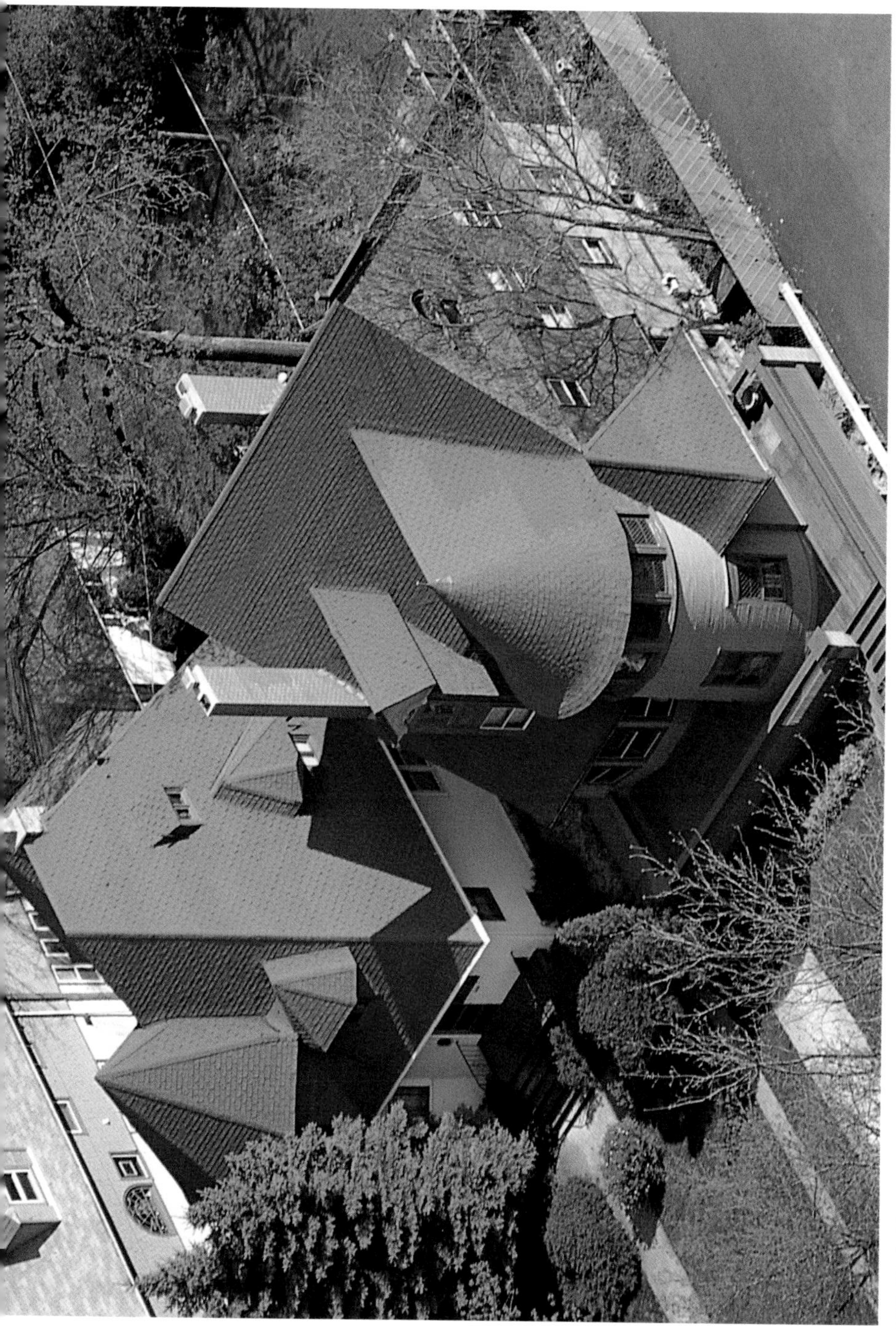

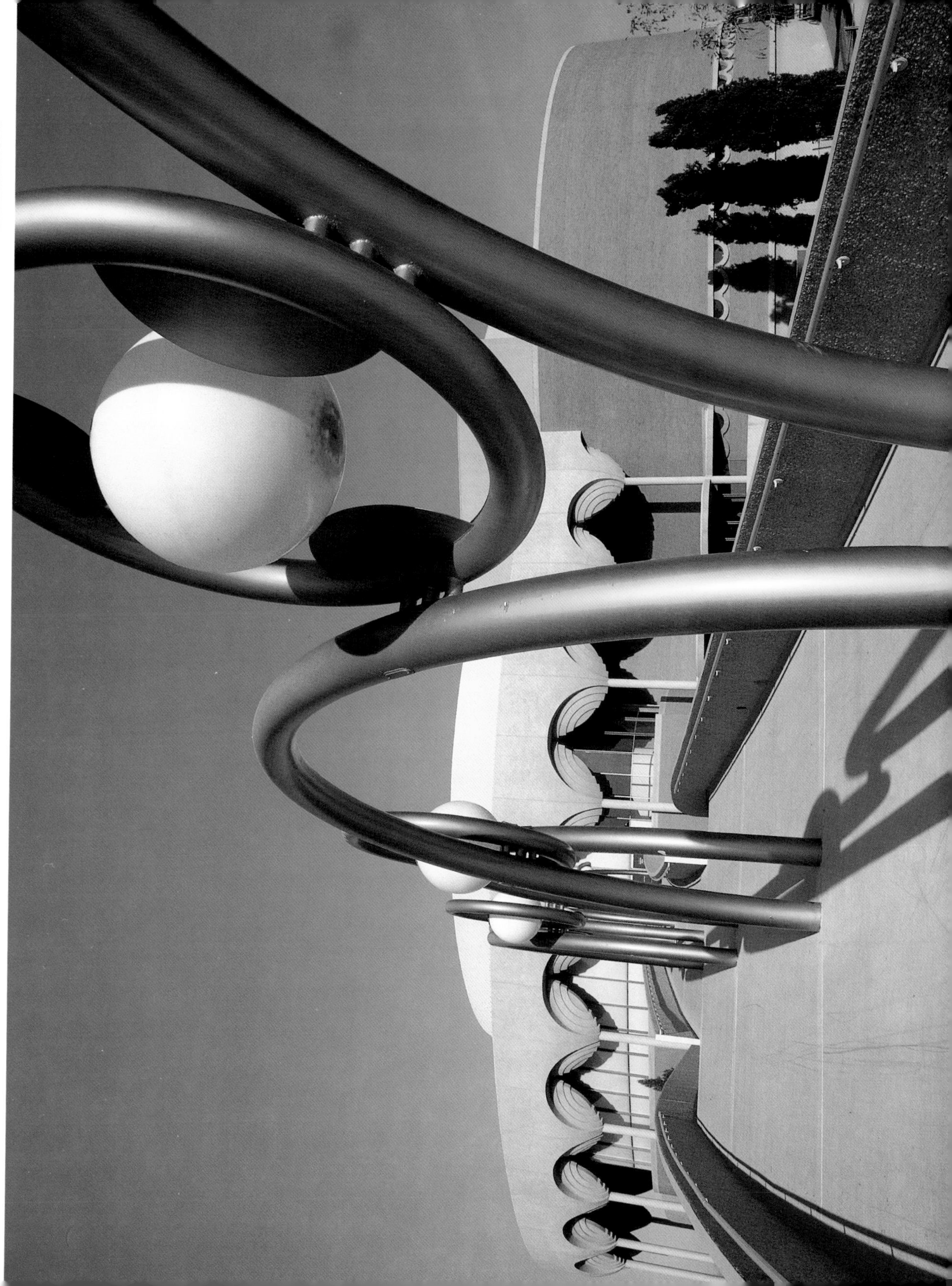

Above: The Grady Gammage Memorial Auditorium.. 50 concrete columns support the outer roof. Exterior walls are made up of brick and marblecrete and have a desert-rose finish giving the building a warm appearance.

Right: The extensive foyer.

Left: There are no center aisles in the auditorium but the rows are widely spaced to provide ease of passage.

Gammage Memorial Auditorium of the Arizona State University at Tempe. It has a circular arcade of 50 tall concrete columns supporting the outer roof. The exterior walls are made of brick and a marble-like composition called marblecrete. A pedestrian bridge takes the audience from parking lot to auditorium. Guided tours are available.

Geneva Inn (designed 1911; demolished 1970)
This **Prairie** style structure commissioned by Arthur L. Richards was of wood frame and the main lobby featured a large Roman brick fireplace.

Genius and the Mobocracy

In this book Wright insisted that "A building can only be functional when integral with environment and so formed in the nature of materials according to purpose and method as to be a living entity." This statement contains the key to Wright's philosophy of architecture.

German, A. D., Warehouse (1915)
A rectangular cube constructed from brick and cast-in-place concrete. The top-story is faced by finely patterned blocks. This is Wright's only work in the town of his birth and the building now houses the **Richland Museum**. Tours by appointment only.

Germany

Wright first went to Germany in 1909 at the invitation of the publisher Ernst **Wasmuth** who produced what became known as the "Wasmuth portfolio," actually entitled *Ausgeführte Bauten und Entwürfe*. It has become a collector's item.

Gerts, George, Duplex (1902)
With a bridged loggia over Birch Brook which flows into

Above and Below: The A.D. German Warehouse. Note the patterned block of the upper story which was designed for cold storage.

Right, above and below: The Eugene A. Gilmore residence — nearby White Lake, this beautiful duplex has had a second-floor sleeping area added.

Gerts, Walter, Cottage (designed 1902; mostly demolished)
The original plan for this house was a rectangular, single-

story board and batten structure with a centrally located fireplace.

Gill, Irving J.
A prominent architect in whose offices Wright's eldest son, Lloyd, worked when he moved to the West Coast. Lloyd **Wright** worked for Gill as a draftsman and delineator until he established himself in independent practice in 1915.

Gillham, Elizabeth Enright
Daughter of Maginel (**Barney**), Wright's sister, a short story writer and author of children's books.

Gillin, John A., House (1950)
A large single-story house which completely avoids any right-angles. The main building material is stone with an unusually large amount of glass. The structure has plaster ceilings and a copper roof.

Gilmore, Eugene A., House (1908) Airplane House
A cruciform plan with a massive sitting room. This house was substantially altered in 1928.

Glasner, W. A., House (1905)
This house features organization of space similar to later **Usonian** designs in that there was no separate dining room. The rough-sawn finish on the wood is typical of

the many **Prairie** style houses with their horizontal board and batten exteriors. The house was renovated in 1926, again in 1938 with further restoration in 1972-73.

Glickman, Mendel

Joined the **Fellowship** at **Taliesin** in 1932 as a teacher in structural engineering, having just returned from Stalingrad, where he had been chief American engineer at a tractor plant. He became firm friends with William Wesley **Peters**.

Glore, Charles F., House (1951)

This is built from an in-line plan and has a children's room opening over the two-story living room. The flues of the fireplaces on both levels share the same masonry core. Building materials include brick, cypress, and salmon **exposed concrete blocks**. The building had a much needed renovation in the 1990s.

Goan, Peter, House (1893)

Wright's preference for wood construction of board and batten, laid horizontally, can be clearly seen in this house. The structure has, over the years, lost its original front

terrace and second-story porch which gave the house the horizontal character much favored by Wright at the time.

Goddard, Lewis W., House (1953)

Goddard's single-story brick and wood house has an extended carport and a substantial living room glazed on its north, east, and south-facing sides.

Goetsch-Winckler, House (1939)

This **Usonian** house was built for two ladies from the **University of Michigan** Art Department. It was the only one built of a development known as Usonia I, which was to have been a venture between various teachers at what was then called the Michigan Agricultural College. It has an 18-foot cantilevered carport roof and the bedrooms open out onto a private, enclosed, veranda.

Goodrich, Harry C., House (1896)

This two-story house still has the original light-colored clapboards. The second story windows are located directly below the eaves and the lower boards conceal a

basement built partially above the ground. The original open porch has now been enclosed.

Gookin, Frederick

An authority on Japanese prints who collaborated with Wright to present a collection of Hiroshige prints at Chicago's Institute of Art, Gookin and Wright became good friends. After his visit to **Japan** in 1905, Wright had acquired a valuable collection of Oriental art and became a considerable expert on Japanese works in particular, especially the prints which he so loved. Gookin, an enthusiastic fan of all things Japanese, was convinced that his friend was the only man who could design and build the new **Imperial Hotel** in Tokyo, so he used his contacts to influence the decision.

Right: The Glore house from the air, showing the house's in-line construction.

Below left: The Goetsch-Winckler house. Behind the wall is an enclosed, private veranda.

Below: The Goodrich house in Oak Park, IL.

Gordon, Conrad E., House (1957)

A T-plan **exposed concrete-block** structure with a two-story living room, the head of the T incorporates sleeping quarters with balconies over the kitchen utilities.

Gordon, Elizabeth

Editor of Hearst's *House Beautiful* and an influential figure in **New York**'s magazine world. She and Wright became friends after she ran an article critical of the **International Style** and received a telegram from Wright. She was made welcome at **Taliesin** and offered the services of the house staff. Elizabeth Gordon proved a valuable ally to Wright.

Granger, Alfred H.

An architect, Granger wrote the commentary that accompanied the presentation of Wright's own house and studio in **Oak Park**, published in the influential Chicago magazine *House Beautiful*. Granger's praise of Wright reveals how the young architect was regarded by his contemporaries even at this early stage of his career.

Grant, Douglas, House (1946)

This is a long I-plan two-story house built from local stone with a reinforced concrete roof, flagstone floors, and a copper fascia. It is built on a slope so the entrance is on the second story.

Great Britain

In 1939, Wright was invited to London to give a series of lectures for the Royal Institute of British Architects and two years later he was presented with the Royal Gold Medal for Architecture by the same august body. Wright also addressed the **Arts and Crafts** Society where 40 years earlier he had given his famous lecture "The Art and Craft of the Machine."

Great Depression

During the Depression, when all of Wright's commissions had dried up, he turned to lecturing and writing, most notably *An Autobiography*. It was during the Depression that Wright founded his **Fellowship** at **Taliesin**. Wright thought that it made sense to have 20 or 30 young men available to provide a steady pool of enthusiastic, if unskilled, labor.

Greenberg, Maurice, House (1954) Stonebroke

This house is cantilevered from the brow of a hill, constructed from brick and concrete with a wood-trim. Work began in stone but cash ran out and the bedroom wing was never completed.

Greene, William B., House (1912)
The plaster surface, wood trim, and hipped roof are all
common elements of Wright's work in **Illinois**. The
house was extended in 1926, and an enclosed porch was
added in 1961.

Above: The William B. Greene house. The enclosed porch is a
1961 addition by the son of the original client.

Gridley, A.W., House (1906)

A **Prairie** style house of cruciform plan on the ground floor with a T-plan at the second story. It has a plastered surface with stained wood trim and the large open porch has no upper level.

Griffin, Marion Mahony and Walter Burley

The second woman to receive a degree in architecture from the Massachusetts Institute of Technology, **Mahony** joined Wright's **Oak Park** studio in 1895 and became indispensable as his delineator. Many of the designs for Wright's 1910 **Wasmuth Portfolio** were actually drawn by her and at least some of the designs for interior furnishings, mosaics, stained glass, and murals, for which Wright took complete credit, are now thought to have been created by Mahony. After she left Wright's studio she joined the office of Walter Burley Griffin,

another architect who had been apprenticed to Wright, and soon married him. Walter Griffin was part of the **New School of the Midwest**, and had a distinguished architectural career in Australia.

Griggs, Chauncey, House (1946)

This house was built to an L-plan with a two-story facade on the inside. The roofing and sidings are of cedar planks laid diagonally and horizontally giving the house the feel of a log cabin.

Gropius, Georg Walter Adolf

The brilliant young **German** architect and founder of the **Bauhaus**. By 1914 he had already built the "Fabrik," a model factory and office building, at an exhibition in Cologne, which was clearly influenced by Wright's designs published by **Wasmuth** three years before.

Above and Below: The Prairie style Gridley house in its idyllic rural setting.

Left: Walter Gropius (left) and his wife (center) take tea with Le Corbusier.

Guggenheim, Harry S.

Harry S. Guggenheim was appointed president of the eponymous museum's Foundation in 1950, the year after the death of his uncle, Solomon R. **Guggenheim**. Harry fully supported Wright in his endeavours.

Guggenheim, Solomon R.

Wright signed a contract with the multi-millionaire Guggenheim on June 29, 1943, to design a museum which would house his art collection. However, it was to take nine months for the museum to obtain a site. The battle to build the museum (see Robert **Moses**) took 16 years and when Guggenheim died in November, 1949, the project was in jeopardy for a time until his bequest was settled.

Guggenheim Museum (completed 1956)

Wright was engaged in a battle, primarily with New York Commissioner Robert **Moses**, for 16 years to build the museum. Over such a long period of time the costs naturally escalated, and the plans were, accordingly, revised many times. Building work on the Guggenheim finally began in the summer of 1956, and it opened to the

The monumental Guggenheim Museum is one of Wright's buildings to be retained by the A.I.A. as an example of his architectural contribution to American culture.

132 A VISUAL ENCYCLOPEDIA OF FRANK LLOYD WRIGHT

public on October 21, 1959, six months after Wright died. The museum is a reminder of the architect's creative originality and ability to shock. Built around an ascending spiral ramp — it would run into fire safety problems because it was all one floor! — it is notable for the inventive use of concrete and its bold geometric form. The museum has normal opening hours.

Gurdjieff, G. I.

Philosopher, mystic, and spiritual adviser to Olgivanna Lazovich **Wright**. Gurdjieff first came to **Taliesin** in the summer of 1934 and, after his visit, Wright wrote a short essay about him comparing him to Gandhi and Whitman and praising his solid, fatherly manner. Gurdjieff was one of the few men Wright seemed to recognize as an equal.

Gutheim, Frederick

The distinguished architectural historian who first visited **Taliesin** in the winter of 1928. The year 1941 saw publication of an anthology of Wright's writings, *Frank Lloyd on Architecture*, edited by Gutheim. Gutheim also suggested the retrospective exhibition of Wright's work — **Sixty Years of Living Architecture** — the premiere of which opened to great acclaim in Florence in May, 1951.

Guthrie, William Norman

Episcopal minister for a small church in **New York**, Guthrie commissioned Wright to design a cathedral that would hold a million people in numerous churches and chapels, all under one roof.

▶ **Guthrie Church**, New York

Wright had moved his studio back to Chicago early in 1925 and commissions were scarce, so he was particularly excited by Guthrie's proposals. Wright set to work on an idea for a triangular glass and steel pyramid which would stand 1,000-foot high and have cathedrals and chapels grouped around its base to form a hexagon. He called it the "Steel Cathedral." It was never realized but some of the plans were published by the Dutch architect **Wijdeveld**, the founder and editor of the architectural magazine *Wendingen*.

Right: Exterior of the Guggenheim museum. Wright's philosophy and principles were esteemed by Hilla Rebay and he was deemed a fitting architect to enclose some of the world's finest examples of modern art. This "ziggurat" is an astonishing building in which Wright took great pride and care. While incorporating the requirements of the building commissioners, he also expressed his own artistry yet was conscious of the work of others and altered the angle of the exterior walls several times in order that the paintings would have the best possible light.

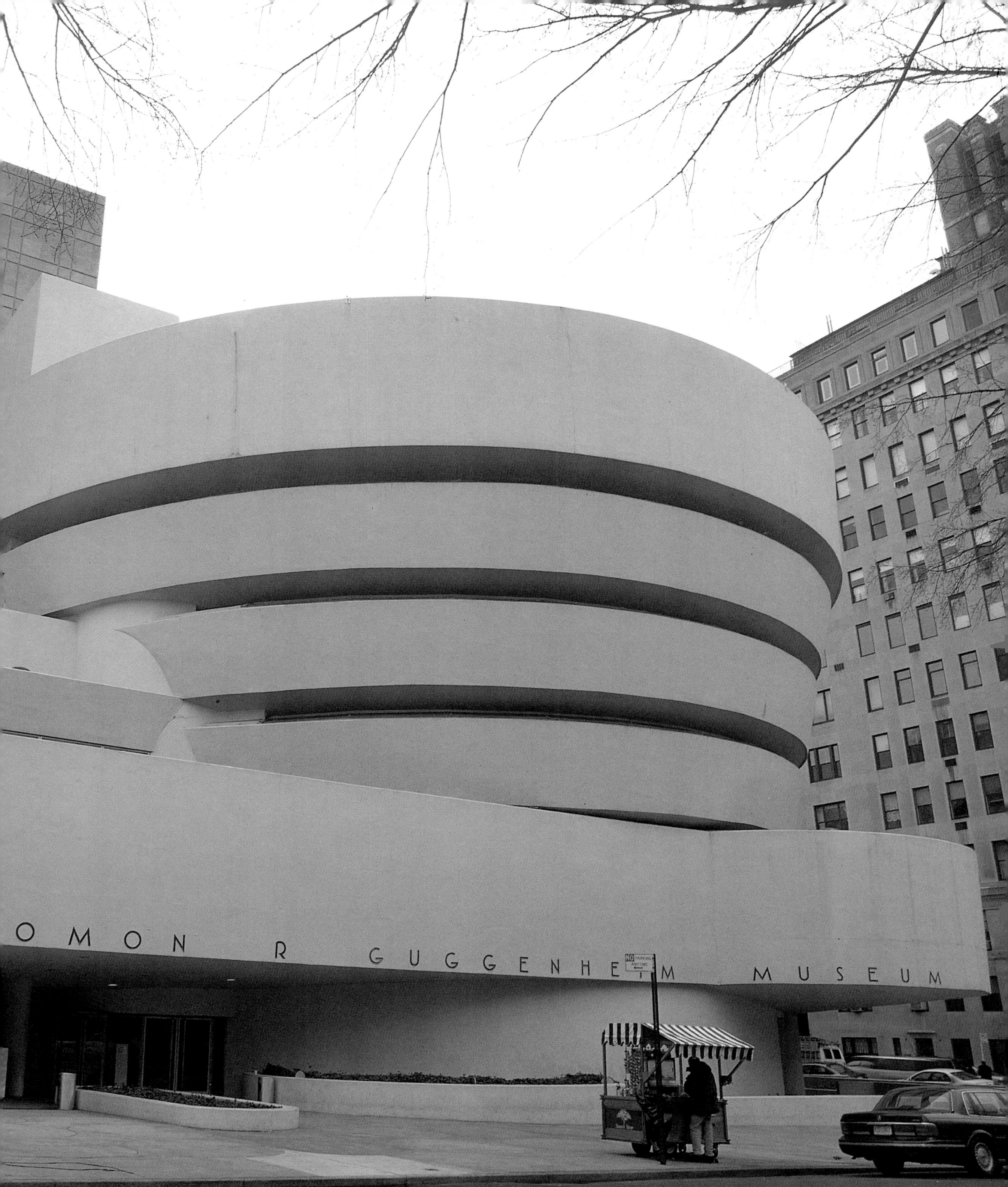
OMON R GUGGENHEIM MUSEUM

Hagan, I. N., House (1954)
This house employs hexagonal modules and there are no right angles to it at all. It is built from local sandstone, quarried at the site, and Tidewater red cypress. Tours are available by appointment.

Hanks, David A.
An authority on Wright's decorative designs and objets d'art.

Hanna, Dr. Paul R. and Jean
Wealthy clients of Wright, they were opposed to modernism as defined by the **Bauhaus**. They were both college professors who earnestly desired to build to the highest principles and who had rejected the **International Style**'s purism and austerity. Their involvement with Wright would lead to a masterpiece.

Hanna, Dr. Paul R. & Jean, House (1936) Honeycombe House
One of the 17 buildings designated to be retained by the **A.I.A.**, the Honeycombe House is now maintained by

Stanford University. Brick-built externally, many of the internal walls are wood and were designed to be moveable in order to change the layout of the playroom as the Hannas' children grew up. The **Usonian** building originally had a copper roof (since replaced) and was Wright's first in the Bay area.

Hardy, Thomas P., House (1905)
This house on Lake Michigan for the one-time mayor of Racine features a living room with an upper-story balcony and a terrace one story below street level.

Harlan, Allison, House (designed 1892; demolished 1963)
One of the **"bootlegged"** projects, it was probably the discovery of his involvement in this house that led to Wright's split from **Adler & Sullivan**.

Pages 136/137, Above, and Above right: The Honeycombe House.

Right: Thomas P. Hardy house.

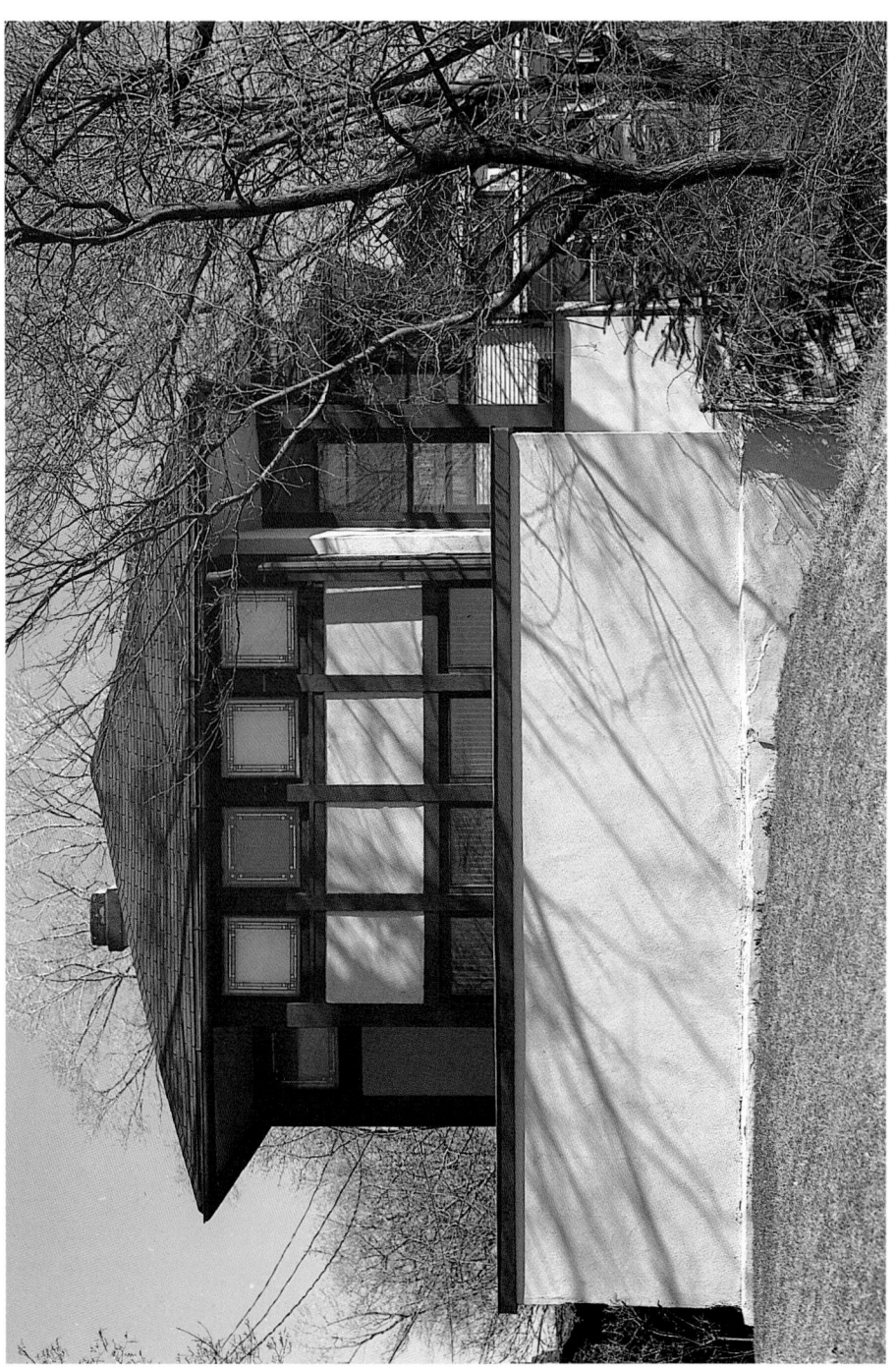

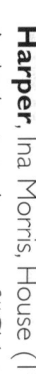

Harper, Ina Morris, House (1950)
A single-story house of "Chicago common" brick, over-looking Lake Michigan. The living room opens out onto a west-facing terrace. Mrs. Harper had read about Wright in an article in **House Beautiful.**

Haskell, Douglas
A writer for the Architectural Record who published a spirited defence of Wright in the *Nation* in 1930 when it seemed that plans for the building of the Chicago World's Fair in 1933 would not include the architect. Later, Haskell became editor of *Architectural Reform,* and the magazine continued to support Wright consistently. However, even Haskell could not publish Wright's vitriolic article attacking the **International Style.**

Heath, W. R., House (1905)
A T-plan **Prairie** style house, it is primarily constructed with dark red brick. The living room opens to the south and it has a large open porch on the eastern side.

Hayashi, Aisaku, House (1917)
Remodeling of the Tokyo house of the Imperial Hotel's manager — the man who got Wright the new hotel commission.

The Heath house. Although 1905 was the year of Wright's first visit to Japan there is little evidence of his trip in this traditional Prairie house.

Details of the Heath house. The large
eastern porch is an entrance to a living
room which has windows to the south.
The north wall of the living room is
dominated by a fireplace and the east wall
has doors which open out onto the
veranda. A sandstone mantel above these
doors is inscribed with the following:

The reality of the house is order.
The blessing of the house is contentment.
The glory of the house is hospitality. Full
crown of the house is coolness.

Henderson, F. B., House (1901)

This is a T-plan building, its hipped roof suggesting a **Prairie House**. The plan was a collaboration with Webster **Tomlinson**.

Heurtley, Arthur

In 1902, Heurtley commissioned what would become one of Wright's most famous houses in **Oak Park**, as well as the remodeling of a cottage in northern **Michigan**. Heurtley was so impressed that he wrote to a notable **German** architect, informing him that Wright was one of the most remarkable men he had ever met.

Heurtley, Arthur, House (1902)

This is a typical square-plan **Prairie** style house, with a sweeping roof, living quarters on the second floor, and a wealth of windows.

The Arthur Heurtley residence. From a distance the Roman brick looks similar to board and batten. As can be seen below the house is built on a square plan.

Above and Below: Hiroshige's style had a marked influence on Western artistic movements and Wright was a particular fan, as was Whistler as exemplified in this detail of Variations in Flesh Colour and Green (**below**).

Right, above and below: Aerial and front view of the Edward R. Hills house. After the remodeling of the original Victorian structure the Hills lived here for 45 years. However, by the time that the DeCaro family acquired it in 1975 it had passed through the hands of two other owners and fallen into a state of disrepair.

Heurtley, Arthur, Summer Cottage remodeling (1902)
On the shores of Lake Huron, this cottage was remodeled by Wright at the same time as he was involved with the Heurtley House in **Oak Park.**

Hicks, Andrew J.
Father of Maude Miriam Noel, Andrew J. Hicks, M.D., was son of one of the wealthiest plantation owners in western **Tennessee.**

Hickox, Warren, House (1900)
This house illustrates Wright's move to the **Prairie** style where the wood timbers become less obvious than the previously popular Tudor style.

Hill, James
Judge James Hill was a lawyer and old friend of Wright's who, in 1926, advised him to go to the Bank of Wisconsin to solicit a new mortgage for **Taliesin** during his acrimonious divorce wrangling with Miriam Noel **Wright.**

Hills, Edward R./**DeCaro,** House (1906)
A **Prairie House** bought by Nathan Moore as a present for his daughter Mary and her husband Tom and Irene DeCaro bought it in 1975 and restored it so substantially that it was officially renamed the Hills/DeCaro house.

Hillside Home School
The Hillside Home School, established in **"The Valley"** in 1886, had been conceived by Nell and Jane **Lloyd Jones** — known as the "Aunts." The school took children of all ages from kindergarten through to high school. As soon as **Unity Chapel** opened, the "Aunts" used it as a temporary school while they built larger quarters. By 1907, Hillside was said to contain nearly a hundred teachers and pupils, most from Chicago.

Hillside Home School I (designed 1887; demolished 1950) and **II** (1902)
Wright's aunts Nell and Jane **Lloyd Jones** taught in this school for many years. In 1903, a larger structure was built. After much restructuring it eventually became part of the **Taliesin Fellowship** complex.

Hinzenberg, Vlademar
A Russian architect, the first husband of Olgivanna **Wright** and father of her daughter Iovanna. Olgivanna and Hinzenberg separated because he felt that her intense involvement in the **Gurdjieff** movement, and her unwillingness to set up a separate household with him, had doomed their marriage from the start.

Hiroshige

A Japanese artist who is considered to have had great influence on the West. Wright much admired him and returned from his first visit to Japan with over two hundred wood-cuts by Hiroshige. He subsequently lent them to the Art Institute of Chicago for the first *ukiyo-e* exhibition to be held in that museum.

Hitchcock, Henry-Russell

The dean of American architectural historians. He was one of the promoters of the **International Style** in the early 1930s and, as such, fell out with Wright although they would later collaborate on *In the Nature of Materials*.

Hoffman, Josef

Founder of the *Wiener Werkstatte*, a Viennese center for the decorative arts. Hoffman rejected both the Classical Academic tradition and the influence of Art Nouveau but shared the **Arts and Crafts** ideals of simplicity and integrity that Wright so vigorously espoused.

Hoffman, Maximilian, House (1955)

A single-story L-plan design, the house is constructed from stone, plaster, and cedar shakes — all trimmed with a copper fascia. The long leg of the L comprises the large living room, kitchen, and bedrooms. The short leg contains the entrance and continues on to the garage and servants' quarters. In 1972, the **Taliesin Associated Architects** added another wing, leading directly to the living room, providing an improved kitchen, a den, a laundry, and additional servants' quarters.

Hoffman Auto Showroom (1954)

A concrete ramp circles around the main display floor. Some of the interior walls are surfaced with glass, as are the structural uprights of the **skyscraper** which houses this ground floor showroom.

Holcomb, Permelia

The first wife of Frank's father, William Carey **Wright**, by whom he had three children. She died in 1864.

Holden, Arthur

The architect who acted as Wright's liaison during construction of the **Guggenheim Museum**.

Holliday, Philip L.

A **Taliesin** apprentice, later a graphic designer, who was elected to serve as a teacher for Olgivanna Lazovich **Wright**'s daughter Iovanna.

The Hoffman Auto Showroom. Alterations were carried out in the 1980s by Wes Peters, Cornelia Brierly and Morton Delson to give more room for additional sales staff.

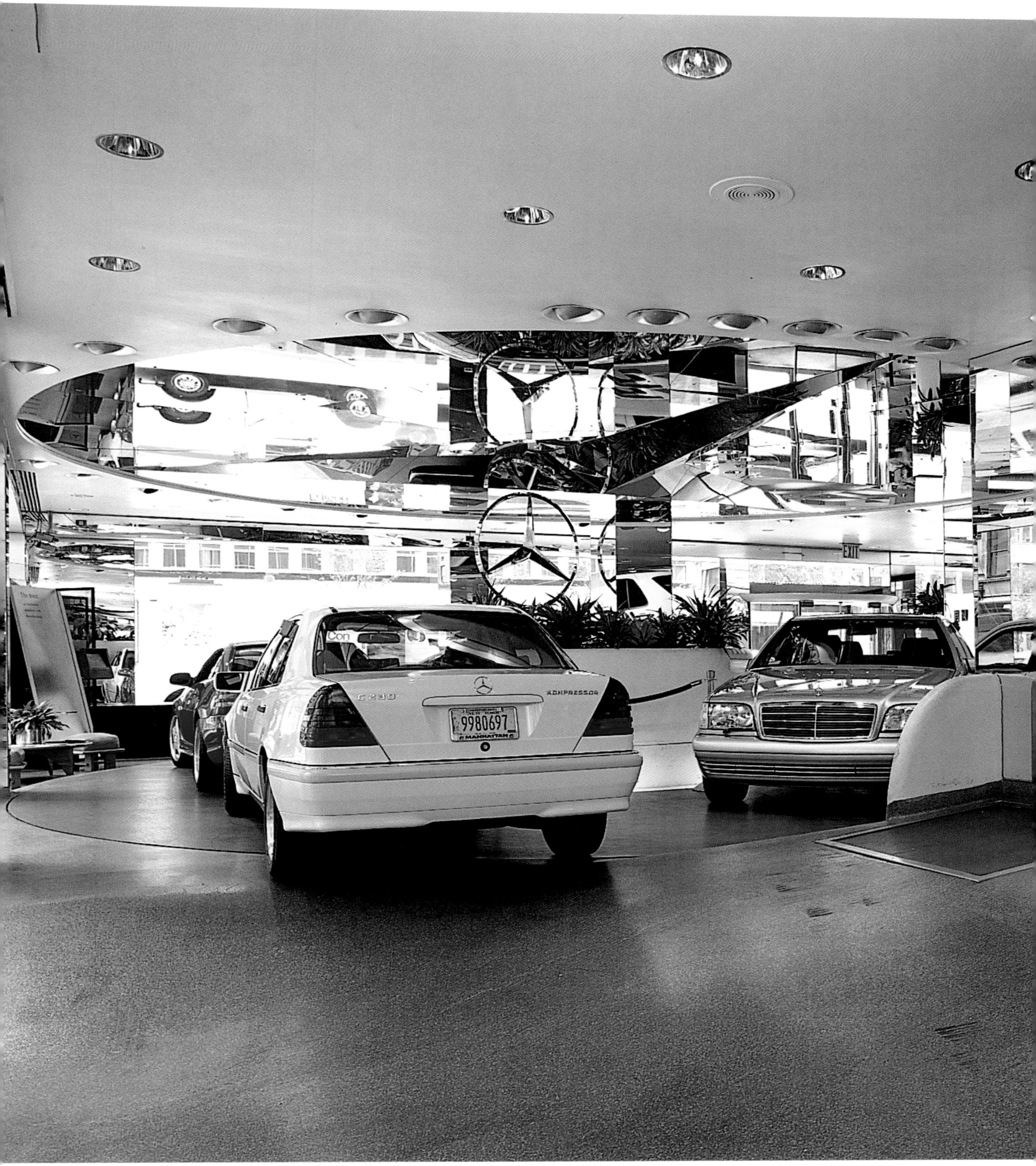
EXIT
C 230
KOMPRESSOR
9980697
MANHATTAN

culture and is undoubtedly one of his great masterpieces. It has been a public park since 1927, when owner Aline Barnsdall gave it to the City of **Los Angeles**. Tours are available.

Holmes, John Haynes

Unitarian of the Community Church in **New York** City. He was a founder and active member of both the National Association for the Advancement of Colored People and the American Civil Liberties Union and was much admired by Wright.

Horner, L. K., House (designed 1908; since demolished) Very similar in plan to Mrs. Thomas **Gale's** residence in **Oak Park**.

Horseshoe Inn, Estes Park (designed 1908; since demolished)

No documentation remains on this building, but it probably resembled the **Como Orchard Summer Colony** project built for Willard Ashton.

House Beautiful

An American journal founded in the winter of 1896–97 to promote the ideals of the **Arts and Crafts Movement**. The journal published the last **Prairie House** designs of Wright's in 1914. In 1953, the magazine famously attacked the **International Style** of architecture.

House Beautiful Book

The second book published by the **Auvergne Press** of which Wright was the chief designer. It was a reprint of a sermon by a close friend of Jenkin **Lloyd Jones**, and it inspired the founding of the journal (see above).

Howe, John H.

Howe entered the **Taliesin** circle in 1932 and soon became a vital member of Wright's drafting-room staff, taking over from Henry **Klumb** as chief draftsman in 1934. He had the rare ability to perceive what Wright wanted from the sketches of outlines and around 90 percent of the drawings from the 1930s that are credited to Wright were actually made by Howe. Another indispensable attribute of Howe's was that he was extremely well organized and made sure that work was finished on time.

Hoyt, D. P., House (1906)

This is another **Prairie** style house in **Illinois** built to a square plan, with a plastered surface, stained wood trim, and an interesting trellised porch.

Hubbard, Elbert

A prominent member of the American **Arts and Crafts Movement** who was co-founder of the **Larkin Company** for which Wright would design one of his most famous buildings. It was from Hubbard that Wright adopted the broad-brimmed hat, the cane, and the swirling cape with which he strode through his life. Hubbard had joined forces with his British counterparts to reject the drab and sober uniformity of Victorian attire.

Hughes, J. Willis, House (1948) Fountainhead

A **Usonian** house with two wings splayed at 120-degrees to each other. Fountainhead was built of poured concrete. The name derives from the pool and fountain off the western bedroom wing. The northern wing ends in a glazed living room and terrace. Serious remedial action had to be taken in the 1980s after many years of neglect but, happily, it is now restored.

Hull House, Chicago, **Illinois**

Hull House was founded as an **Arts and Crafts** social settlement by Jane **Addams** in 1889.

Hunt, Myron

A gifted young architect who worked for Wright when he set up on his own after leaving **Adler & Sullivan**. He eventually left Wright's employ and moved to **Los Angeles** in southern **California**.

Hunt, Stephen M. B., House (1907)

The best built example of **"A Fireproof House"** (as advertised in 1907). It is a square-plan wood and plaster **Prairie** style house, although it was originally planned to be built of the concrete which would have made it fire-proof. Renovation has seen the terraces enclosed but the oak woodwork and the Tiffany brick fireplace have been fully restored.

Hunt, Stephen M. B., Second House (1917)

This single-story house is from American System Ready-cut prefab plans of 1911. It was landscaped by Lloyd Wright.

Hunter, John

Hunter was the associate editor of the *Madison Capital Times* who published the article concerning the exhumation of Wright's body, its cremation, and the removal of his ashes to **Scottsdale**, **Arizona**. This was carried out secretly, with great alacrity by some members of the **Fellowship** and there was a public outcry when Hunter published the story.

Husser, Joseph, House (designed 1899; demolished 1926)

Forerunner of the **Prairie House** and a notable loss. As with the Prairie Houses, with their living quarters above ground level, this building had the basement at ground level with the house rising two stories higher — partly as protection against flooding by nearby Lake Michigan. The furniture, designed by Wright, was saved, and the dining room (complete with table and chairs) was auctioned in 1987 for $1.6 million.

Right: The Hoyt residence, a typical square plan Prairie house. The final cost of this building was around $5,000 and it features a highly unusual entrance directly into the main living room. It has been suggested that this indicates that the design was by some-one else in Wright's office.

Below: The Hunt house.

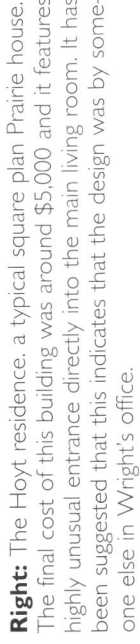

Iber, Frank, House (1956)

A Marshall **Erdman** Company No. 1 Prefab this is an L-plan brick building with a masonry core, painted horizontal board, and batten siding on the bedroom wing.

Idaho

Wright's only work in Idaho is the Archie Boyd **Teater** Studio in Bliss, built above the banks of the Snake River.

Illinois

Illinois was where Wright spent most of his working life and, consequently, the state — especially in Chicago and Oak Park — has more examples of his work than any other. Illinois also boasts many of his most important, and beautiful, designs.

Today, the starting point of any examination of the works of Frank Lloyd Wright is the first extant house of his career: his own house and studio in Oak Park. Built 1889-1909, it is one of 17 of Wright's buildings designated by the **A.I.A.** to be preserved as examples of his architectural contribution to American culture. He set up his own office in Chicago and his first independent

commission after leaving **Adler & Sullivan** was the William H. **Winslow** House in **River Forest,** another of Wright's buildings to be listed by the A.I.A. In fact, including this and his home and studio, there are five listed Wright houses in Illinois, the others being the first

Prairie House, which was built for Ward W. **Willits,** the **Unity Temple** — the first significant American piece of architecture to use poured concrete — and the **Robie** House, which is considered to be Wright's best example of Prairie masonry with its precise Roman brickwork. At the turn of the century Wright's work began to move in the direction of his Prairie style houses, the first of which were those built for Harley **Bradley** and his brother-in-law, Warren **Hickox,** in Kankakee, Illinois. At this time Wright was working with Webster **Tomlinson,** the only partner he ever had, and one of their collaborations was the first of Wright's Prairie style houses to be built in Oak Park — the Frank

Pages 156/157: Aerial view of the Imperial Hotel, Japan.

Above and Right: Examples of Wright's work in Illinois, the Ward Willits House (**above**) and a detail of the Unity Temple (**right**).

the few buildings to survive the great Kanto earthquake of 1923 which leveled everything else around it. On demolition the entrance lobby was moved to Nagoya.

Indiana

Wright's building in Indiana, only five houses, spans five decades. The earliest, the **DeRhodes** House in South Bend, is a **Prairie** House best known for its living room — as is the 1948 **Mossberg** House. The strangest is the "teepee"-like structure of the Richard **Davis** House which derived from a 1920s project.

Ingalls, J. Kibben, House (1909)
This building is the last of Wright's existing work in **River Forest**. It is a typical **Prairie** style house of plastered surface and wood trim.

Ingraham, Elizabeth Wright
Daughter of Wright's son John, an architect in her own right, and chairman of **Unity Chapel** Inc., a family corporation established to restore the chapel and tend the burial grounds.

International Style

Exponents of the International Style — sleek, austere, steel-and-glass edifices — included **Le Corbusier, Mies van der Rohe**, J. J. Oud and Walter **Gropius**. Albert H. Barr, Jr., founder of the Museum of Modern Art in **New York**, is generally accredited with naming the movement.

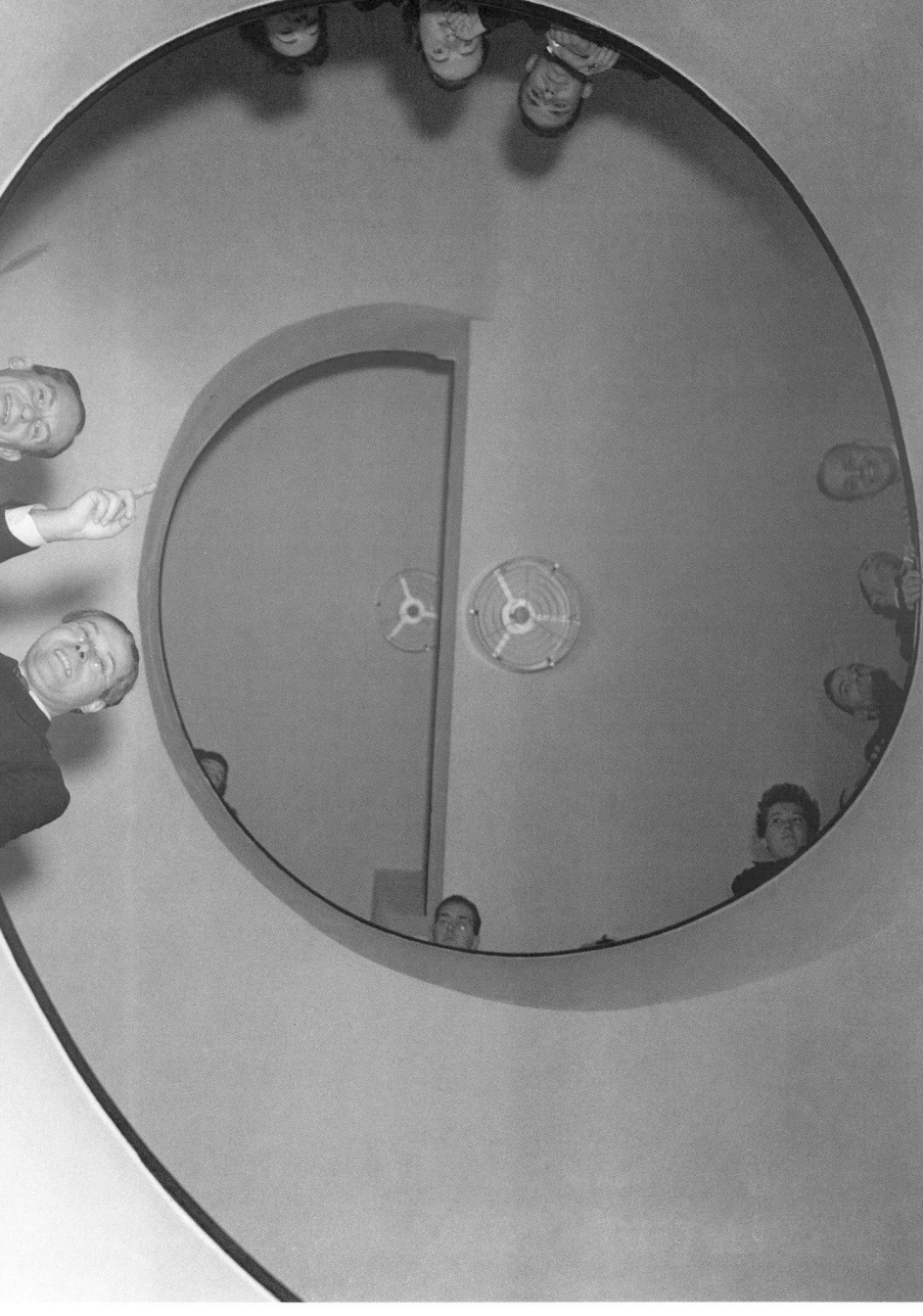

Above: French architect, Le Corbusier.

Above right: The Ingalls house is a compact Prairie structure.

Below right: The Chapel of Notre Dame Haut by Le Corbusier.

Below: Gropius (bottom left) at the Chicago Bauhaus School.

A VISUAL ENCYCLOPEDIA OF FRANK LLOYD WRIGHT 163

Wright variously described the style as an "evil crusade" and a "manifestation of totalitarianism." These attacks led the exponents of the style to the belief that Wright should be relegated to the background.

Iowa

Wright designed two buildings in Iowa before he left for Europe with Mamah **Cheney**. The first — the **Stockman** House — was one of the houses which developed from his article **"A Fireproof House for $5000"** that was published in the *Ladies' Home Journal* in April 1907. A year later, in Mason City, he started work on the **City National Bank and Hotel**, a job he left to be finished by William **Drummond**. It would be nearly 40 years before he saw another of his designs built in Iowa, a time gap caused by the opprobrium surrounding his personal life, the **Great Depression**, and the building restrictions enforced during the Second World War. Indeed, it would not be until 1950 that the **Walter** House, designed in 1945, could be lived in. His other buildings in Iowa are all private residences, the construction of the final few taking place after Wright's death in 1959.

Irving, E. P. House (1909)
This house had as many as three designers. It has been suggested that it is too tall to be a true Wright design.

Italy

It was in 1909-10, while Wright was designing a typical Tuscan house in **Fiesole** near Florence, that his imagination seems to have been galvanized and brought to bear on the challenge of designing a house for himself that would express everything that he thought and believed in — the idea of **Taliesin**. Over 40 years later, in May 1951, the exhibition **"Sixty Years of Living Architecture"** was an immediate success when it opened in Florence, and this success led to Wright's designs for the **Masieri Memorial**.

Right and Pages 166 and 167: Interior of the Walter residence in Iowa. This house is a typical Wright dwelling and blends with the natural verdant Iowa environment. As can be seen this landscape is reflected in the residence and windowed walls allow the scenery to flow into the house.

Jackson, Arnold, House (1957) Skyview

A Marshall **Erdman** Company No. I Prefab, this house was originally at 2909 West Beltway and was moved in 1985. Dr. Jackson was Wright's doctor in the 1950s. It is an L-plan brick building with a masonry core, painted horizontal board, and batten siding on the bedroom wing.

Jackson, Harold

Miriam Noel Wright's Chicago attorney at the time of her acrimonious divorce from Wright. The lawyer was also acting for Olgivanna's divorced husband **Hinzenberg** over fears that their daughter (Svetlana) was to be taken out of the country.

Jacobs, Herbert and Katherine

Herbert Jacobs was a **Wisconsin** journalist whose daughter would become an apprentice at **Taliesin**. The house that Wright built for the Jacobs' was so full of trend-setting ideas that Katherine wrote a book about it. They were so besieged by visitors that Herbert decided to give tours at 50 cents a time. He calculated that by

the time that they sold the house this modest charge would pay back the architect's fees. Later, when the Jacobs wanted a larger house, they were to be Wright's guinea pigs for his latest experiment — the **solar hemicycle**.

Jacobs, Herbert, First House (1936)

Considered — despite the claims of the M. E. **Willey** House — to be the first **Usonian** house. Designed to an L-plan, the building materials were typical of future Usonian houses: brick and redwood.

Jacobs, Herbert, Second House (1944)

A two-story solar hemicycle with its back set into the ground (entry is via a tunnel through a wall of earth.) It has a glass facade opening onto a sunken terrace.

Pages 168/169: The Johnson's Wax complex of buildings.

Above and Right: The first Jacobs house.

The house Wright built for Herbert Jacobs in 1956 is the first of the Usonian houses. Internally the red brick and three-inch redwood battens create a warm appearance.

Japan

Wright's interest in **Japanese art** was kindled in the 1890s and several authorities claim to see a connection between the Japanese temple that Wright saw at the World's Colombian Exposition of 1893 and some of his own buildings. When Wright lost his appetite for work in 1905 he left for a three-month stay in Japan and returned invigorated. Wright returned to Japan in 1913, staying for six months, while he formulated preliminary plans for the **Imperial Hotel**. The completed hotel was one of Wright's favorite buildings and he boasted about it all his life. He was to make frequent visits to Japan, a country that he loved, and spent the bulk of his time there from 1919 to 1922.

Japanese Architecture

After the Philadelphia Centennial Exposition of 1876, where Japanese pavilions had been built, and especially after publication of the first English-language book on Japanese architecture in 1886, American architects focused their attention on this aspect of Japanese culture. For Americans, including Wright, who were oriented toward the **Arts and Crafts Movement, Japan** offered "the example of an indigenous culture that embodied the organic quality they found in the middle ages." (Richard Guy Wilson).

Japanese Art

Wright was passionately interested in the subject of Japanese prints and sometimes dealt in them when times were hard — he would talk endlessly about them. His original collection was sold to pay off debts.

Jekyll, Gertrude

The English landscape architect, a contemporary of Wright's, was leading a revolution in landscaping in England, just as he was in architecture in America. Wright was keenly aware of her work and a great admirer.

Jenny, William Le Baron

Sullivan received some firsthand instruction in "Chicago construction" at the office of William Le Baron Jenny, an architect-engineer and leading figure in the design of the structural iron skeleton as well as the invention of the **"floating foundation"** that would answer the acute problems caused by Chicago's muddy soils. These techniques were put to good use in the construction of Wright's **Imperial Hotel**.

The Jacobs second house is the first of Wright's solar hemicycles. Laid out in circular segments, each of six degrees, in front of its glassed facade is a private open terrace.

Jensen, Jens
A distinguished landscape architect whose help Wright solicited when formulating his ideas of the Fellowship at **Taliesin** — Wright wanted him to run the school. Jensen was Wright's personal secretary until 1933 when he was replaced by Gene **Masselink.**

Johnson, A. P., House (1905)
A symmetrical tongue-and-groove-sided **Prairie** style house which was extensively restored in the 1970s. It retains the original Roman brick fireplace and leaded windows.

Johnson, Albert
An uninspiring businessman whom everyone at **Taliesin** was eager to please in 1924 because he was about to commission Wright to design a **skyscraper** for the National Life Insurance Company in Chicago — and Frank needed the work!

Johnson, Herbert F. ("Hib")
Hib was the grandson of the founder of Johnson's Wax and the man who commissioned Wright to design a new administration building for his Racine, **Wisconsin,** company, S. C. Johnson & Sons. The two men, after a stormy start to their relationship, became great friends. After Johnson's second wife, Jane, died he married the actress Irene **Purcell** and brought her to live at **Wingspread** — the house that Wright had designed for him.

Johnson, Herbert F., House (1937) Wingspread
Like the **Hollyhock House,** this is another of Wright's large scale designs with a central core and four wings leading off — each separating a set of functions from the others: so, one contains the master bedrooms, the others guest and children's rooms, the services, and garages. This pinwheel plan, a variant of the cruciform, extends from a central three-story high octagon. The architect himself called the Johnson House the "last of the **Prairie Houses**" and considered it to be his best and most expensive house to date.

Johnson, Jane Roach
Hib **Johnson** (see above) divorced his first wife when his first-born, Samuel C. **Johnson,** was six years old and married Jane Roach, who already had two sons of her own. This led Hib to commission Wright to build him a large house — **Wingspread** — which would be the biggest private residence that Wright ever built. Jane expressed reservations about the house after a spell in hospital but Wright typically dismissed them. She died of alcoholism before the house was completed.

Johnson, Karen, House (1954)
Karen Johnson was the daughter of the Johnson Wax company owner, H. F. Johnson. Her house saw additions in 1961 by John H. **Howe.**

Johnson, Philip
An early collector of modern art, Johnson was an intellectual and a wealthy connoisseur who was fascinated by the new European modernists as exemplified by work at the **Bauhaus.** Johnson persuaded Wright to exhibit at the first exhibition of modern architecture to feature the **International Style** at the museum of Modern Art in New York. When Wright pulled out at the last minute, Johnson is credited with quipping that Wright was "America's greatest nineteenth century architect." Johnson himself went on to become one of America's top architects.

Johnson, Samuel C.
The first-born son of Hib **Johnson.** Regarding the day that the **Johnson Administration Building** opened Samuel wrote, "We achieved international attention because that building represented and symbolized the quality of everything we did . . ."

Above right: Karen Johnson house. This brick house has a central atrium dominated by a two-story section.

Below right and Below: Herbert Johnson's Wingspread.

Pages 180/181: Further views of Wright's domestic masterpiece, Wingspread.

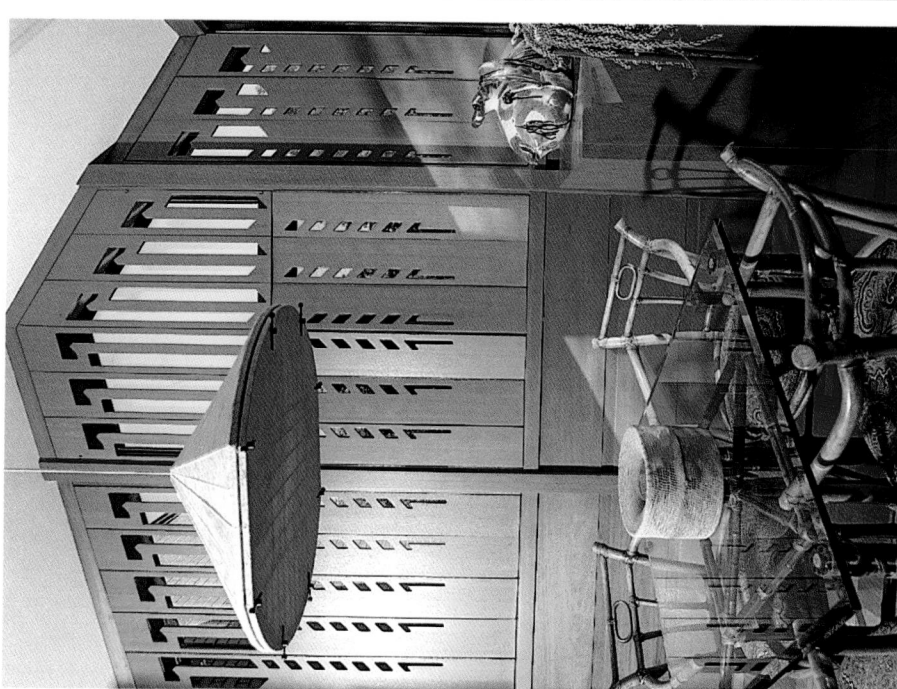

Further views of Wingspread, including the central octagon that is three stories high (**right**). Wright was particularly pleased with the building as many thought the site to be unpromising until the house was finished.

Johnson Administration Building (1936) and Research Tower (1944)

The Administration Building and the Tower have been designated by the **A.I.A.** as two of the 17 buildings designed by Wright to be retained as supreme examples of his architectural contribution to American culture. The main offices were completed in 1939 and have columns capable of supporting six times the weight imposed on them. Both of the buildings are constructed from brick and tubular glass — not panes. The tower is totally enclosed. Guided tours are available.

Johnson & Son Wax Company Administration Center (1936-50)

This construction was based on forms borrowed from nature, and the intentions were clearly romantic and intensely personal to Wright. This building contains many unusual and innovative features, the best known being the slender, mushroom columns in the central hypostyle

Panoramic views of the Johnson's Wax buildings. The brick and glass Administration Building and the Research Tower are now national landmarks.

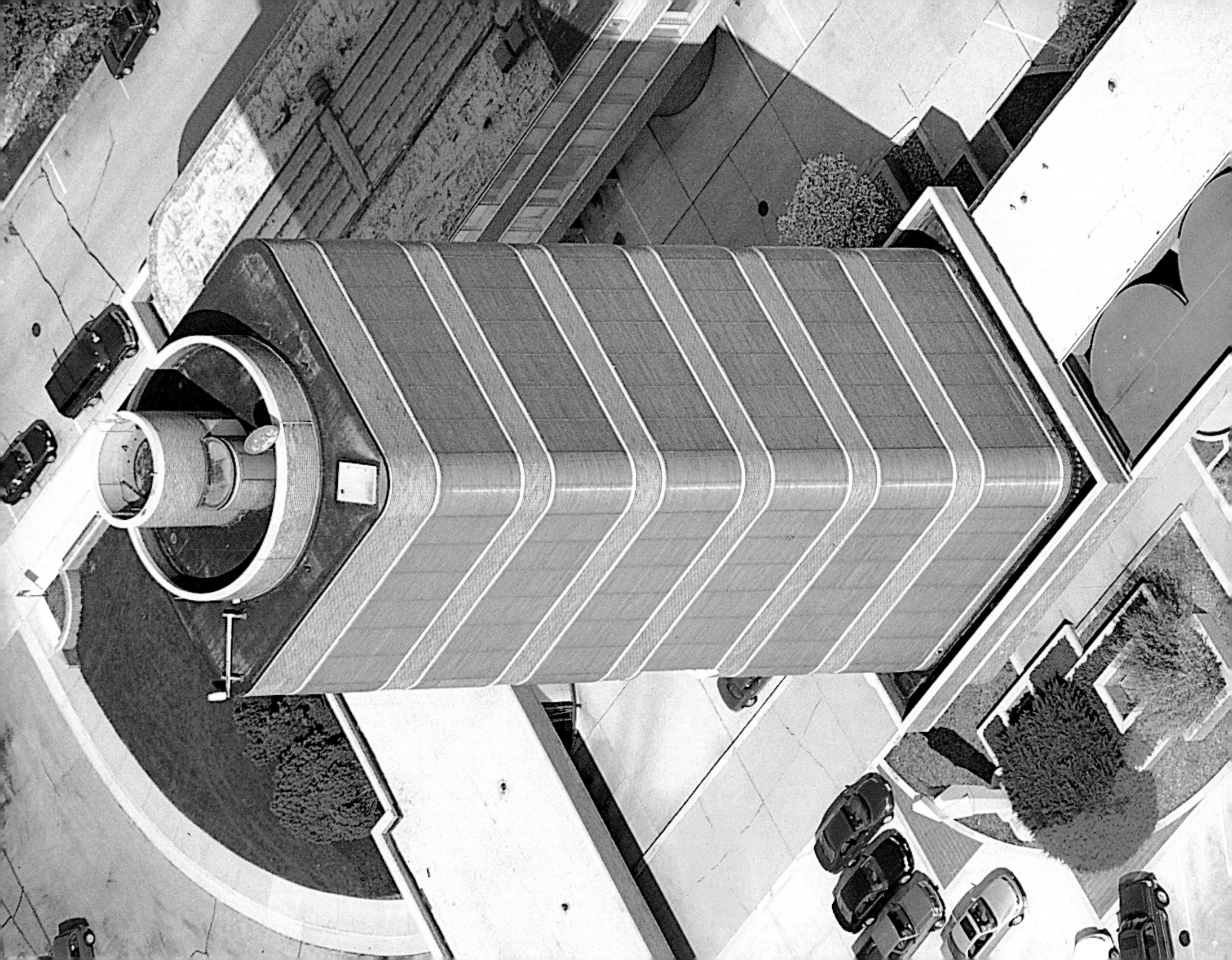

hall. The use of lighting tubes in horizontal bands, set in conjunction with a brick facing to admit light during the day and illumination at night, provides a brilliant warmth to the interior. This building is generally recognized as one of the most remarkable structures built in the inter-war period.

Jones, Anthony
A former director of the Glasgow School of Art who became director of the Art Institute of Chicago art school and author of a book about the Welsh chapel.

Jones, Fred B., House (1900) Penwern
Wright built the house, a gate lodge, a barn with stables, and a boathouse. The exterior is of board and batten siding, while the inside features a large Roman brick fireplace. The living room has a staircase leading to a balcony which overlooks it and other rooms. It has distinctive arches on the front veranda and at the *porte-cochère*. This is the most extensive of the **Lake Delavan Projects.**

Jones, Owen
Owen Jones's *The Grammar of Ornament* was the first book that Wright went to in his search for mastery of drawing, ornamentation, and design while working for Joseph **Silsbee.** The book reflected the central concepts of the **Aesthetic Movement,** and Jones espoused the notion that what made the ornamental designs of previous periods so unique was that they somehow reflected the needs and values of their times.

Jones, Richard Lloyd, House (1929) Westhope
Constructed from glass and **textile block,** the building is two stories high for one third of the plan, and encloses a raised inner courtyard with pool.

Juvenile Cultural Study Center (1957)
The only design by Wright to be built in the **Corbin Education Center.**

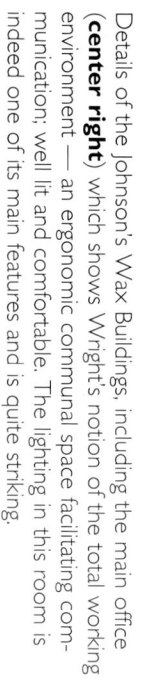

Details of the Johnson's Wax Buildings, including the main office **(center right)** which shows Wright's notion of the total working environment — an ergonomic communal space facilitating communication; well lit and comfortable. The lighting in this room is indeed one of its main features and is quite striking.

Kahn, Ely Jacques
Architect in whose office Alyn **Rand** was working in order to learn about architecture first hand. Alyn Rand made plans to meet Wright through introductions from Kahn.

Kahn, Louis
The American architect most influenced by **Le Corbusier** and an associate of Alyn **Rand**.

Kahn Lectures (1930 — Princeton University)
In the late spring of 1930, Wright was invited to give the famous Kahn Lectures on art, archaeology, and architecture at **Princeton** (published in book form the following year) and with that went the privilege of mounting an exhibition of his work that would then travel around the country. It was Wright's volume of Princeton lectures that so impressed Dr. and Mrs. **Hanna**.

Kaim, Lydia
A member of staff at the elegant nineteenth century **New York** town house where Wright received the gold medal for architecture from the **American Academy of Arts and Letters**. Although Wright was in his 80s, she was quoted as saying "how wonderful he looked."

Kalil, Toufic H., House (1955)
This **Usonian automatic** house is built to an L-plan, extended to a T with the addition of a carport.

Kansas
Examples of Wright's work in Kansas span 40 years. The state can boast a substantial residence in the form of the Henry **Allen** house, and an impressively utilitarian university building — the **Juvenile Cultural Study Center** at the Wichita State University.

Pages 188/189: The famous Kaufmann house — Fallingwater.

Above: Kansas City Community Christian Church.

Right, above and below: The Kalil residence. This building has no large windows; instead light is admitted throught the pierced blocks.

Kansas City Community Christian Church

(1940)

There were problems during the construction of the church, generally caused by differences of opinion between the client and Wright, who wanted to use pressure-sprayed concrete. The "light-towers" were blacked out during wartime, but can still be seen working. Open to the public, guided tours are available by appointment.

THE COMMUNITY CHRISTIAN CHURCH

CHAPEL

The Kansas City Community Christian Church. Due to the input of conservative local "experts," who were unfortunately allowed the final say over this building, there is little resemblance to

Wright's original drawings and the ambitious plans of Rev. Dr. Burris Jenkins. However, the light towers (**far left**) survived the restructuring of the plans and are still in working order today.

Karfik, Vladimir

A young Czech architect who worked for Wright during the architect's hard times following the **Great Depression**. Karfik remembers accompanying the Wrights to the Czechoslovak Art Shop in Chicago to buy some Yugoslavian clothes for Olgivanna.

Karl Kundert Medical Clinic (1955)

Pierced wood panels with glass inset (like those used on the 1955 Randall **Fawcett** House) make up the clerestory and admit patterned light. Wright wanted to build in **textile blocks** but planning laws forbade this.

Kassler, Elizabeth

An early apprentice at **Taliesin** who was invited to stay at the Fellowship while she was experiencing a traumatic divorce. Wright's generosity and understanding was still deeply moving to her 40 years later.

Kaufmann, Edgar J.

The Pennsylvanian department store owner was one of Wright's most important clients. He commissioned Wright for both his private domain, **Fallingwater**, and his public working environment in the luxuriously appointed **Kaufmann Office**. Kaufmann's decision to make Wright "his" architect in 1935 came at a fortuitous time for Frank as his former patron, Darwin D. **Martin**, died in the same year.

Kaufmann, Edgar J. Sr., House (1935) Fallingwater

In 1935, Wright further developed his philosophy of **organic architecture** with Fallingwater. An extraordinary cantilevered house in an idyllic setting, it is based on forms borrowed from nature and the intentions were clearly romantic. The house is boldly cantilevered over a waterfall, its glass walls permitting interior and exterior to mingle without detracting from the emphatically horizontal composition of the suspended concrete slabs. The feeling of nature is continued internally by carrying the character of the stonework in floors and walls in opposition to the trees which can be seen surrounding the building through the almost uninterrupted glass. The inventiveness that Wright showed in all aspects of the design ensures that Fallingwater occupies a unique place in modern architectural history.

Kaufmann, Edgar J. Sr., Office (1937; since removed from situ)

This office for the Kaufmann Department Store was reassembled in London, England, in the Victoria and Albert Museum. Wright's chairs and other furniture are complemented in the museum display by a cypress plywood mural in relief.

Fallingwater is a luxurious and beautiful testimony to Wright's genius. The stone so evident in its construction is known as Pottsville sandstone.

Kaufmann, Edgar J. Jr.

An early apprentice at **Taliesin**, the son of wealthy Pittsburgh department store owner Edgar Sr. He was a persuasive advocate for Wright and his father soon wrote to ask whether he would be interested in collaborating on a number of civic projects for Pittsburgh that were being planned at the end of 1934. To Wright's disappointment, Kaufmann Jr. did not stay at Taliesin long before he left to join his father's business.

Kaufmann, Liliane

Edgar J. Sr.'s wife who committed suicide with a rifle a short distance from **Fallingwater**.

Kentucky

Wright's only work in Kentucky is said to have been secured while he was in Europe with Mamah **Cheney**, when they met Presbyterian minister Jessie **Ziegler**. The Ziegler house is a two-story **Prairie** style structure.

Key, Ellen
The Swedish feminist whose translated writings, especially those having to do with free love and "The Woman Movement," were published by Frank and Mamah **Cheney** in 1913.

Keys, Thomas E., House (1950)
A single-story house built from **exposed concrete block** with pine wood-trim. The 1971 additions enlarged the living room and converted the former carport into an *en suite* guest room.

Kier, William F., House (1915)
Located in the **Ravine Bluffs Development**. This square-plan house has a hipped roof and its porch has been modified.

Kimball, Fiske
Curator at the Philadelphia Museum of Art who, in his history of architecture (*American Architecture, 1928*) had referred to Wright and complained about the shameful neglect of this giant in the field.

Kingswood School for Girls
Saarinen's school, built on the **Cranbrook** campus from 1929 to 1931, is generally acknowledged to have been inspired by the **Prairie** style buildings that Wright had built in **Oak Park** a quarter of a century before. It is also reminiscent of Wright's design of **Hillside** from 1903.

Kinney, Patrick, House (1951)
This single-story house was built on triangular modules with Kinney acting as his own contractor. A stone and wood building detached from the main structure, the northeast wing, was added in 1964.

Kinney, Sterling, House (1957)
Built to a T-plan with a separate porch which forms an L around the north and west facades of a sunken living room. The main building material is red brick.

Kissam, Lute F., House (1915)
Located in the **Ravine Bluffs Development**. The main square of the house has an open porch attached.

Klumb, Henry
Sometime chief draftsman for Wright, a native of Cologne, **Germany**, Klumb joined the Fellowship early in 1929 and worked on **San Marcos** and then supervised a traveling exhibition that went to Amsterdam, Berlin, Stuttgart, Antwerp, and Brussels. It was the first such review of Wright's work since 1909. Klumb went on to have a major career as an architect in Puerto Rico.

Kraus, Russell W. M., House (1951)
A **Usonian** house with interesting art-glass manufactured by the owner. There is both a lanai — a veranda — and a substantial walled terrace.

Krynska, Madame
Miriam Noel **Wright**'s Russian friend to whom she claimed Wright was attracted. In a tempestuous incident it appears that Miriam pulled a gun and threatened to kill Madame Krynska or herself or both, and Frank had to wrestle the weapon from her.

Kundert Medical Clinic (1955)
Commissioned by two doctors — Kundert and Fogo who knew of Wright as they had come from La Crosse, **Wisconsin**, and **Richland Center** respectively — the design of this clinic of Ophthalmology is based on **Usonian** principles. It is open during working hours.

Left: The William F. Kier house. A version of the "Fireproof house for $5,000."

Right: A picturesque view of the idyllic Fallingwater. The house appears to be an organic extension of its surroundings and is surely one of the most beautiful private homes in the world.

Ladies' Home Journal

It was through Wright's drawings in the journal that he became known nationally at the end of the nineteenth century. Particularly significant was his design "A Home in Prairie Town," published in 1901.

La Follette, Philip F.

In 1927, Wright engaged La Follette, member of a prominent **Wisconsin** family, as his lawyer in dealings with the Bank of Wisconsin, when it looked as though he might lose **Taliesin**. La Follette later went on to serve two terms as Governor of Wisconsin.

Lafond, Dr. Ed, House (1960)
An **Erdman Prefab No. 1**.

La Jolla, California

In 1928, Wright and Olgivanna moved to La Jolla and, as 1929 began, Wright was commissioned by the Rosenwald Foundation to design one of the schoolhouses that this philanthropic organization was building for black children in the town.

Lamberson, Jack, House (1948)

A spectacular brick and redwood single-story building near the **Alsop** House. A notable feature is the big triangular carport.

Lamp, Robert M.

Wright's boyhood friend who had been crippled by polio. Their friendship went on into adulthood, and Frank designed a small, square, brick house with its own roof garden, in **Madison**, especially suited to Robie's physical needs.

Lamp, Robert M., House (designed 1893; since demolished)

Though living in **Oak Park** at the time, Wright maintained contact with the area around Madison, his birthplace. This house was built for a boyhood friend.

Pages 198/199: Interior of the Lovness house.

Above, Right, and Pages 202 and 203: Details from the *Ladies' Home Journal* showing Wright's article "A Home in Prairie Town."

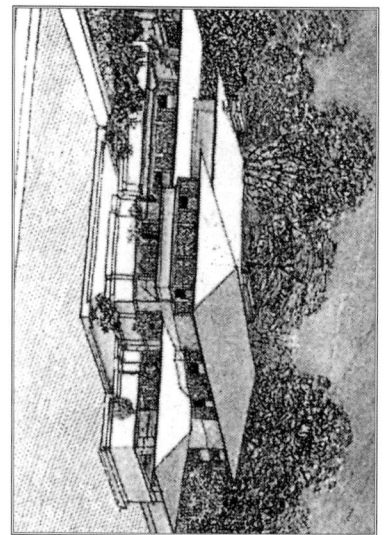

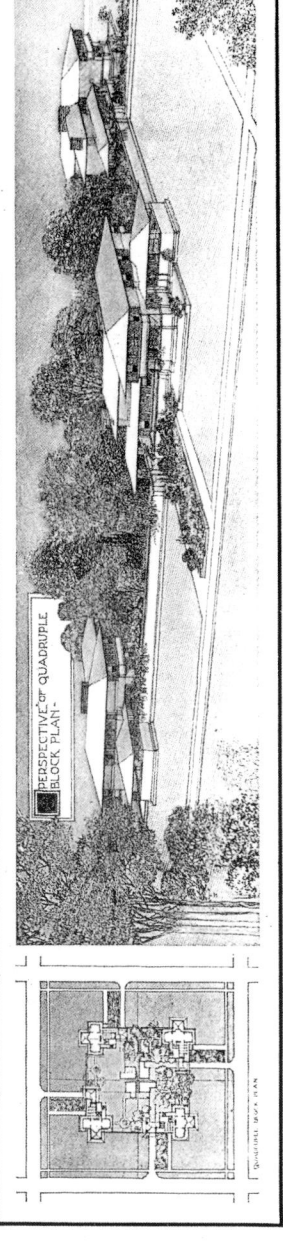

PERSPECTIVE OF QUADRUPLE BLOCK PLAN

A Home in a Prairie Town

BY FRANK LLOYD WRIGHT

This is the Fifth Design in the Journal's New Series of Model Suburban Houses Which Can be Built at Moderate Cost

A CITY man going to the country puts too much in his house and too little in his ground. He drags after him the fifty-foot lot, soon the twenty-five-foot lot, finally the party wall; and the home-maker who fully appreciates the advantages which he came to the country to secure feels himself impelled to move on.

It seems a waste of energy to plan a house happhazard, to hit or miss an already distorted condition, so this partial solution of a city man's country home on the prairie begins at the beginning and assumes four houses to the block of four hundred feet square as the minimum of ground for the basis of his prairie community.

The block plan to the left, at the top of the page, shows an arrangement of the four houses that secures breadth and prospect to the community as a whole, and absolute privacy both as regards each to the community, and each to each of the four.

T HE perspective view shows the handling of the group at the centre of the block, with its foil of simple lawn, omitting the foliage of curb parkways to better show the scheme, retaining the same house in the four locations merely to afford an idea of the unity of the various elevations. In practice the houses would differ distinctly, though based upon a similar plan.

The ground plan, which is intended to explain itself, is arranged to offer the least resistance to a simple mode of living, in keeping with a high ideal of the family life together. It is arranged, too, with a certain well-established order that enables free use without the sense of confusion felt in five out of seven houses which people really use.

The exterior recognizes the influence of the prairie, is firmly and broadly associated with the site, and makes a feature of its quiet level. The low terraces

and broad eaves are desi[gn]ed to accentuate that quiet level and complete the h[armo]nious relationship. The curbs of the terraces an[d fi]nal inclosures for extremely informal masses of [fol]iage and bloom should be worked in cement with the walks and drives.

Cement on metal lath is suggested for the exterior covering throughout, because it is simple, and, as now understood, durable and cheap.

The cost of this house with interior as specified and cement construction would be seven thousand dollars:

Masonry, Cement and Plaster	$2800.00
Carpentry	3100.00
Plumbing	400.00
Painting and Glass	325.00
Heating — combination (hot water)	345.00
Total	$6970.00

I N A HOUSE of this character the upper reach and gallery of the central living-room is decidedly a luxury. Two bedrooms may take its place, as suggested by the second-floor plan. The gallery feature is, nevertheless, a temptation because of the happy sense of variety and depth it lends to the composition of the interior, and the sunlight it gains from above to relieve the shadow of the porch. The details are better grasped by a study of the drawings. The interior section in perspective shows the gallery, as indicated by dotted lines on the floor plan of the living-room.

The second-floor plan disregards this feature and is arranged for a larger family. Where three bedrooms would suffice the gallery would be practicable, and two large and two small bedrooms with the gallery might be had by rearranging servants' rooms and baths.

The interior is plastered throughout with sand finish and trimmed all through with flat bands of Georgia pine, smaller back bands following the base and casings. This Georgia pine should be selected from straight grain for stiles, rails and running members, and from figured grain for panels and wide surfaces.

All the wood should be shellacked once and waxed, and the plaster should be stained with thin, pure color in water and glue.

EDITOR'S NOTE — As a guarantee that the plan of this house is practicable, and that the estimates for cost are conservative, the architect is ready to accept the commission for preparing the working plans and specifications for this house to cost Seven Thousand Dollars, providing that the building site selected is within reasonable distance of a base of supplies where material and labor may be had at the standard market rates.

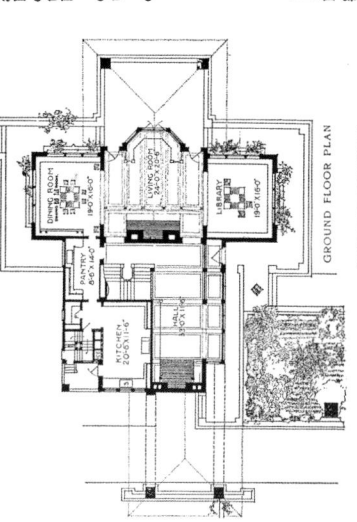

GROUND FLOOR PLAN

SECOND FLOOR PLAN

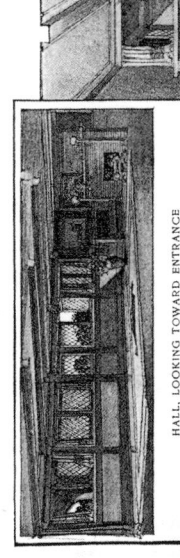

HALL, LOOKING TOWARD ENTRANCE

THE LIBRARY

THE DINING-ROOM

LIVING-ROOM AND GALLERY

INTERIOR VIEW OF THE FIRST FLOOR OF THIS HOUSE

Lamp, Robert M., House (1904)
Built for an old friend and overlooking **Madison**'s lakes, this is a simple rectangular brick **Prairie House**. The third story has been enclosed.

Landon, Alfred M.
From **Kansas**, Landon was a candidate for the Republican presidential nomination to run against Roosevelt. Richard **Lloyd Jones** was one of the organizers of the Grass Roots Republican convention (1935) in **Springfield, Illinois**, and ran Landon's pre-convention campaign.

Larkin, John D.
Founder of the Larkin Company in Buffalo, **New York**.

Larkin Company Administration Building
(designed 1903; demolished 1949–50)
Wright got this job through his friendship with William E. **Martin**, from **Oak Park**, whose brother, Darwin D. **Martin**, worked with Larkin. This strikingly innovative structure was one of the finest buildings of Wright's early period and was notable for its monolithic structure and large atrium. The Larkin building also used plate glass and air conditioning — a first in commercial buildings. For the internal spatial distribution Wright introduced a central court rising to the full height of the building, with side gallery offices illuminated both from the central court and from the side windows between the brick piers. The austere exterior was enlivened with sculpture by Wright's regular collaborator, Richard **Bock**. This building was of considerable architectural importance and its destruction in 1949 was a significant loss to the history of the developing modern movement.

Larson, Alfred
Grandfather of Herbert **Fritz** who had been a farmer-mason from Norway and had built most of **Taliesin**.

Laurent, Ken, House (1949)
This is a single-story **Usonian** solar hemicycle constructed from common brick and cypress. The plan incorporates special access facilities for the disabled owner, Ken Laurent.

Lautner, John
A **Taliesin Fellowship** apprentice who witnessed the historic first pencil drawings of **Fallingwater** in 1935. In 1938, he wrote an angry letter to Henry Russell **Hitchcock**, the architectural historian, after he had referred to Wright in the past tense.

Above: The Robert M. Lamp house. The third story is a later addition (not by Wright) and the original brick has been painted over in white. These changes have done little to augment the aesthetics of this building.

Above right, Below, and Right: The Kenneth Laurent house. The living room opens out onto a slope which leads down to Spring Creek.

Lazovich, Ivan
The father of Olgivanna Lloyd **Wright,** he was chief justice of the tiny principality of Montenegro.

Lazovich, Militza
Mother of Olgivanna and wife of Ivan (see above). She was the daughter of a famous general, a man of almost legendary courage, who had been commander in chief of the Montenegrin army.

Lazovich, Olgivanna (see Olgivanna Lloyd **Wright**)

Lazovich, Sophie
"Aunt Sophie" was the wife of Olgivanna's brother Vladimir (see below). The couple lived with the Wrights after the Second World War.

Lazovich, Vladimir
"Uncle Vlad" was the brother of Olgivanna; he and his wife Sophie lived with the Wrights after the Second World War.

Leerdam Glass-fabriek
At the beginning of 1929, Wright signed a life contract with the Leerdam Glass-fabriek of Holland to design on a royalty basis.

Lemmon, Lawrence C.
Larry Lemmon, a practicing landscape architect with several years' experience, found himself out of work in 1937, with a wife and baby to support, and applied for a job as cook at **Taliesin.** His application was accepted and he became a Taliesin apprentice. Lemmon was on the first expedition to build **Taliesin West.**

Levin, Robert, House (designed 1948; extended 1960)
A single-story house built with **textile blocks** and cypress. There is a later (1960) addition by John H. **Howe** of the **Taliesin Associated Architects,** who was also the construction supervisor of the other Wright homes at **Parkwyn Village.**

Lewis, George, House (1952)
This two-story residence is Wright's only private house to be built in **Florida.** The lower story of the hemicycle building is of **exposed concrete block** and the upper is wood-sheathed.

Lewis, Lloyd and Katherine
An old friend of Wright's, he met the architect in 1918 in Chicago while he was a sportswriter for the *Chicago Daily News* (he later became its editor.) During Wright's

years of crisis he hired Lewis to keep his name *out of the* newspapers. Lewis and his wife Katherine's friendship with Wright was stretched to breaking point over troubles in the construction of the house that they commissioned him to build but eventually these problems were resolved.

Lewis, Lloyd, House (1939)

A two-story building with the living room and a balcony above the ground level bedroom wing and entrance. The building is constructed from brick and cypress. A poultry shed built to Wright's 1943 design was added later.

Lilien, Marya

Professor Marya Lilien came to know Wright in the 1930s when she was an apprentice at **Taliesin**. She was exiled from Poland and came to regard Taliesin as her second home.

Lindblom, David

A landscape gardener who sat down to lunch at **Taliesin** on the day of the **murders**. He died of burns and axe wounds.

Lindholm, R. W., Service Station (1957)

Wright's only built service station, it is constructed from painted cement block with a terne metal roof and cantilevered canopy. Open during working hours. Tours available by appointment.

Lindholm, R. W., House (1952)

Built before his service station, the Lindholm house has a T-plan that opens the bedrooms and living room to the west. It is constructed from painted **exposed concrete block** and wood-trim.

The Lindholm Service Station. Wright utilized his design for the "Broadacre City Standardized Overhead Service Station" for this building, although contrary to the design the actual pumps here are on the ground rather than overhead.

Little, Francis W.
A former client of Wright, and a dedicated collector of Japanese prints, Frank borrowed $10,000 from Little to buy the American rights to the **Wasmuth Portfolios.** Little held a portfolio of Wright's Japanese prints as collateral.

Little, Francis W., House (1902)
Wright was commissioned to design a brick T-plan house with a separate, spacious, stable. The house was enlarged in 1909 when additions elongated the original T-plan. The porch has subsequently been enclosed with glass.

Little, Francis W., Second House (designed 1912; demolished 1972) Northome
This house boasted the most spacious interior of Wright's **Prairie** period with its 55-foot living room. At the time of the building's demolition, various museums removed sections for later reconstruction. The living room was reconstructed at the Metropolitan Museum of Art (**New York** City), while the library was reconstructed at the Allentown Art Museum (Pennsylvania). This was Wright's first building in **Minnesota.**

Lloyd Jones, Enos
Born in 1853, the youngest son of Richard **Lloyd Jones** and Mary Thomas, uncle of Frank Lloyd Wright. Enos died in 1942 at the age of 88.

Lloyd Jones, Georgia Haydn
Wife of Frank Lloyd Wright's cousin Richard **Lloyd Jones,** they had three children Richard, Jenkin, and Florence.

Lloyd Jones, James
Born in 1850, the son of Richard **Lloyd Jones** and Mary Thomas, he was Frank Lloyd Wright's favorite uncle. Frank got to know his cousins when he and his sister spent the summers on his uncle's farm in **The Valley** in **Spring Green.** It was here that Frank found an interest in nature and the feel of the land.

Views of the first Francis Little house in Peoria, Illinois. The house contains a large amount of beautiful gold-tinted art glass (as can be seen in the skylights **right.**) The design of the building has proved so successful that little upkeep has been required.

Lloyd Jones, Jenkin

Born in Llanwenog, Wales, in 1843, Frank Lloyd Wright's uncle, the Reverend Jenkin Lloyd Jones, "Our Jenkin," was a famous Unitarian minister in Chicago. It was while his uncle was pastor of All Souls' Church in Chicago that Wright met the notable architect Joseph Lyman **Silsbee** who was working on a new building for the Church. The role that Jenkin Lloyd Jones played in Wright's life cannot be ignored. "Uncle Jenk" provided Frank with a positive example of what a bold and militant radical can accomplish when his or her reformist zeal is channeled into constructive directions. A great many of Jenkin's beliefs, which were topics of debate around the dinner table when Frank was an adolescent, would find their echoes in the architect's own speeches in later years.

Lloyd Jones, Jennie (Jane)

Jennie was born in 1848, Wright's maternal aunt for whom, with her sister Nell, he designed and built the **Romeo and Juliet Windmill** in **Spring Green, Wisconsin**. Jennie and her sister Nell were always referred to as the "Aunts."

Lloyd Jones, John

Born in Llanwenog, Wales, in 1832. The second son of Richard **Lloyd Jones** and Mary Thomas and uncle of Frank Lloyd Wright.

Lloyd Jones, Margaret

Born in Llanwenog, Wales, 1835. Eldest daughter of Richard **Lloyd Jones** and Mary Thomas, and aunt of Frank Lloyd Wright.

Lloyd Jones, Mary

Born in Llanwenog, Wales, 1836. Second daughter of Richard **Lloyd Jones** and Mary Thomas, and aunt of Frank Lloyd Wright.

Lloyd Jones, Mary Thomas

"Ein Mam," the wife of Richard **Lloyd Jones** was Wright's maternal grandmother, "Mallie," the mother of 11 children. She died in 1870 when Frank was three years old.

Lloyd Jones, Nanny

Born in Llanwenog, Wales, 1840. Daughter of Richard **Lloyd Jones** and Mary Thomas, she died at the age of three as the family was crossing the United States on their emigration from Wales.

Lloyd Jones, Nell

Wright's maternal aunt for whom, with her sister Jane, he designed and built the **Romeo and Juliet Windmill** in **Spring Green, Wisconsin**. Together with her sister Jane they were always referred to as the "Aunts."

Lloyd Jones, Orin

Cousin of Frank Lloyd Wright who helped at the funeral of Mamah **Cheney** at the **Unity Church** in **Spring Green** in 1914.

Lloyd Jones, Ralph

Cousin of Frank Lloyd Wright who helped at the funeral of Mamah **Cheney** at the **Unity Church** in **Spring Green** in 1914.

Lloyd Jones, Richard (cousin)

Wright's cousin, the founder and publisher of the *Tulsa Tribune*, for whom Wright built a house in Tulsa, **Oklahoma**. This was the only work that Wright had after the stock market crash of 1929. Richard and Frank's political views were diametrically opposed and the house project was a battleground for old grievances and resentments. However, the house, Westhope, is now on the National Register of historic buildings.

Lloyd Jones, Richard (grandfather)

"Ein Tad," founder of the clan, Wright's maternal grandfather who was born in Wales before the turn of the nineteenth century.

Lloyd Jones, Thomas

Born in Llanwenog, Wales, in 1830. The eldest child of Richard **Lloyd Jones** and Mary Thomas, Frank Lloyd Wright's uncle.

Lockridge Medical Clinic (1958)

Built in Whitefish, Montana after Wright's death.

Los Angeles

At the prompting of his sister Catherine, Wright moved his offices to the West Coast in the spring of 1923. The venture was short-lived, however, and he returned to Chicago barely two years later. Wright, with a contingent of assistants, however, continued to work on the West Coast and there are many examples of his work in southern **California**.

The house of Richard Lloyd Jones, cousin to the architect — Westhope — is on the National Register of historic buildings and its beauty belies the tempestuous relationship between the two cousins.

Lovness, Donald, House (1955) cottage (1958–76)
This single-story structure is one of the last **Usonian** houses. It is constructed from stone and wood. The master and guest bedrooms form separate wings. The cottage is a square plan "one-room cottage" with a central fireplace in the living room.

Luccock, Rev. George M.
In 1910, it was the Reverend George Luccock of First Presbyterian Church in **Oak Park** who made a damning sermon on the theme of adultery. This did nothing to enhance Wright's already dwindling reputation in the area or improve his chances for work.

Lykes, Norman, House (1959)
Wright's last residential design to be built, the central living room is of circular plan with all the other parts of the house planned as circular segments. The building is constructed of **exposed concrete-block** and was supervised by a member of the **Taliesin Fellowship**. Building work took place between 1966 and 1968.

Views of the Lovness house. The building is one of the last of the Usonian homes and is primarily built of Dolomite, a local hard limestone. As can be seen in the pictures on this spread, the house is a small treasury of Wright design, in both construction and fittings.

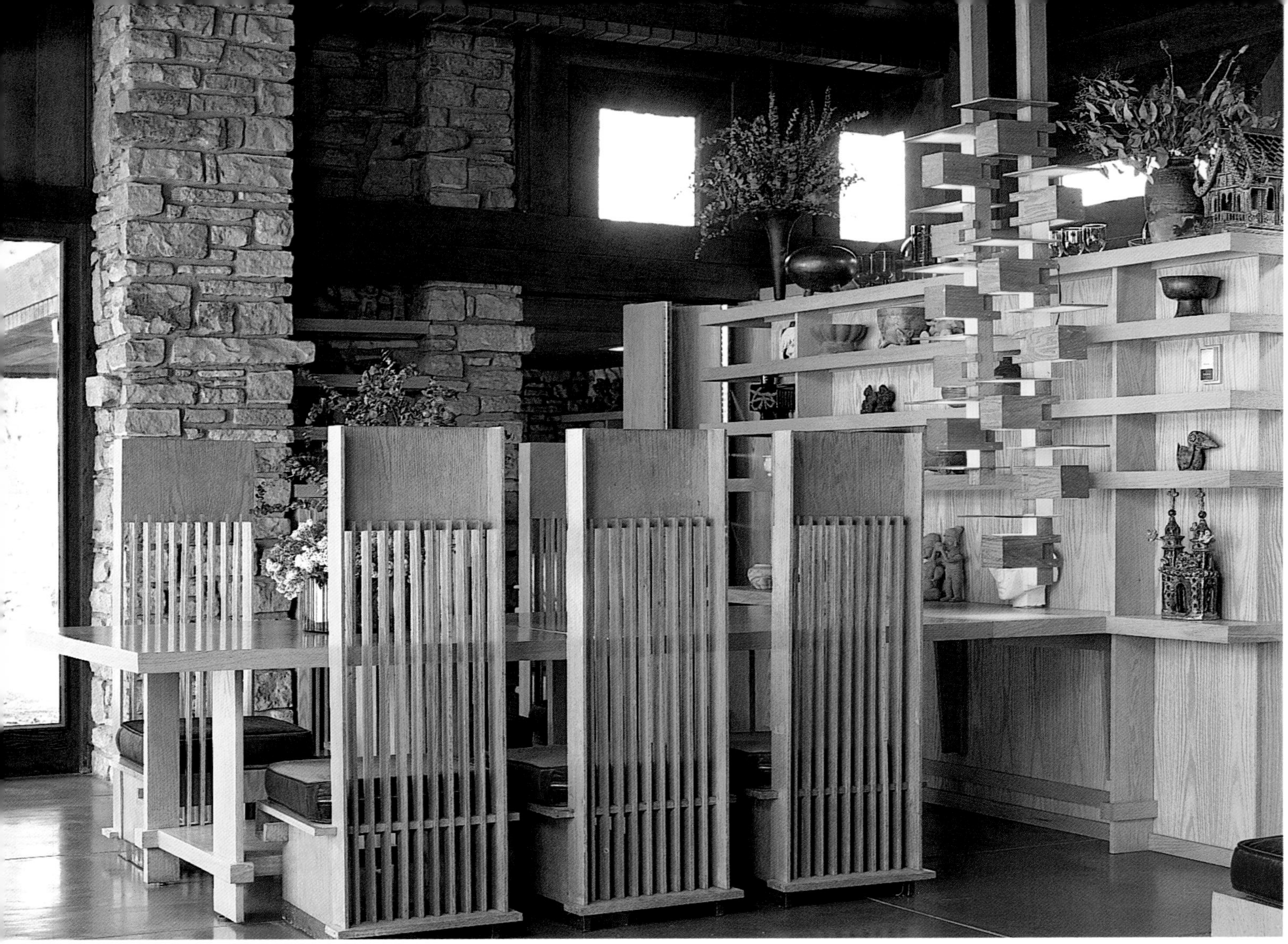

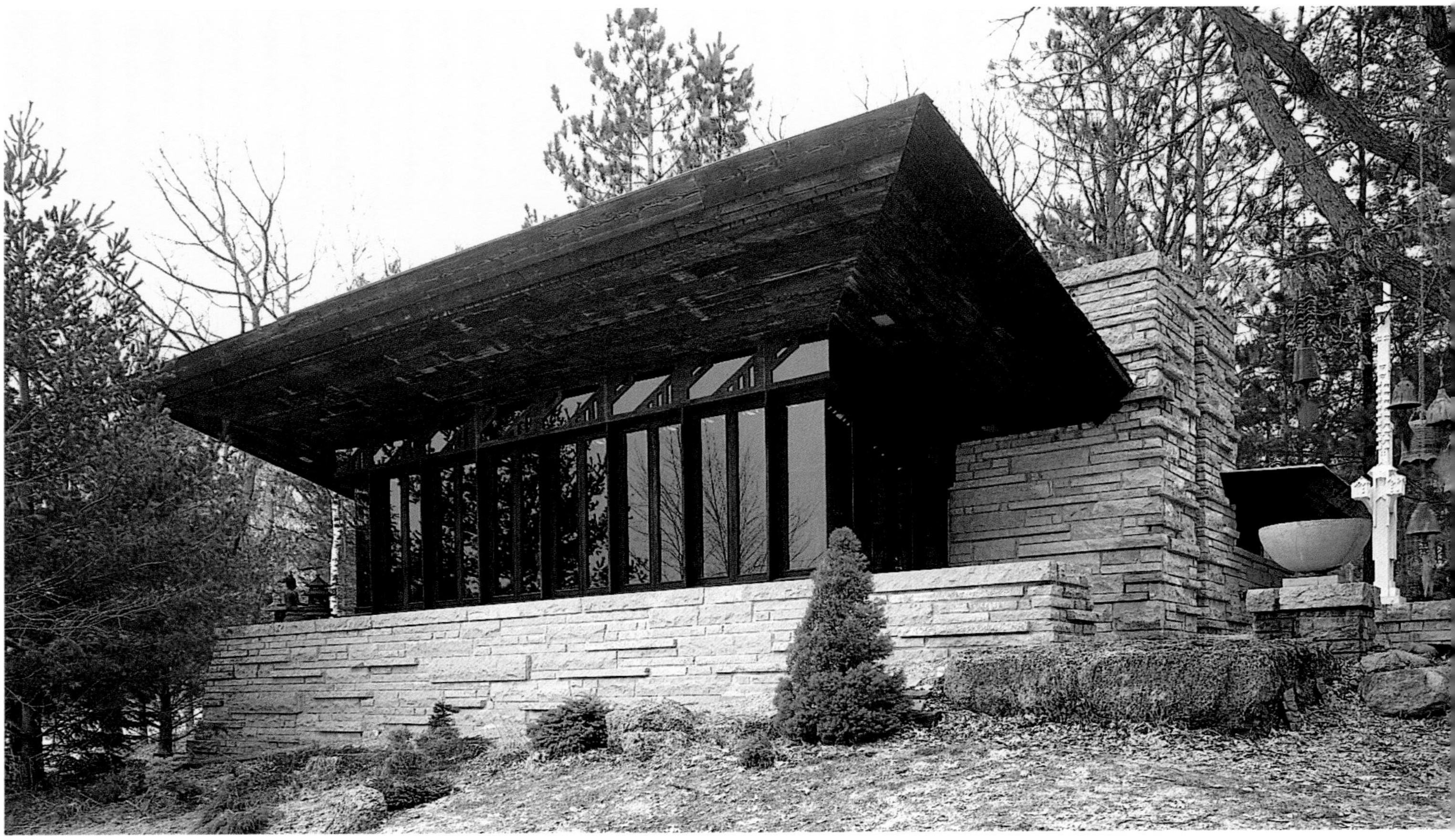

Interior and exterior photographs of the Lovness house, including the elegant furniture that was designed for the residence. The house blends extremely well with its environment and the windowed walls offer views out onto surrounding woodland.

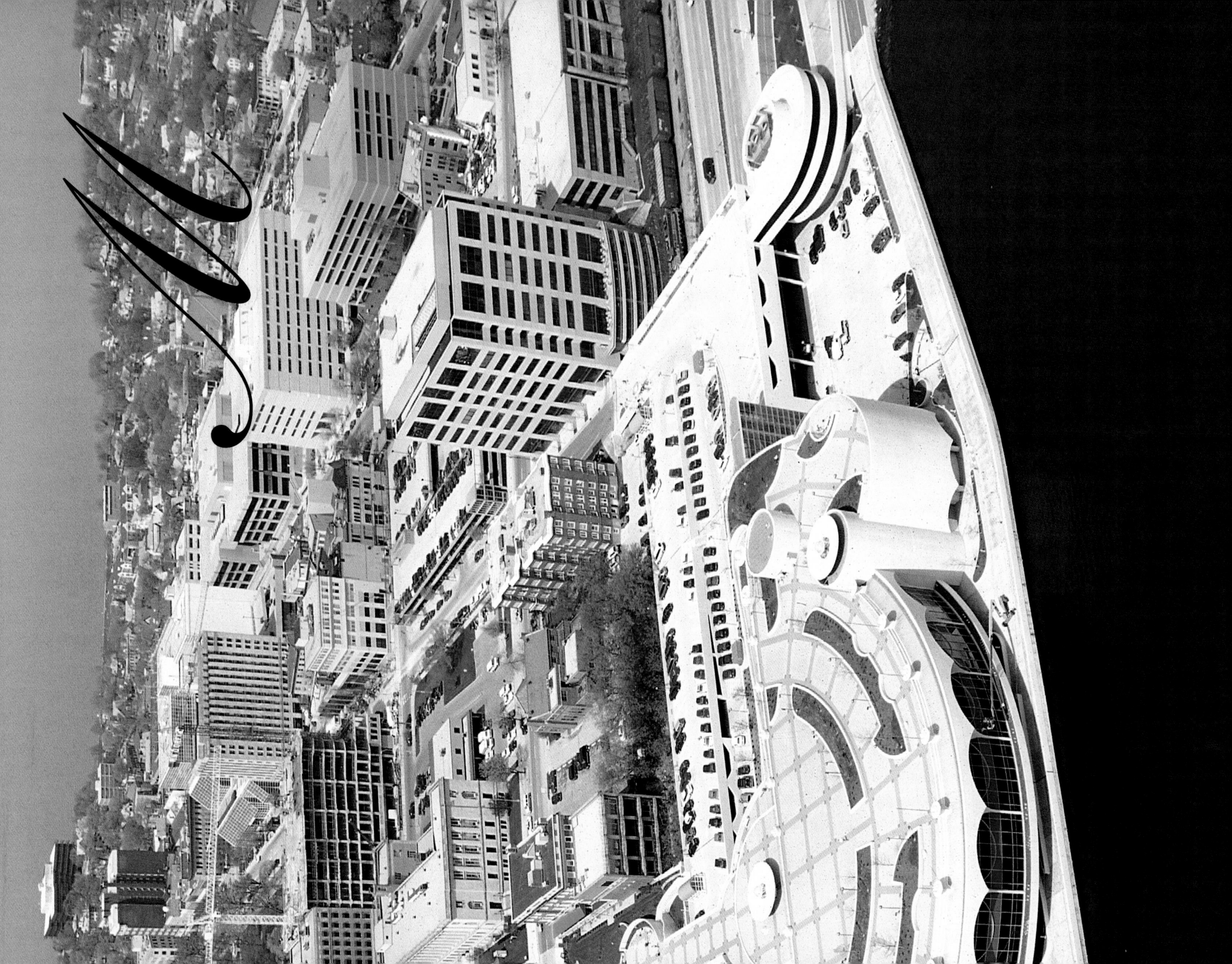

MacArthur, Alfred

A publisher in Chicago, and an old friend of Wright's from his **Oak Park** days, whom Frank turned to during his troubles in 1926 with Miriam Noel **Wright**. MacArthur later became a banker and financed the house for Lloyd and Katherine **Lewis**. Alfred had two famous brothers — Charles, a playwright, and John, who established the MacArthur Foundation.

Macbean, James B., House (1957)

One of the Marshall **Erdman** Company No. 2 Prefabs, this house, set into a hillside, is essentially a square-plan "one-room house." It is constructed from **exposed concrete block** and painted horizontal board and batten.

MacKintosh, Charles Rennie

Scottish architect whose designs for a museum Wright admitted copying for his own designs submitted to a competition for a new public library and museum in Milwaukee in 1893. MacKintosh shared Wright's fondness for linear, abstract design, and there are many interesting parallels to be found in their work.

Madison, Wisconsin

The house in Madison where Wright's parents moved in 1879 was the first house they ever owned and they lived in it for several years. The house made an impression on Frank and he frequently wrote about it. The move to Madison, closer to **The Valley**, brought them into the **Lloyd Jones**'s sphere of influence, particularly Jenkin, James, Enos and the "Aunts," Jennie and Nell.

Maher, George Washington

A distinguished architect who worked with Wright in Joseph **Silsbee's** office. When Wright left **Adler & Sullivan** he and **Corwin** moved into an 11-story building where Washington and his partners were set up. Washington would become one of the **New School of the Midwest**, who Wright believed were "throwing up sordid little imitations of his work all over the Midwest."

Pages 216/217 and Above: Monona Terrace.

Right: Hill house is considered to be Charles Rennie MacKintosh's finest domestic achievement. Margaret MacDonald, his wife, assisted him with the interior decor.

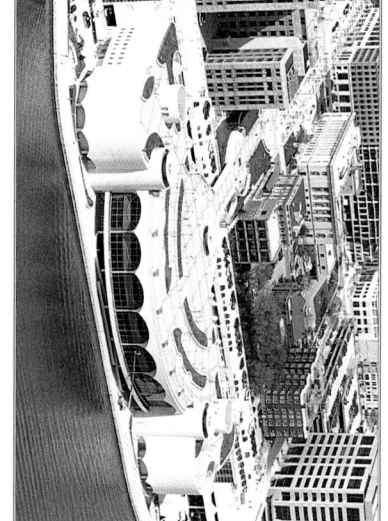

Mahoney, Marion

See **Griffin**, Walter Burley and Marion.

Mann, James Robert

The Chicagoan who sponsored the White Slave Traffic Act, also known as the **Mann Act** (see below) which was named after him.

Mann Act (1910)

This act of Congress was passed as part of an international effort to suppress the world-wide trade in prostitutes and provided stiff penalties for the interstate transportation of women for "immoral purposes" — in short, anyone who took an unmarried woman across a state line. Wright fell foul of this act during his acrimonious divorce with Miriam Noel **Wright** and charges could be brought every time that he and Olgivanna went from Chicago to **Spring Green.**

Manny, Carter H. Jr.

Director of the Graham Foundation for Advanced Studies in the Fine Arts in Chicago. After initially being turned down, he joined the Fellowship in **Arizona (Taliesin West)** just after the Second World War and his dexterity with a hammer and a saw soon convinced his employer that he was capable of living down his Harvard background.

Manson, Charles L. House (1938)

This brick-built house is sheathed and partitioned by regular board and batten walls. A second story, barely higher than the first, is accommodated by a dropped ceiling in the children's bedrooms.

Marcus, Stanley

Owner of Neiman-Marcus, a famous Dallas department store, who commissioned Wright to build a house for him after he had visited the architect's studio at **Taliesin** in 1935. It has been suggested that this encouraged the competitive Edgar **Kaufmann** to commission Wright to design **Fallingwater.**

Marden, Luis, House (1952)

A block and wood hemicycle that suffers from lack of light in the living room, which faces west by northwest.

Marin County Civic Center (1957)

When Wright died in 1959 he was working on plans for the Civic Center, a complex that included offices, libraries, and spaces for social activities. The project was the nearest he got to realizing his dream of a utopian city (see also buildings). Wright's sole works for the U.S.

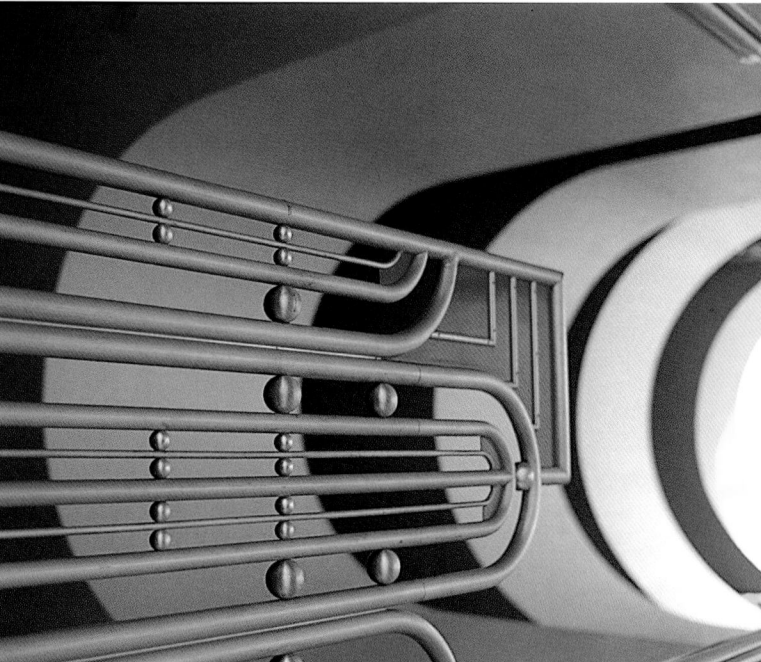

Above and Below: The Marin County Civic Center. The pylon (**below**) which dominates the building was intended to serve as both a radio transmitter and ventilating tower.

Above right: The Manson house. This house is interesting in that it sees Wright attempting to move away from the hard 90 degree angles of the L-plan home and here he investigates the possibilities of triangles and parallelograms.

Below right: View along one of the galleries of the Marin County Civic Center.

Pages 222/223: Views of the Marin County Civic Center including interior detail.

Government are contained in this complex. The post office is a nearly circular structure of exposed con-crete block and forms. The Hall of Justice and the Administration building are also of concrete blocks. The most spectacular part of the design, the pylon, which was intended to be a radio tower, is a dramatic exclamation point in the design of the futuristic development. The design and construction of this complex was underway when Wright died in 1959 and it was finished under the aegis of Aaron **Green**, William Wesley **Peters**, and the **Taliesin Associated Architects**. It gives us a vision of what Wright's dream city — **Broadacre** — could have been, and also exemplifies how innovative Wright's architectural designs were even into his 90s. Open to the public.

Martin, Darwin D.

Darwin D. Martin had a pivotal role in sustaining the talent of Frank Lloyd Wright as his chief benefactor. He was chief executive of the **Larkin** Company when Wright first met him in 1902, and it was Martin who commissioned Wright to design the famous **Larkin Company Building**. Throughout his life, after meeting Wright, Martin was to be the architect's friend, confidante, financial adviser, and above all his patron and private Croesus. He was one of the seven of Wright's friends and clients who contributed between them some $57,000 to defend him and get him back to work again at **Taliesin** in the 1920s.

Martin, Isabel, House (1904)

This building, with its original conservatory, is a large T-plan **Prairie** style house. It was constructed from russet Roman brick with oak trim. The glass work was by Orlando **Gianinni** who collaborated with Wright on many projects at this time.

Martin, Darwin D., Gardener's Cottage (1905)

A house constructed from plaster on wood frame. The plans for this building were not in the **Taliesin** archives and it has been suggested that it was designed by one of the draftsmen in Wright's employ.

Martin, Darwin D., Summer House and Garage (1927) Graycliff

Built close to the cliffs that drop down to Lake Erie, this structure originally had a plaster surface with wood trim but has been resurfaced. The fireplaces and chimney are of stone.

Martin, William.E.

Elder brother of Darwin (see above). W. E. Martin of

Oak Park, with his brother, owned a small business in Chicago, the **E-Z Polish Factory** and he was the first member of the family to commission Wright.

Martin, William E., House (1902)

A three-story house of plaster and wood-trim and a precursor of the **Prairie Houses** to come. The building was restored to a single family house in 1945 after many years of being split into three apartments. Originally landscaped by Burley **Griffin**, little of this now remains.

Maryland

There are only two examples of Wright's work in Maryland and both show his talent for drawing the best from difficult terrain and locations. The **Euchtman** house was built on a run-down lot. Wright built into the slope, effectively presenting the neighbor to the north with a view of carport and the rear of the house, freeing the private southern arc. For his son Llewellyn's house, he made the best use of a ravine running around the southwest of the property to provide a dramatic profile.

Masefield, Howard

An art collector of the Metropolitan Museum of Art in **New York City** for whom Wright bought **Japanese art** to supplement his income while working in Tokyo on the **Imperial Hotel** project.

Masieri Memorial

Masieri was a young Italian architectural student who had seen Wright's **"Frank Lloyd Wright in the Realm of Ideas"** exhibition in Florence (1951) and was killed in a car accident on his way to visit Wright in **Arizona**. His family decided to commission Wright to build a memorial to their son in the form of a small architectural library. The memorial was greeted with a very mixed reception and the Venetian Committee on Tourism finally exerted such pressure on the project that it was abandoned.

Massachusetts

Wright's only work in Massachusetts is the Theodore **Baird** House, a typical **Usonian** brick house with horizontal cypress board and sunk batten.

Top right: William E. Martin house. This building has a distinctive pergola which was designed by Walter Burley who also supervised construction of the house.

Right and Far right: Darwin D. Martin residence. The building is one of the largest of Wright's Prairie structures and features beautiful glass ornamentation by Orlando Gianinni.

Masselink, Eugene

Born in South Africa of Dutch parents, Gene was Wright's inuncio and personal secretary, and one of the pivotal figures in the smooth functioning of **Taliesin.** Over the years Masselink, a talented artist, created Wrightian murals and paintings for clients, helped establish the Taliesin Press, and designed programs, stationary, and invitations.

Mathews, Arthur C., House (1950)

A brick-built house with two parallel wings emanating from a central dining area segment which produced an enclosed terrace and garden area.

Matthews, J. B.

Former chief investigator for the House Un-American Activities Committee and former staff director of the Senate Investigations Subcommittee. He wrote a seven-page dossier on Wright accusing him of communist sympathies which was presented when the architect appeared before the Marin County board of supervisors to sign a contract for a new civic center.

May, Meyer, House (1908; extended 1920)

A superb T-plan two-story **Prairie House** built with Roman brick. Its interior boasts much art-glass and a Niedecken mural. May was Amberg's son-in-law and suggested Wright for the **Amberg** House. Restored 1987-88, it is now open to the public.

McAndrew, John

Curator of architecture at **New York City**'s Museum of Modern Art. In the autumn of 1937 he was one of the first visitors to spend a weekend at **Fallingwater.** He returned full of praise and organized a photographic exhibition at the museum. Of all the events that were conspiring to bring Wright back to the public eye, this backing by the Museum of Modern Art has to be considered one of the most important.

McArthur, Albert Chase

To this day it is stated in brochures published by the **Arizona Biltmore Hotel** that its architect was McArthur, a former Wright apprentice from the **Oak Park** days. McArthur claims that Wright licensed him to make use of the **textile block** method acted as advisor during the construction, criticized the plans and details, made sketches of the decorative designs, and was paid for those services — that was all.

The Meyer May house is finely detailed and features leaded art-glass ceiling windows. The tan brick complements the red Belgian roof tiles and copper detailing.

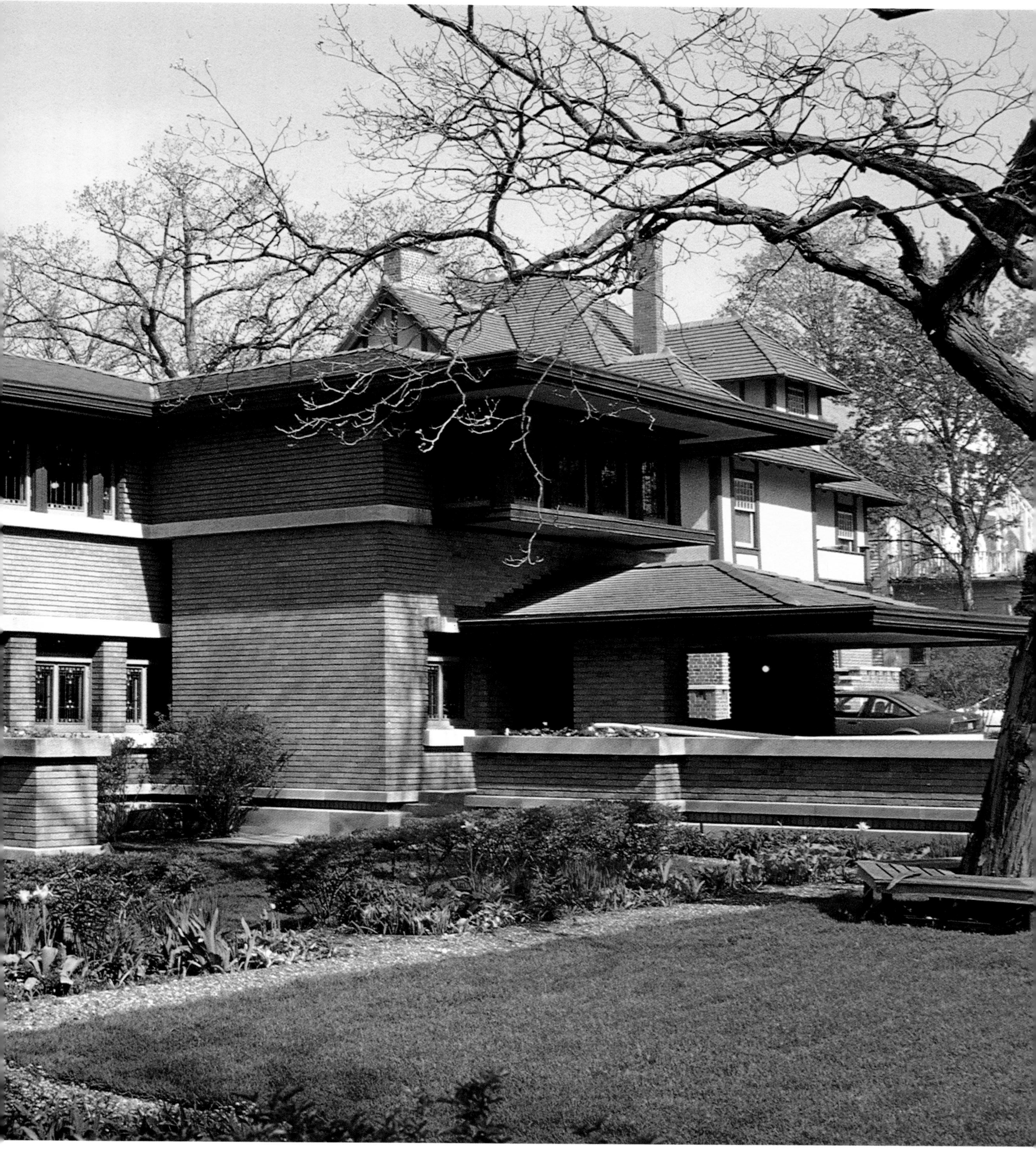

McArthur, Warren, House and Stable (1892)
In the house, Roman brick was used up to the windowsill and plaster above. Both house and stable were remodeled in 1900. Warren McArthur's son Albert was the project architect on the **Arizona Biltmore Hotel.**

McCartney, Ward, House (1949)
One of the **Parkwyn Village** house. Designed on a diamond (double equilateral triangle) module, the single-story house is built with Wright **textile blocks** and mahogany. Although the enclosure of the north portal and a carport came later, they were part of Wright's original plan.

McCormick, Harold and Edith Rockefeller
The failure by Wright to capture the prized commission of designing a mansion for the McCormicks, heirs to two of the country's greatest fortunes, has sometimes been given as one of the reasons that Wright left his wife and six children to run off with Mamah **Cheney**. Harold was, however, one of the seven of Wright's friends and clients who contributed between them some $57,000 to defend him and get him back to work again at **Taliesin** in the 1920s.

McHarg, W. S., House (designed 1891; since demolished)
This house was the first of Wright's nine **"bootlegged"** designs, created while he was working for **Adler & Sullivan.**

McKim, Charles F.
His design for the Chicago World Fair of 1893 was based on the **Villa Medici** in Rome, and he had a great ambition to found an American Academy in Rome to solidify American interest in the classical tradition. He wrote to **Burnham** about setting up some Chicago Fellowships and this led to Burnham's offer to Wright which the latter turned down (see Daniel Burnham).

McKim, Mead & White
A famous New York architectural firm whose published house plans are said to have influenced Wright's early designs. **Hitchcock** saw clear resemblances between Wright's first important design for **Adler & Sullivan,** the **Charnley** House (1891), and a McKim, Mead & White design, a **New York** town house, built seven years before.

Meija Mura
In the Carnegie Museum of Art is Wright's Field Office from San Francisco, rebuilt as a museum exhibit. There are other similar museum exhibits around the world — in **Japan's** Meija Mura museum is the rebuilt lobby of the **Imperial Hotel**; in the Metropolitan Museum of Art, **New York** City, there is the living room from the second Francis W. **Little** house; and London's Victoria and Albert Museum has on display the office of **Fallingwater** owner Edgar J. **Kaufmann,** Sr.

Meiklejohn, Alexander
A respected educator who was brought to the **University of Wisconsin** in the late 1920s to head their Experimental College. Wright had hoped that Meiklejohn might become the director of the **Hillside Home School** for the Allied Arts.

Mendelsohn, Erich
Within a matter of days after the **Imperial Hotel** survived the earthquake it became an object of praise and Wright was hailed as its architect. Young architects world-wide wanted to meet Wright and one of them, Erich Mendelsohn, a gifted young German architect, was completely overwhelmed after a meeting at **Taliesin** in 1924.

Meudt, Edna
A **Wisconsin** poet who was a childhood friend of Mamah **Cheney's** children when they visited **Taliesin.** Her poem, *A Summer Day That Changed the World* was about the horrific **Taliesin murders.**

Kenneth L. Meyers Medical Clinic (1956)
A single-story **Usonian** brick structure with a circular laboratory in the center of the medical section of the building. At an angle of 120 degrees from this is the rectangular waiting room. Open to the public.

Above left: The Warren McArthur house. Another of Wright's "bootlegged" projects, it was remodeled in 1900, eight years after construction, and a garage was added. Though not as radical as the architect's later work, this house is typically elegant and the interior is well laid out and spacious. Today, its remarkably good state of repair is the responsibility of David and Ruth Michael, the third owners of the house.

Above, Right and Below: The Curtis Meyer house.

Meyer, Curtis, House (1948)
A **Galesberg Country Home**, it's an east-facing solar hemicycle built from **exposed concrete blocks**.

Michigan

Because of Michigan's proximity to **Illinois** where Wright studied, lived, and did most of his early work, there are a great many examples of his buildings in the state. Wright's first work in Michigan was the George **Gerts** Duplex (Bridge Cottage) in Whitehall which was built in 1902. The only two-story **Usonian automatic** house is in Michigan: it was built for Dorothy and Dr. H. **Turkel**. The state also contains two estate developments which show well the way which Wright's designs lent themselves to mass-production, both in the simplicity of their construction — for example, the use of **exposed concrete blocks** — and in the way that basic designs could be modified to suit individual requirements and the geography of the site. The two estates were the **Galesburg Country Homes**, the concept of a group of chemists working together in a company in Kalamazoo, and **Parkwyn Village**, created by some of the same people involved with the Galesburg plan but who decided that a site nearer their work was in order. Unfortunately, few of the planned houses were built, but from what was constructed we can get a small idea of how the residential sections of **Broadacre City** would have looked.

Midway Gardens (designed 1913; demolished 1929)

Among many of the unfortunate consequences of Prohibition in America was the destruction of the Midway Gardens less than ten years after its opening. Conceived by **Edward C. Waller Jr**, this huge restaurant-cum-entertainment complex occupied an entire city block and appear to have been something between a pleasure park and a beer garden. It was notable for its patterned **exposed concrete blocks** as well as its brick work and the whole complex seems to have been used by Wright for a bold experiment in form and decoration. Much of the decoration was inspired by Mayan sources and included abstract and Cubist compositions in the form of murals. It was eventually sold to a Chicago brewer who was put out of business by Prohibition.

Mies van der Rohe, Ludwig

An architect who was an exponent of the **International Style** of sleek, austere, steel-and-glass edifices. Wright's rallying cry of perpetual renewal put him temperamentally in opposition to Mies whose goal was to polish his particular style to a high gloss.

Mikkelsen, M. A.

The editor of the *Architectural Record* who was sympathetic to Wright's work and mission. In 1926 he commissioned the architect to write a series of five articles and

offered to pay him $500 for each. These earnings brought Wright a much needed revenue at a time when he was especially financially pressed.

Miliyanov (or Milanoff) Marco

Maternal grandfather of Olgivanna Lazovich **Wright** (see Militza **Lazovich**).

Millard, Alice, House (1923) La Miniatura

Arguably the finest of its kind, this was the first example of a **textile block** house to be designed and has become known as La Miniatura. It was constructed by stacking concrete blocks adjacent to and on top of each other without visible mortar joints. The supervision of the construction of the house, with its two-story high living room, was undertaken by Lloyd Wright. Today, in its overgrown gardens the effect of intimacy and nature makes it seem like a half excavated Central American monument.

Millard, George Madison, House (1906)

A board and batten two-story **Prairie House** built to a cruciform plan.

Miller, Alvin, House (1946)

Situated on the Cedar River, this is a single-story, L-plan house with a clerestory.

Minnesota

Wright's earliest extant building in Minnesota, the 1933 Malcolm E. **Willey** House, represents a major link between Wright's **Prairie** and **Usonian** styles. Another interesting building, in Stillwater, is the Donald **Lovness** House; built in 1955, this was one of the last Usonian houses to be constructed. Minnesota can also lay claim to the only service station constructed from Wright's designs, the R. W. **Lindholm** building. The design derives from the **Broadacre City** Standardized Overhead Service Station of 1932, except that ground-based pumps are used instead of the overhead fuel lines envisaged by Wright. In Rochester in 1957, the James **MacBean** House, one of Wright's designs of a prefabricated structure for the Marshall **Erdman** Company, was built. Wright conceived three different prefabricated designs with Marshall Erdman, but only two were ever realized, albeit in reasonable numbers, and this house represents the original of the second of those — a

Right: The Alice Millard house — La Miniatura — the first of four textile block houses to be constructed in the Los Angeles area and often cited as the finest. Its quiet, natural environment and superb detail combine with Wright's organic philosophy to create a serene dwelling which overlooks a lovely pool.

wood two-story structure with a balcony outside the bedrooms above the living area.

Mississippi

In 1890, while Wright was working for Louis **Sullivan**, he was delegated to undertake the work for Sullivan's Summer Residence at Ocean Springs. Sullivan had acquired the land from his friends (and clients) the **Charnleys**, for whom the **Adler & Sullivan** company undertook a Chicago townhouse as well as a summer house — like Sullivan's, looking out towards the Gulf of Mexico. They were to be Wright's only commissions in Mississippi until the post-war years when, in 1948, he designed the **Hughes** House, Fountainhead, in Jackson. This is a house which gives the only example of modern Wright architecture in the state. The building represents a complete demonstration of organic principles in design. Wright proclaimed that the structural principles found in natural forms should guide modern American architecture and put his words into practice with Fountainhead.

Missouri

Wright's buildings in Missouri are split neatly into two eras — immediately pre-war and the early 1950s. The **Bott** House is certainly the most dramatic of the mainly residential commissions, and the **Community Christian Church** in **Kansas** City the most disappointing when compared to Wright's original drawings.

Mock, Rudolph

A pioneer student at **Taliesin** from Switzerland who, in 1932, was sharing quarters with Herbert **Fritz** and other young apprentices.

Mollica, Joseph, House (1958)

This is an L-plan Marshall **Erdman** Prefab four-bedroomed house and garage. Its main construction material is stone.

Monona Terrace (designed 1938; built 1997)

Planned in 1938 as a building with offices, courtroom, jail, and a railroad station, none of the plans came to fruition until after Wright's death. Thus, today, his home town of Madison, Wisconsin, has a reminder of its greatest son.

Montana

50 years separate Wright's two buildings in Montana — the substantial but ill-fated **Como Orchard** project and the **Kundert Clinic** of Ophthalmology.

Montooth, Charles and Minerva

Fellowship members at **Taliesin West** in the 1950s.

Charles Montooth assisted another Fellowship member, Arthur **Pieper**, in the construction of his house using Wright's new block system — the **Usonian automatic**.

Moore, Nathan G., House (1895)

A Roman brick house which is essentially Tudor in style was rebuilt above the first floor after a fire in 1922. It was half timbered in the original design and, although the original

form has been retained, the present building is, in its outward appearance, closer to Wright's designs of the late 1920s, particularly in the use of carved brick and stonework. Wright also built the stable. It's open to the public and guided tours are available during summer months.

The Nathan G. Moore Tudor house is an early testament to Wright's flexibility.

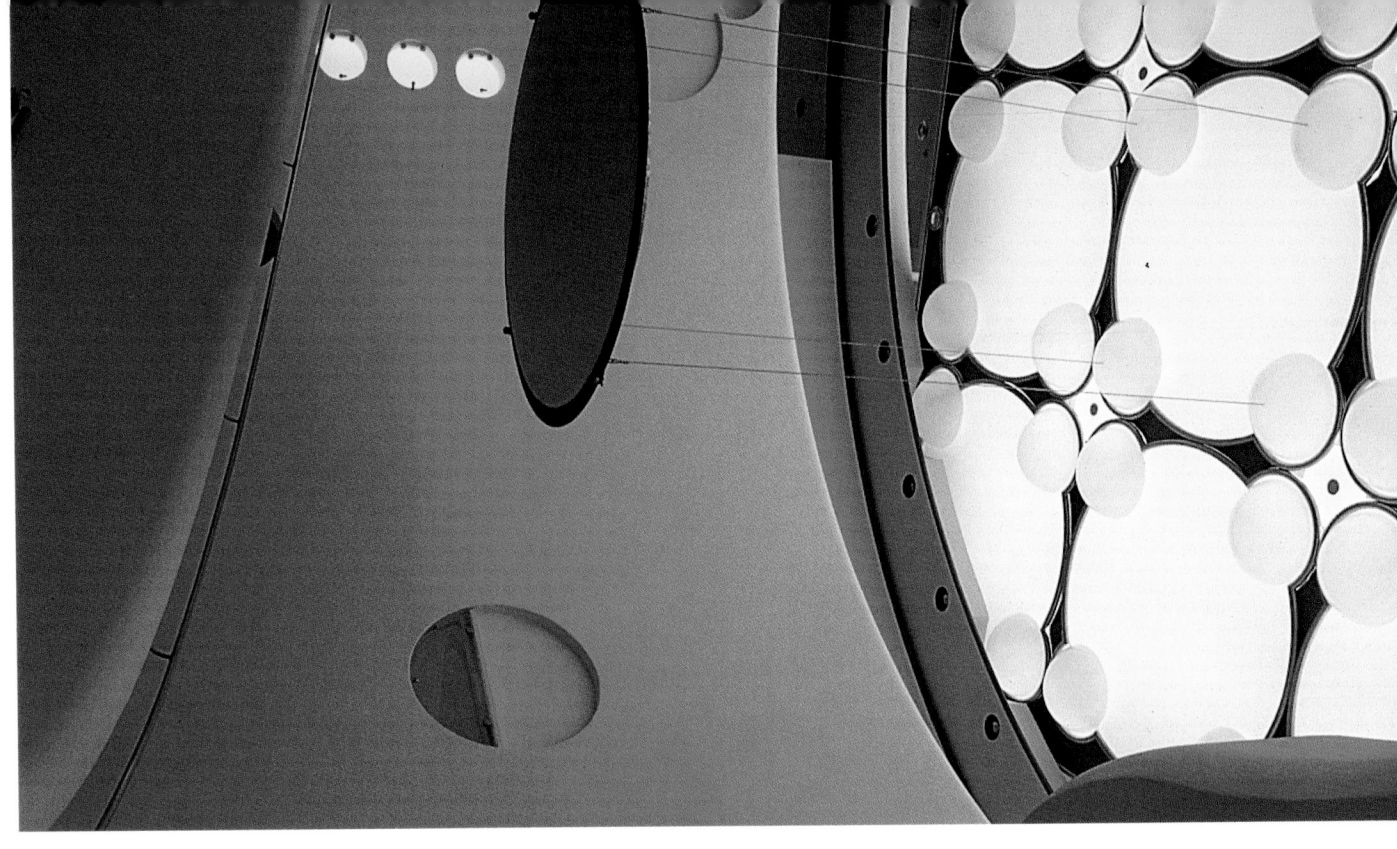

Morris, William
Acknowledged leader of the **Arts and Crafts Movement** as it evolved in Britain in the 1880s.

Mori Oriental Art Studio (1914; since demolished)
Wright decorated the interior of a corner room on the eighth floor of the Fine Arts Building on Michigan Avenue for use as an art studio.

(V. C.) Morris gift shop (1948)
One of the 17 buildings designated to be retained by the **A.I.A.** Circular forms are employed and with its brick facade, Romanesque splayed portal arch, and circular ramp, it is a **Guggenheim** in microcosm. Originally a gift shop, it has been renovated and variously used as a dress shop and art gallery. Open to the public.

Mueller, Paul
A young **German** engineer who handled all the mechanical details and worked directly under Wright when Wright was with **Adler & Sullivan**. Later, Mueller was Wright's contractor for the **Imperial Hotel** as well as a number of other major projects.

Mossberg, Herman T.
The construction of Mossberg's house in South Bend, **Indiana**, was the first building that Jack **Howe** was allowed to supervise.

Mossberg, Herman T., House (1948)
A two-story L-plan house. It is constructed of red brick and cypress with cedar shingles. The L-wing contains sleeping quarters on the second floor whilst the living room forms the largest segment of the plan. It is built on a corner lot and the L encloses a patio.

Mosher, Bob
Mosher was witness to one of the most famous moments in architecture when Wright sat down to begin the drawings for **Fallingwater**. Mosher was also the senior apprentice who was charged with overseeing the construction of it.

Moses, Robert
New York City Commissioner Robert Moses was the bane of Wright's life during the designing and planning of the **Guggenheim Museum**. The two men were cousins by marriage, but intellectually their minds had no meeting point: Moses had plans for New York which included building high-rise, high-density housing. Wright, in complete contrast, saw dispersed low-level homes as the only answer to housing the urban masses. The conflicts resulted in Moses doing all he could to obstruct the building of the museum.

Moser, Werner
The Swiss architect Werner Moser and his wife Silva visited **Taliesin** in 1924 and their son, Lorenz, was born there during their stay. As well as being an architect, Moser was on the faculty of Zürich's architectural school and devoted a great portion of his life to education. It was Werner Moser who met and looked after Richard and Dione **Neutra** when they first arrived at **Taliesin** in the summer of 1924.

Moser, Karl
An Austrian architect under whom Richard **Neutra** had briefly studied in Zurich. He was also the father of **Taliesin** apprentice Werner **Moser** (see below).

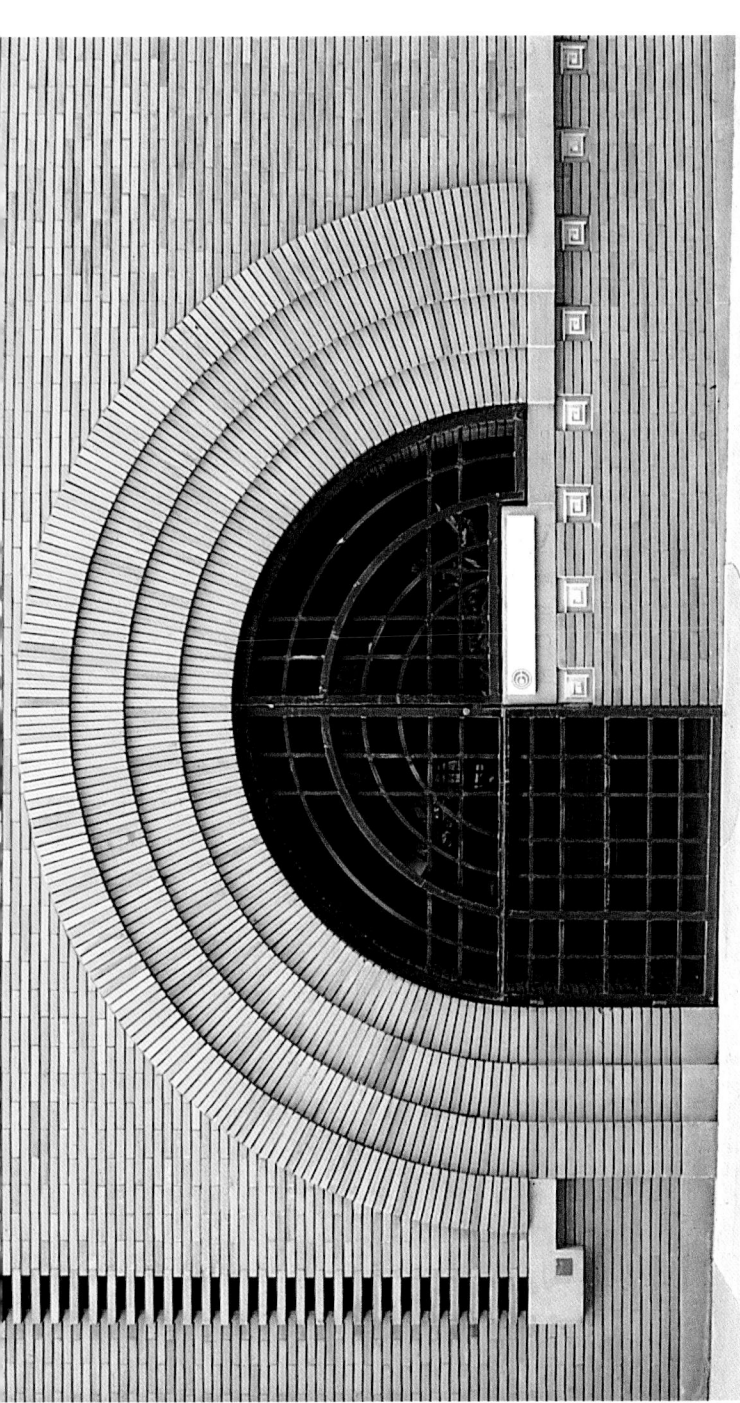

Mueller, Robert, House (1909)
The basic design of this house belonged to Wright; the interior treatment of the living and dining spaces were the work of **Von Holst** and **Mahony**.

Muirhead, Robert, House (1950)
An elongated plan built on a four-foot module. The main building materials of this one-story house are common brick and cypress.

Mumford, Lewis
The great American social philosopher, city planner, and architectural critic who was an early champion of Wright in the face of an avalanche of approval for the new styles of architecture, including the **International Style**. Later, Wright and Mumford were to have a serious falling out over the issue of Wright's pacifism during the Second World War.

Myers, Howard
The editor of the *Architectural Forum* who approached Wright in 1936 requesting publishing rights to the new S. C. **Johnson Administration Building** in Racine, **Wisconsin**. In the years that followed, a strong and affectionate relationship developed between the two men until Myers's death in 1947.

Municipal Boathouse (designed 1893; demolished 1928)
Wright won a Madison Improvement Association competition for design of the boathouse. Its large, lake facing arch was to be featured in later Wright designs.

Munkwitz, Arthur, Duplex Apartments (designed 1916; since demolished)
These buildings were the result of Wright's designs for his American System Ready-Cut structures with their pre-fabricated construction essential to the concept. They were based on the American Model A4 home, with two bedrooms and a large living room. Two Model A4 units were built, one above the other to form a duplex. The term "quadraplex" comes from the joining of two of these duplexes with a common entryway.

Top and Above: Details of the Morris gift shop. The interior of displays the use of the circular form which runs through the building. Wright's red square signature tile is shown **above.**

National Institute of Art and Letters

The institute made Wright a member in 1947 and later presented him with the gold medal for architecture. The house that Wright designed for his son, David, in Phoenix, **Arizona**, was put on exhibit at the institute in 1953.

National Life Insurance Company, Chicago

In the 1920s Wright was asked to design a 32-story **skyscraper** for the company and, although the project did not materialize, it resulted in a brilliant design that he would adapt later for an even more ambitious project in New York City — **St. Mark's-in-the-Bouwerie Tower.**

Nebraska

The Harvey P. **Sutton** House, a 1905 **Prairie House** built in McCook, is Wright's only work in Nebraska. It has been restored extensively by Donald J. **Poore.**

Neils, Harry J., House (1949)
This house on Cedar Lake was commissioned by some-one who worked in, and could acquire, metal and stone

— which accounts for Wright being able to use building materials like scrap marble and aluminium window fram-ing. The house is dominated by a large chimney and the east-facing terrace which opens off the living room.

Nelson, William E.
An inventor of **concrete blocks** and holder of two U.S. patents, he claimed that Wright's **textile block** system violated his own.

Neutra, Dione
Wife of Richard (see below). Dione could sing and play the cello at the same time. Wright found this quite outstanding and the musical evenings held at his house were a model of the intellectual, bohemian way of life that Wright would later perpetuate in his **Taliesin Fellowship.**

Pages 236/237: The Frederick Nichols house.

Above and Right: Wright was a complete designer and even the smallest detail did not escape him. His typeface — Eaglefeather — is always associated with him. This memorial is at Taliesin East.

Neutra, Richard

Born in Vienna, Neutra was inspired to go to America by Wright's **Wasmuth Portfolios**. He worked in Chicago where he met **Sullivan**, and it was at Sullivan's funeral in 1924 that he met Wright who offered him a job at **Taliesin**. Neutra spent nine constructive months in Wright's studio working on several major projects and he and his wife were ideal additions to life at Taliesin. After Neutra left, Wright became disenchanted with his former student as by 1931 he had become one of the leading practitioners of the **International Style** on the West Coast.

New Hampshire

The Isadore J. **Zimmerman** house and Toufic H. **Kalil** house are the only two examples of Wright's work in the state and were built within shouting distance of each other.

New Jersey

The four examples of Wright's work in the state of New Jersey are all private houses and span a period of 14 years from 1940 (the **Christie** House in Bernardsville.) to 1954 (the **Wilson** House in Millstone.) In between these was the **Richardson** House (1941) in Glen Ridge and the **Sweeton** House (1950) in Cherry Hill.

New Mexico
The only example of Wright's work in the state of New Mexico is the Arnold **Freeman** house, Fir Tree, a summer residence in Pecos.

New School of the Midwest (see **Prairie School**)

New York, City & State
Examples of Wright's work in New York State range from private homes, including a Prefab, to an auto showroom, and one of his best-known and greatest achievements — the **Guggenheim Museum**. His

The Zimmerman house in New Hampshire is one of only two examples in this state. The verdant scenery is complemented by the common brick and cypress structure.

earliest work is in Buffalo with four private residences built between 1903 and 1908. His next New York commission, Graycliff, a summer house and garage for Darwin D. **Martin**, at Lakeshore, Derby, was in 1927 and a further ten years elapsed before the Ben **Rebhuhn** house. Between 1948 and 1951, three **Usonian** houses were built closely together in wooded, hilly countryside within commuting distance north of New York City. This was **Pleasantville** — the **Usonia Homes** complex, for which Wright was engaged to design himself, or approve the design of, all the houses proposed for the estate. In New York City the **Hoffman Auto Showroom** features the interior remodeling of a ground floor corner of a curtain wall **skyscraper**. New York City also houses the **Guggenheim**, one of the 17 buildings designated to be retained by the **American Institute of Architects** as an example of Wright's architectural contribution to American culture. While discussing New York, mention must be made of **Taliesin East** — or Taliesin the Third — created in the **Hotel Plaza**, a three-room suite which Wright remodeled for his own accommodation while overseeing the Guggenheim project.

New York City Exhibition (designed 1910; since demolished)
For the Universal Portland Cement Company.

Nichols, Frederick, House (1906)
This is a cube design built with stained lapped wood. Often referred to as the "Nicholas" House because of a Wrightian misspelling.

Nineteenth Century Women's Club
Wright's mother Anna was a founding member of the club and it was here that Mamah Borthwick **Cheney** met Catherine **Wright**. Grace Hemmingway, Ernest's mother, was also a leading light of the club.

Noel, Corinne
Youngest daughter of Emil **Noel** and Miriam Noel **Wright**.

Noel, Emil
First husband of Miriam Noel **Wright**, whom she married at the age of 15, the son of a wealthy Southern family.

Noel, Miriam (see Miriam Noel **Wright**)

Noel, Norma
The eldest daughter of Emil **Noel** and Miriam Noel **Wright**.

Noel, Thomas
The son of Emil **Noel** and Miriam Noel **Wright**.

The Nichols house has seen several alterations — including a porch to the southeast — though these have been carefully structured and the house looks similar to the original design. Heating has also been added — the house was originally intended as a summer golf retreat only.

Olbrich, Jose Maria

A Viennese architect and a contemporary of Wright. Resemblances have been noted between Olbrich's work and Wright's design for **Unity Temple**. Olbrich was one of the European designers who rejected both the Classical Academic tradition and also the influence of Art Nouveau.

Olfelt, Paul, House (1958)

This small house is built into a hillside; the living room opens out to a downhill aspect, and the west-facing deck off this room is therefore supported from below. Construction was completed by the **Taliesin Associated Architects** after Wright's death.

Olive Hill, Los Angeles

The 36-acre tract of land that Aline **Barnsdall** bought in 1919. It was a prominent local landmark at the edge of the **Los Angeles** Basin with unimpeded views of the city to the southeast, the San Gabriel Mountains to the north, and the Pacific Ocean in the distance. Barnsdall's plan was to turn the whole hill into an artists' encampment with a grand house for herself.

Olmsted, Frederick Law,

The famous landscape architect who, along with Henry Sargent **Codman**, drafted the preliminary plan for the 1893 Chicago World's Fair.

Oregon

The only example of Wright's work in Oregon is the T-plan Conrad E. **Gordon** House on the Willamette River.

Organic Architecture

Wright believed passionately in the principle of "organic architecture", although he never gave a precise definition of the term. The central principle of this concept maintains that a building should develop out of its natural surroundings. He extolled the virtues of an architecture that would use reinforced concrete in the configurations found in seashells and snails and would construct **skyscrapers** in the same the way that trees are "built"—that is with a central "trunk" deeply rooted in the ground, and floors cantilevered from that trunk like branches. Spaces within such buildings would be animated by natural light allowed to penetrate the interiors and to travel across textured surfaces as the incidence of sunlight and moonlight changed. From the outset he exhibited bold originality in his designs for both private and public structures and rebelled against the ornate neo-classic and Victorian styles favored by conventional architects. Wright was vehemently opposed to the

mechanical imposition of preconceived styles. He believed that the architectural form must ultimately be determined in each case by the particular function of the building, its environment, and the type of materials employed in the structure. Wright's phrase "the nature of materials" meant to him the sympathetic employment of natural or structural materials, with an understanding of their colors and textures, individually or in combination. His interiors emphasize the sense of spaciousness, which derives from open planning with one room flowing into another. This concept was particularly evident in his early single-family houses, the so-called **Prairie Houses**.

The Price Tower embodies Wright's notions of organic architecture. It stands like a tree in the rolling hills of eastern Oklahoma, constructed around a central trunk from which the floors are cantilevered out like branches.

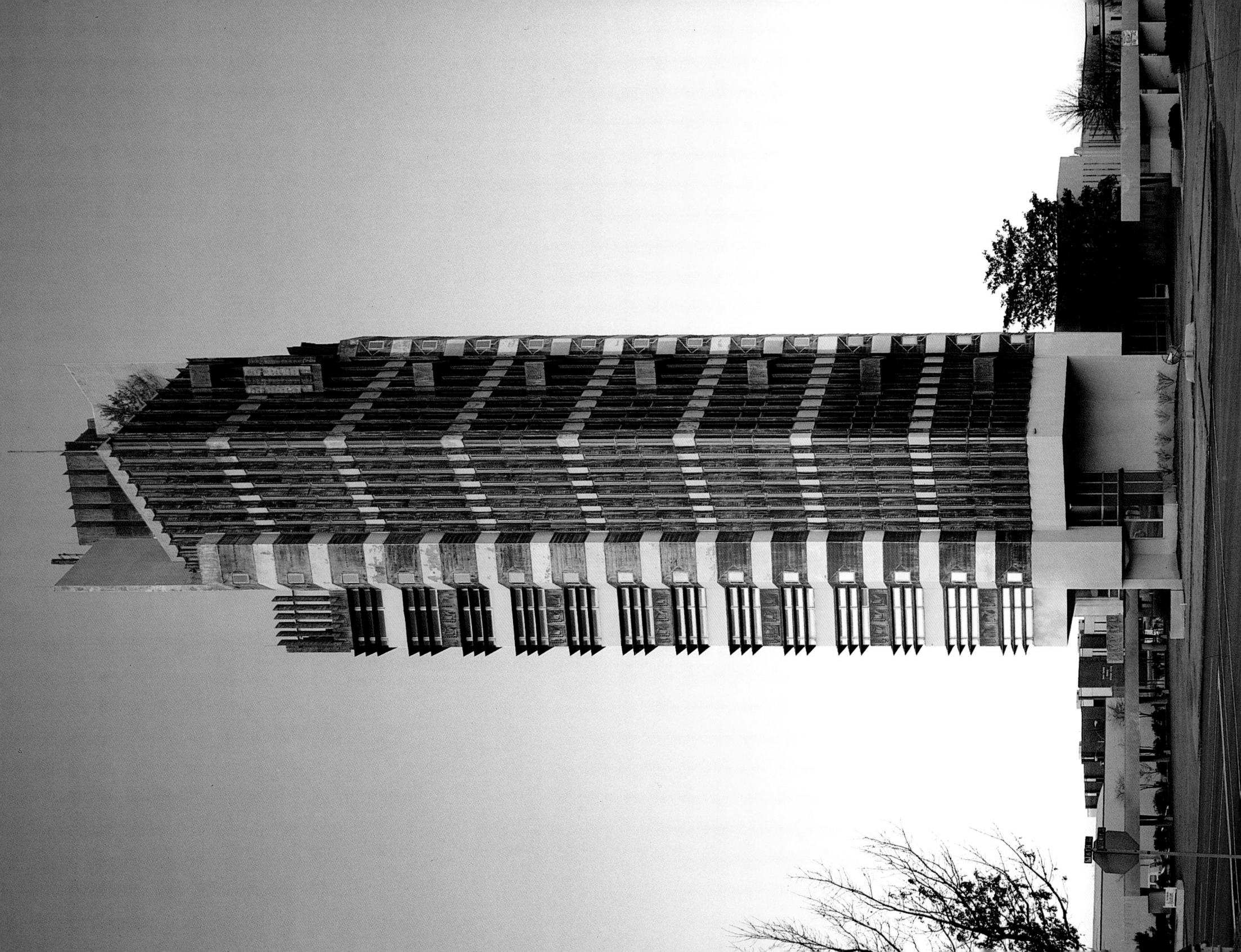

Page, Benjamin Eldridge
A Chicago businessman who took over the running of Wright's financial affairs from Philip **La Follette**. He was one of the seven of Wright's friends and clients who contributed between them some $57,000 to defend him and get him back to work again at **Taliesin** in the 1920s. Page met Catherine **Wright** when she was 59, at some point during the year 1929-30, a romance developed and they married. When the stock market crashed, he was dropped from Wright's inner circle, ruining Page, he was dropped from Wright's inner circle, Catherine split up from him and they were later divorced in 1937.

Palmer, William, House (1950)
Bill Palmer was Professor of Mathematics at the **University of Michigan** when he chose Wright to design his home. He received a single-story **Usonian** house, built to a triangular plan that complements perfectly the hilltop on which it rests.

Pappas, T.A., House (1955)
A **Usonian automatic** design, constructed from salmon-tinted blocks which the owner assembled himself.

Park Ridge Country Club (Remodeling 1912; since demolished)
The country club was both altered and added to by Wright.

Parker, George
George Parker, of Parker Pens, was one of the seven of Wright's friends and clients who contributed between them some $57,000 to defend him and get him back to work again at **Taliesin** in the 1920s.

Parker, Robert P., House (1892)
Identical to the Thomas **Gale** House at 1019 Chicago Avenue, **Oak Park**.

Parkwyn Village, Michigan
Created by people involved with the **Galesburg** plan but who wanted a site nearer their work.

Pauson, Rose, House (designed 1939; destroyed 1942)
Constructed from desert rubblestone, this in-line house burnt down and only the vast chimneybreast remains.

Pages 252/253, Above, and Right: The William Palmer house.

Pleasantville projects

After the Second World War, between 1948 and 1951, three **Usonian** houses were built closely together in wooded, hilly countryside within commuting distance north of **New York City** at **Pleasantville** — the **Usonia Homes** complex. Wright was engaged to design himself, or approve the design of all the houses proposed for the estate.

Poore, Donald J.

The Harvey P. **Sutton** House, a 1905 **Prairie House** built in McCook, is Wright's only work in **Nebraska**. It has been restored extensively by Poore.

Pope-Leighey House (1939)

A **Usonian** house of typical horizontal sunk cypress batten dry-wall construction around a brick core. Here the Usonian idea can be seen at its simplest and most functionally efficient. The house is open to the public from March to December.

Porter, Andrew Taylor

Frank Lloyd Wright's brother-in-law, a Canadian businessman who had married Frank's sister **Jennie**. He became business manager for **Hillside School** in 1907. The school's finances were in a parlous state and, although Porter worked tirelessly without salary for two years, Hillside declared bankruptcy in September 1909.

Above, Right, and Pages 262/263: The Pope-Leighey house was moved from its original site to Mount Vernon in Virginia in 1964. Unfortunately, the repositioning was rather careless and many design details and original features were overlooked.

Porter, Andrew, House (1907) Tanyderi

Part of the **Taliesin II** complex, Tanyderi was built for Wright's sister, Jane, and her husband, who was head of the **Hillside Home School**. It is a square **Prairie House** though Wright, on occasion, denied that the design for this shingle-sided house was his.

Porter, Anna

Daughter of Andrew **Porter** and Frank Lloyd Wright's sister **Jennie**.

Porter, Franklin Wright

Born 1909, son of Andrew **Porter** and Frank Lloyd Wright's sister **Jennie**. He was originally christened after his uncle but, when Frank Lloyd Wright did something outrageous, Jennie decreed that the young Frank would become Franklin from then on.

Porter, James Andrew

Son of Andrew **Porter** and Frank Lloyd Wright's sister **Jennie**. James died at the age of 13.

Porter, Mary Jane ("Jennie") Wright
William Carey **Wright** and Anna **Lloyd Jones**'s eldest
daughter; born in 1869. The closeness of their ages meant
Frank had a somewhat uneasy relationship with his sister.
She married Canadian businessman Andrew **Porter.**

Post, Carl, House (1957)
One of the four prefabricated house designs by Wright
for the Marshall **Erdman** Company. This L-plan house
has the kitchen and dining facilities in the short leg with
the living room below the entrance at the inner intersection of the L. The house has a masonry core and is built
of brick with horizontal board and batten siding on the
bedroom wing.

Prairie Houses
Wright believed that the West and Midwest embodied
the "real American spirit" and, acting on this belief, he
designed the houses that were to win him international
renown. His **Prairie Houses** were horizontal, often of
one story, with rooms merging in a continuous open
space. **"Breaking the box"** was the phrase that
Wright used for the development of this style. Massive
brick or stone fireplaces at the heart of the house were
a core to the construction which led to the expansion of
the design outward without defining rooms until the
space and circulation needs were determined. Rooms
were not as before, boxes constrained by interior walls,
but became increasingly open to one another. The overall
configuration of his plans became more and more
asymmetrical, reaching out toward some real or imagined
prairie horizon. The houses with their low, sweeping
rooflines hanging over uninterrupted walls of windows
were derived but extended from the indigenous wooden
style of the early settlers and were designed to suggest
the wide prairie expanses of the Midwest.

Prairie School
Sometimes called the **New School of the Midwest.** A
group of young architects including Walter Burley

The Carl Post house is very similar to the other Erdman Prefab
houses with the exception of the walkway between the kitchen
and garage which is twice as wide in this residence. The term
"prefab" belies the quality of construction and the excellent
design of these homes which are of typical Wright standards as
can be seen in these photographs.

Griffin, George Grant **Elmslie**, Barry **Byrne**, George W. **Maher**, Robert C. **Spencer** Jr., Eben E. **Roberts**, John S. **Van Bergen**, Charles E. **White**, and the architectural firm of **Tallmadge & Watson**. Wright thought this group, whose designs, to the casual eye, looked Wright-inspired and influenced, was "throwing up sordid little imitations of his work all over the Midwest." This view did contain elements of the truth.

"Prairie Town" house
One of Wright's best known designs, that for a small "Prairie Town" house was first published in the *Ladies' Home Journal* of 1901.

Pratt, Eric, House (1948)
One of the **Galesberg Country Homes**. The westernmost block of the homes is a long I-plan **textile block automatic** house with central living room. Pratt was the general purchasing agent for the homes.

Price, Bruce
An American architect. It has been noted that the house Wright designed for himself in 1889 was closely modelled on the "Queen Anne" designs of two houses built by Price in Tuxedo Park, **New York** City, three or four years earlier.

Price, Mr. and Mrs. Harold
Patrons of the **Price Tower** in Bartlesville, **Oklahoma**. Mr. and Mrs. Price were a far sighted couple who had made a fortune in oil and natural gas pipeline construction. Their son, Harold Jr., was also a Wright convert.

Price, Harold, House (1954)
Built for Harold Price Sr., who also commissioned the **Price Tower** in Bartlesville, **Oklahoma**. The most distinctive feature of the design is the central atrium with its roof raised above concrete pillars, thus serving the dual purpose of allowing in cool air but keeping out rain and direct sun. Its construction is of **exposed concrete block** throughout, the central core housing the service elements with the floors cantilevered off from this central trunk. This fell in very much with Wright's views on **Organic Architecture**.

Price, Harold Jr., House (1953) Hillside
Built to a large L-plan with a two-story living room, master bedroom and a hipped roof. A later addition added a playroom to the original design.

Price Tower (designed 1929, built 1953)
This combined office and apartment block is the only **skyscraper** that Wright fully designed. It is a modified, version of the building as Wright originally conceived it — "dignified as a tree in the midst of nature, but a child of the spirit of man." The tower is constructed with reinforced concrete and has cantilevered floors, copper louvers, and copper-faced parapets. It also has a striking gold-tinted glass exterior. While it is not open to the public, guided tours are available.

Princeton University (See **Kahn Lectures**)

Progressive Party
A party with a socialist manifesto formed by Philip **La Follette**, as Governor of **Wisconsin**, and his brother Bob. The Progressives believed in the right of men and women to own their own homes and they also lobbied for public ownership of utilities. This manifesto was essentially that adopted by Wright.

Pugin, A. W. N.
An early-nineteenth century British architect and designer. Pugin was the son of a French artist and one of the leading theoreticians of the **Aesthetic Movement** in the arts, architecture, and interior decor that was in vogue when Wright was growing up. His best-known work can be seen in the furniture and decorations for the Houses of Parliament in London, England.

Purcell, Irene
A film actress, Herbert **Johnson's** third wife. She would infuriate Wright with her redecorations of the Johnson house, **Wingspread**.

Right: The Price Tower is a 19-floor skyscraper and one of the most widely recognized of Wright's works.

Below: The Eric Pratt house. The Pratts made the sand-colored textile-blocks themselves.

R

Rancho Santa Fe
The place where Frank Lloyd Wright and Olgivanna Lazovich were married in August, 1928.

Rand, Alyn
Successful novelist born in St. Petersburg, Russia, in 1905. She wrote the best-selling novel *The Fountainhead* about an idealistic architect. She met Wright at **Taliesin** but their relationship was strained. This, however, has not prevented the continued misconception that Rand's hero in her novel is Wright personified.

Rattenbury, Kay
Member of the **Fellowship** who married another member — Allen L. Davy **Davison**.

Ravine Bluffs Development (1915)
Six houses commissioned by Sherman M. **Booth**. In addition, there are poured concrete sculptures and a bridge marking the northeastern entrance. Five of the houses (**Perry, Root, Kier, Ross,** and **Kissam**) were for rent and are named after their first tenant.

Raymond, Antonin
A Czech who had been educated in Prague, studied painting in **Italy**, and trained as an architectural drafts-man in **New York** City. He came to join Wright as work was being completed on the reconstruction of **Taliesin** in the spring of 1916. Raymond was one of the trusted architects who acted as supervisor of the construction of the **Imperial Hotel** during Wright's absences.

Raymond, Noémi
The French artist, wife of **Antonin**.

Pages 268/269, Above, Right, and Far right: Views from around the Ravine Bluffs Development. The site includes six houses and two poured concrete sculptures (**right**). Each house in the development is named after its first independant tenant. Four are square-plan buildings, developed from the "Fireproof House" concept; the Ross residence is different, having the chimney set to one side rather than being the central feature.

Above right: The Perry house.

Rayward, John L. House (1955) Tirranna Tirranna is a solar hemicycle with an extension added by second owner Herman R. Shepherd. **Exposed concrete block** construction combines with Philippine mahogany and glass. The swimming pool separates the living room from an 18-foot drop to the pond.

Rebay, Hilla, Baroness

A **German** baroness and art connoisseur who was the guiding light of the original decision to build a "temple" to contain her and Solomon R. **Guggenheim**'s collection of paintings — the **Guggenheim Museum**. Rebay was convinced that Wright's buildings had the necessary spiritual qualities to provide a fitting background for the art collection.

Above: The Rayward residence is a complex building in an idyllic woodland setting. The immediate surroundings were landscaped by Frank Okamura, designer of the Brooklyn Botanical Garden.

Right: Wright's signature, the red square symbol.

Rebhuhn, Ben, House (1937)

This **Usonian** house, with its two-story living room, was built to a cruciform plan with cypress board and batten with brickwork used inside and out.

"Red House"

The design for William **Morris**'s home, the "Red House" (1859-60), is considered the prototype for the **Arts and Crafts** concept of the artistic house. This early experiment would be an inspiration for a new generation of British architects and for Frank Lloyd Wright's work from the beginning of his independent practice.

red square symbol

By about 1904 Wright was substituting a new motif for the Celtic cross — the signature symbol on his earlier designs. The new motif was a plain red square with an ochre outline. Most authorities on Wright agree that this new symbol owes its origins to Japanese prints.

Reisley, Roland, House (1951)

This single-story structure with a balcony, wraps around its hillside lot. Construction is of stone with wood siding; it is the last of the **Pleasantville** project buildings.

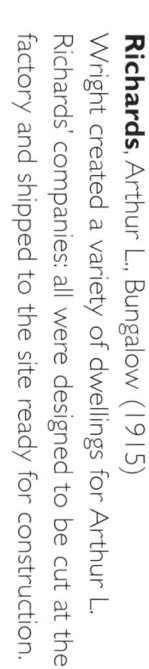

Richards, Arthur L., Bungalow (1915)
Wright created a variety of dwellings for Arthur L. Richards' companies; all were designed to be cut at the factory and shipped to the site ready for construction.

Richards, Arthur L., Duplex Apartments (1916)
These four separate buildings are all from American System Ready-cut prefab plans of 1911. They each had upper and lower apartments and were originally of plaster surface and wood trim (two have since been resurfaced).

Richards, Arthur L., Small House (1915)
This single story flat-roofed house is from American System Ready-cut prefab plans of 1911.

Richardson, Henry Hobson
A major East Coast architect who helped launch the **Shingle Style** that was the height of fashion for the final two decades of the nineteenth century. Richardson was much in demand in Chicago as well as the East Coast and **Silsbee** was one of his most ardent admirers.

Richardson was the architect of the 1885 Marshall Field Wholesale store in Chicago, a building many critics consider to be one of the finest of the nineteenth century. Richardson's work in the 1870s to some extent preempted Wright's early experiments with open floor plans.

Richardson, Stuart, House (1940)
This brick-built **Usonian** house represents an early example of Wright's use of triangular forms.

Above and Below: The Stuart Richardson residence is built of masonry, and the cypress wood evident in these photographs is used as trim rather than being an integral part of the wall. Designs for the house were altered to reduce cost and many features and details do not appear in the finished building.

Above right: The Arthur L. Richards bungalow is an American System-Built Home. These self assemble structures retailed for as little as $2,750.

Below right: The Arthur L. Richards duplex apartments.

Details of the Robie house show the exquisite detail that make this residence such a fine example of Prairie architecture and a National Historic Landmark. Note the fireplace (**above**) which provides the only separation between living and dining rooms and

the beautiful art-glass windows (**right**). The house is now owned by the University of Chicago and guided tours are available by arrangement. Some of the original furniture is in the University's Smart Museum.

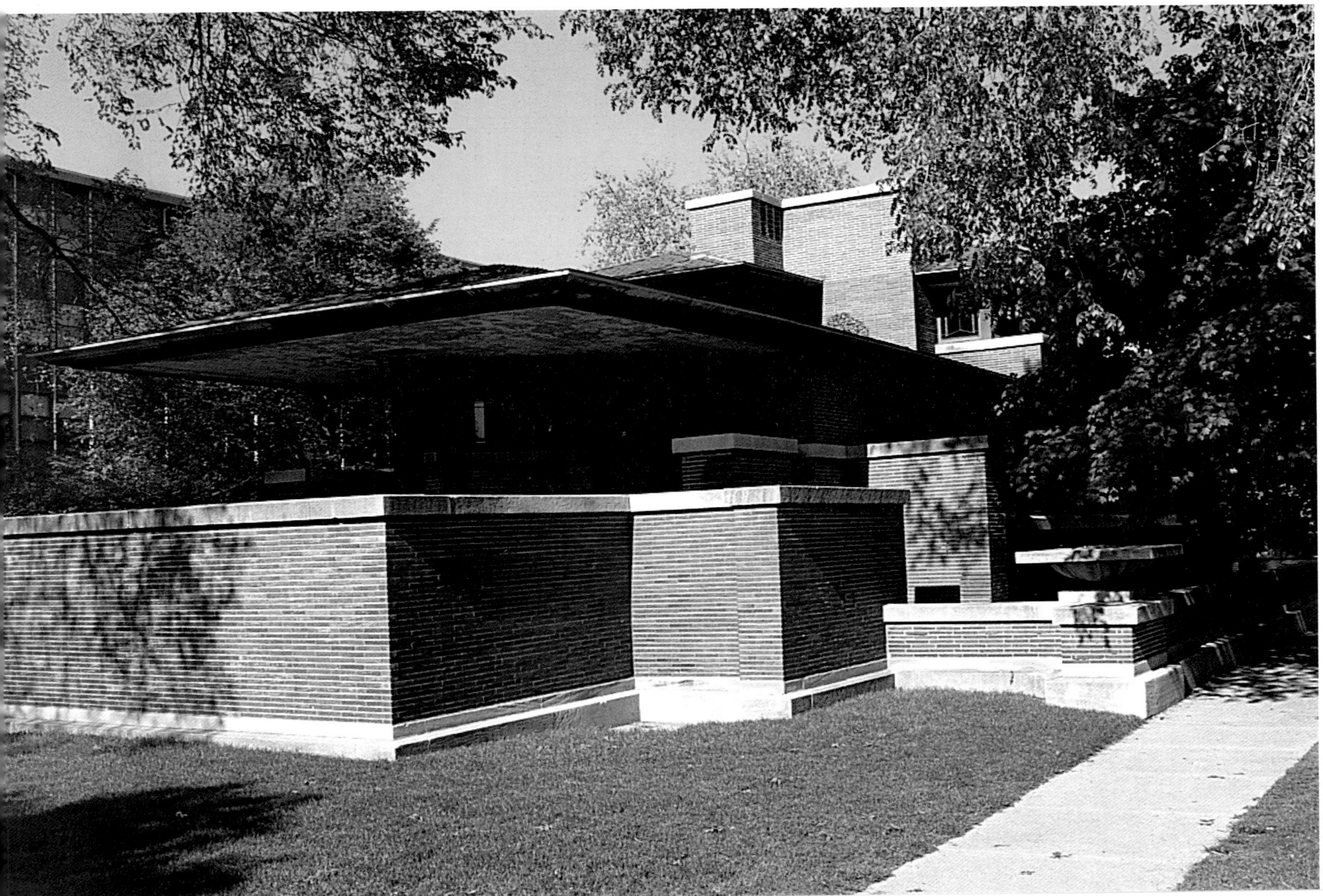

Roloson, Robert, W., Rowhouses (1894)
This was the first of Wright's "apartment" projects and is the only built example of city rowhouses. The brown brick row is noted for its abstract stone work.

Romeo and Juliet Windmill (1896)
The plan for the windmill reveals a diamond interlocked with an octagon. The original wood shingles were replaced with horizontal boards and battens in 1939.

Rookery Building Office, Entrance and Lobby (1905)
The only work that Wright did in this Chicago **skyscraper** was the remodeling of the entrance and lobby. This has been carefully restored over the last few years and is worth seeing.

Root, Hollis R., House (1915)
Located in the **Ravine Bluffs Development** Very similar to the **Perry** House, the Root House was badly neglected until restored sympathetically in the 1980s.

Root, John Wellborn
Partner in the Chicago firm of architects with Daniel H. **Burnham**, the major rivals to **Adler & Sullivan**. He moved to Chicago in 1872 following the great fire and is best known for the tall office buildings he designed in partnership with Burnham during the 1880s.

Left: The Romeo and Juliet Windmill which Wright built for "the Aunts," Nell and Jane. The octagon penetrated by a diamond is symbolic of Shakespeare's lovers embracing. The tower used to have a loudspeaker attatched to its roof through which Wright would play classical music to the cows and apprentices in the fields.

Right: The four Roloson Rowhouses were gutted in 1981 after fire and general decay. Today Wright's work is limited to the exterior of abstract stonework. Nevertheless, this is an interesting example of his early work.

Below: The Root residence is a square-plan house typical of the Ravine Bluffs Development. Restoration work has been carried out and the building is now much the same as when it was originally constructed.

Rorke, Dr Joseph
Wright's private physician who was with him when he
died. He was also the only person present when
Olgivanna **Wright** died. He became a **Taliesin Fellow**.

Rosenbaum, Stanley House (1939)
The only example of Wright's work in **Alabama** is in
Florence — built for Stanley and Mildred Rosenbaum.
This L-plan **Usonian** house was enlarged in 1948 by
Wright himself and was completely renovated in 1970
with internal modifications and the addition of an outside
Japanese garden. The living area built-in furniture was
specially designed by Wright and made from Cypress
wood. The house is open to the public and guided tours
are available by appointment.

The Stanley Rosenbaum house. The building was completely
renovated in 1970 by the Taliesin Fellowship and again in 1990.
The house is now open to the public at certain times.

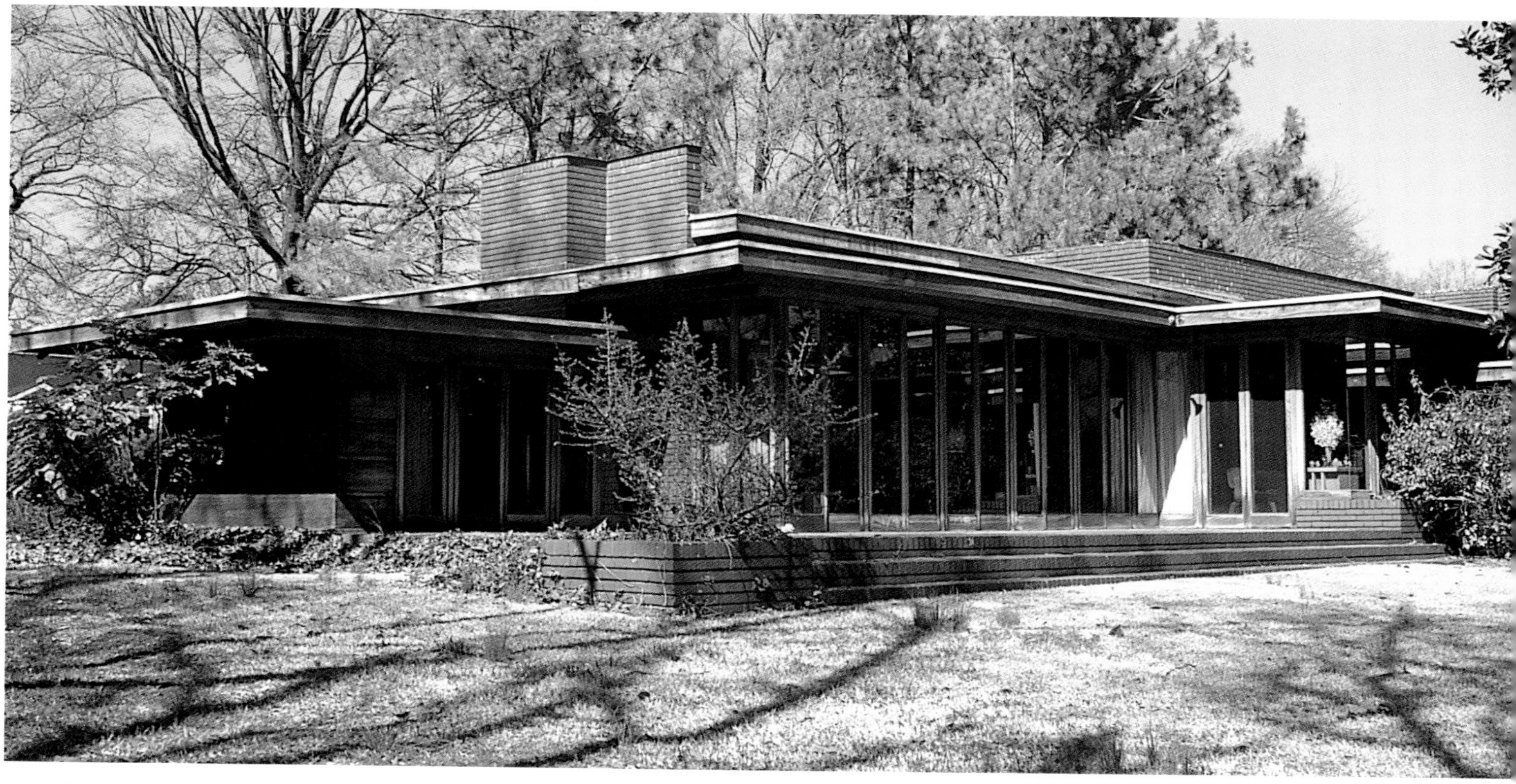

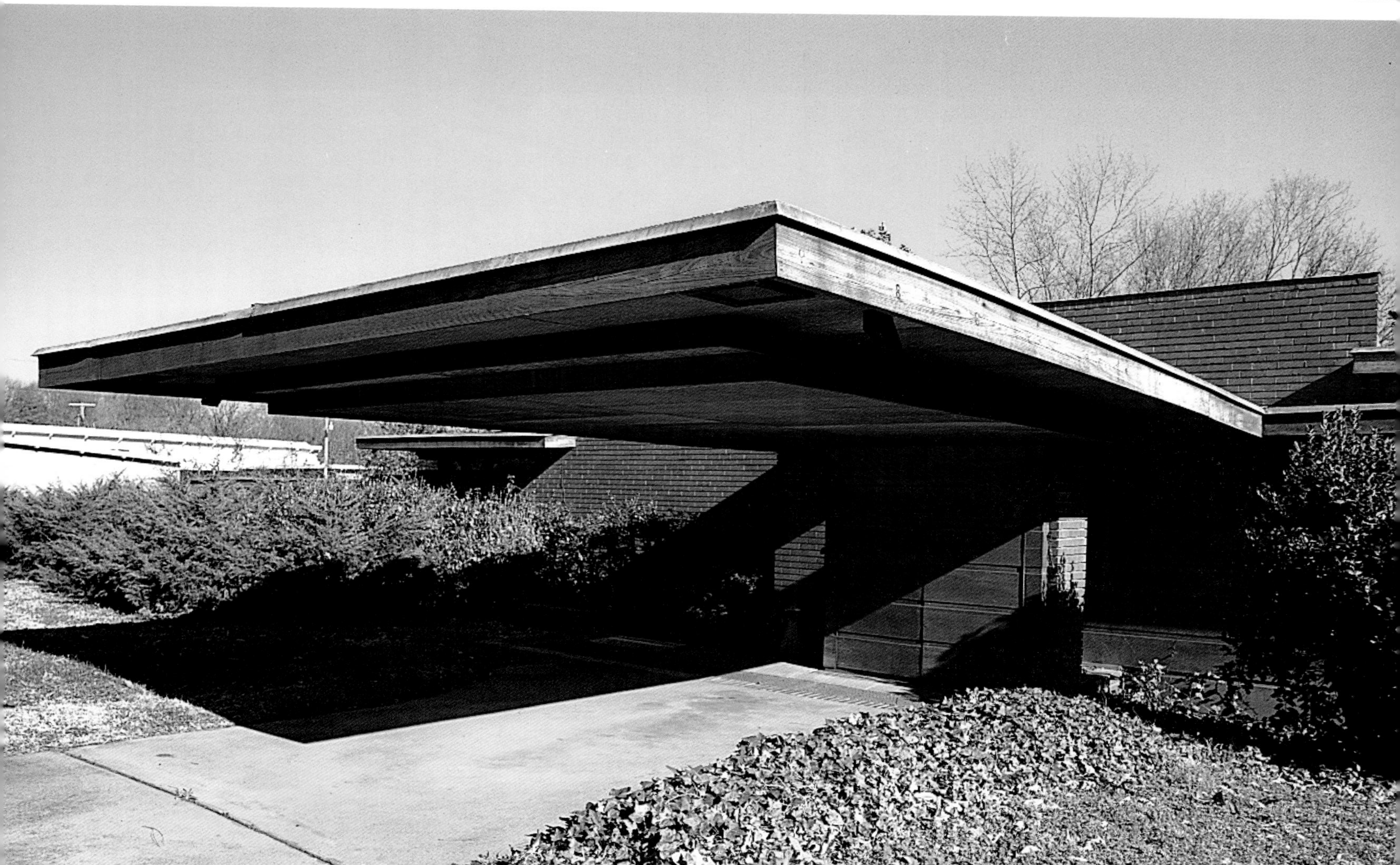

Ross, Charles S., House (1902) Part of the **Delavan Lake Group**. Originally built to a T-plan, this is a typical board and batten **Prairie** style house. A second-story extension — since enclosed — converted the plan to a cruciform.

Ross, William F., House (1915) Located in the **Ravine Bluffs Development**. The house is in its original form apart from an added porch (not by Wright.)

Roycrofters, East Aurora, New York The model **Arts and Crafts** colony that Elbert **Hubbard** established after his pilgrimage to meet William **Morris** in 1893. Hubbard was so successful in promoting his colony that the Roycrofters were obliged to build an inn to house all the people that wanted to buy their produce. There are some evident parallels between Hubbard's experiment at the turn of the century and Wright's own colony at **Taliesin** 30 years later.

Rubin, Nathan, House (1951) Constructed from brick with a horizontal wood siding sheath, the southeast-facing bedrooms and south-facing

aspect of the hexagonal living room open out onto a terrace; a pool is located off the northeast face of the living room.

Rudin, Walter, House (1957) A Marshall **Erdman** Company No. 2 Prefab, this square plan "one-room house" is built with **exposed concrete blocks** and has painted, horizontal board and batten. A balcony outside the sleeping quarters overlooks the large two-story living room.

Ruskin, John The English art critic and writer who inspired the aesthetic ideals of William **Morris**. Wright, while still an adolescent, had been given Ruskin's first book on architecture, The Seven Lamps of Architecture, and had read its sequel, The Stones of Venice. The concept of organic architecture originated with Ruskin.

Below and Right: The Charles Ross house. Now covered with yellow paint, the original structure was originally dark stained wood. Other alterations include additions at the front and rear as well as changes to allow for occupation during the winter.

Saarinen, Eliel
A Finnish architect employed by George **Booth** for the **Cranbrook** experiment. Saarinen's **Kingswood School**, built from 1929-31, is generally acknowledged to have been inspired by the **Prairie** style buildings that Wright had built in **Oak Park** a quarter of a century earlier, and is also reminiscent of the design Wright made for **Hillside** in 1903.

Saint-Gaudens, Augustus
An American sculptor responsible for the statue of Abraham Lincoln in Lincoln Park which Wright admired but wished someone would "kindly remove the chair."

Saint Mark's-in-the-Bouwerie Tower
A Wright commission for a 23-story copper-and-glass apartment tower in **New York** City. The tower was designed as a central trunk with reinforced concrete piers running up it and, like a tree, growing wider as it spread upward. After the stock market crash of October 29, 1929, all work on the project ceased and this, along with **San Marcos-in-the-Desert**, were two

of Wright's most brilliant designs that would never be built. The **Price Tower** in Bartlesville, **Oklahoma**, is a modified version of the great St. Mark's tower.

Sandburg, Carl
A poet and writer, he was a friend of Wright's. It is said that the architect was influenced by Sandburg's story-teller's tone, which he adopted for his own autobiography — *An Autobiography*.

Sander, Frank S. House (1952) Springbough
A brick foundation and core house which juts out from a rocky promontory and is complemented by wood siding. Springbough was restored and freshly landscaped in the 1990s. It is noted for its cantilevered living room.

Pages 286/287: The Sturges house, a remarkable building cantilevered out from the side of the hill on which it rests.

Above and Right: The Donald Schaberg residence overlooks a broad wooded valley. Cedar shakes were used in the roofing of this building and it blends well with the natural surroundings.

Sandova, Manuel
A superb cabinetmaker from Nicaragua who came to **Taliesin** in the early 1930s just as the **Fellowship** was being founded. Sandova became disenchanted as he had come to study architecture from the master but felt that he was kept doing cabinet work for Wright. He was highly paid for this work in the outside world so felt that he was being exploited.

San Marcos-in-the-Desert
Dr. Alexander **Chandler**'s large, elegant, hotel-cum-resort outside the town of Chandler where Wright lived and worked in 1928. This sizeable project gave a convincing demonstration of the large-scale possibilities of the

textile block system. The stock market crash of 1929 brought the commission to an abrupt halt. This project, along with the **St. Mark's-in-the-Bouwerie Tower,** were two of Wright's most brilliant designs that would never be built.

Schaberg, Donald, House (designed 1950, addition 1960s)
A large house which saw the addition of a family room and bedroom designed by original construction supervisor, Wright's ubiquitous assistant, John H. **Howe.**

Schevill, Ferdinand
Professor of history at the University of Chicago. Schevill was one of the seven friends and clients who lent Wright

money in 1926 when he was fighting lawsuits against Miriam Noel **Wright** and trying to keep the Bank of Wisconsin from repossessing **Taliesin.**

Schindler, Pauline
A bohemian artist, the wife of Rudolph (see below). Already upset when her husband left him, Wright was further upset when Pauline organized an exhibition in **Los Angeles** in 1930, "Three Architects of International Renown." Wright took offence at being equated with her husband and Richard **Neutra.**

Schindler, Rudolph M.
Schindler was born in Vienna, and while employed there

Above: The Donald Schaberg house. Over 55,000 hard-burned Maryland bricks were used in its construction; their gold color creates a warm appearance and blends with the cedar shakes on the roof.

saw Wright's **Wasmuth Portfolios.** He moved to America in 1914, and worked for a Chicago firm for three years before joining Wright's office in 1918; there he worked on both the **Imperial Hotel,** Tokyo, and the **Hollyhock House,** for which Wright sent him to **California** to oversee the construction. Schindler went on to become one of the leading practitioners of the **International Style** on the West Coast.

Schultz, Carl, House (1957)

Completed by the **Taliesin Associated Architects** after Wright's death, the Schultz House was built with reused bricks from the owner's other properties in the area. It looks out over the St. Joseph River and has a massive cantilevered terrace as well as a large basement.

Schuyler, Montgomery

He was a journalist for *The New York Times*, a critic and historian of American architecture, and one of the founders of *The Architectural Record*. Schuyler was an early advocate of Wright's work when others were not so keen.

Schwanke, Bill

A master carpenter from **Spring Green** who came to **Taliesin** in the early 1930s just as the **Taliesin Fellowship** was being founded.

Schwartz, Bernard, House (1939)

An early **Usonian** house built of red brick with horizontal cypress board and sunk batten, it overlooks the East Twin River. The building derives from Wright's idea of a home "for a family of $5,000–$6,000 income" as published in *Life Magazine* (1938). It actually cost $18,000.

Scott, M. H. Baillie

A British **Arts and Crafts** architect who had pioneered experiments with open-plan living although Wright has been given credit for the concept. Wright's famous all-encompassing roofs with broad overhangs were another concept that may have evolved from the work of Baillie Scott, among others.

Scoville Park Fountain (1903)

The original fountain was demolished and a replica can now be found in **Oak Park**.

Self-build houses (see **Usonian automatic**)

Serlin, Edward, House (1949)

The second of the **Pleasantville** projects is a **Usonian** house built from stone with some horizontal siding. The projected east and west extensions of Wright's original design were never built.

The Carl Schultz house. A feature of this house is the large cantilevered terrace which has a dramatic view of a ravine off the bank of the St. Joseph River.

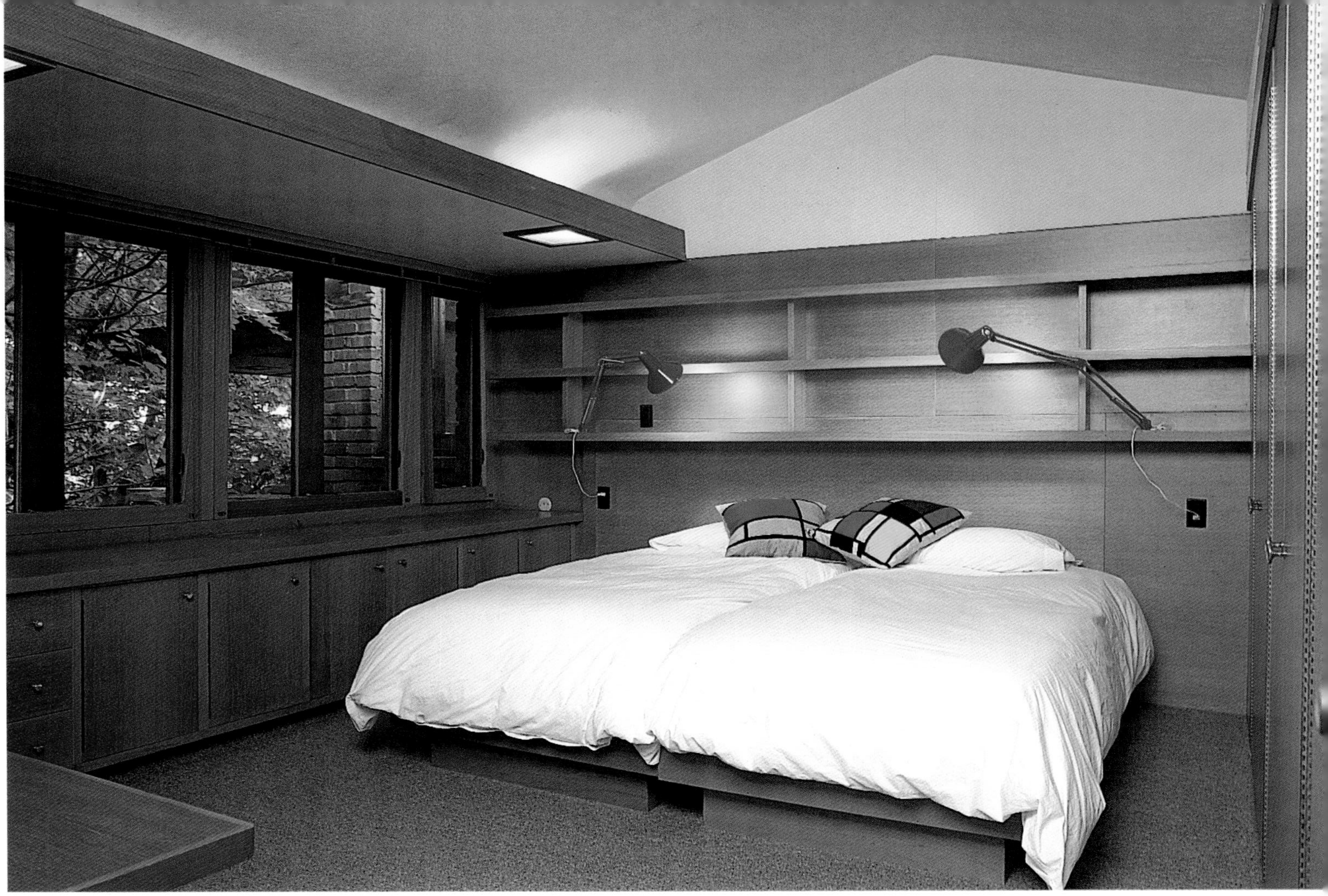

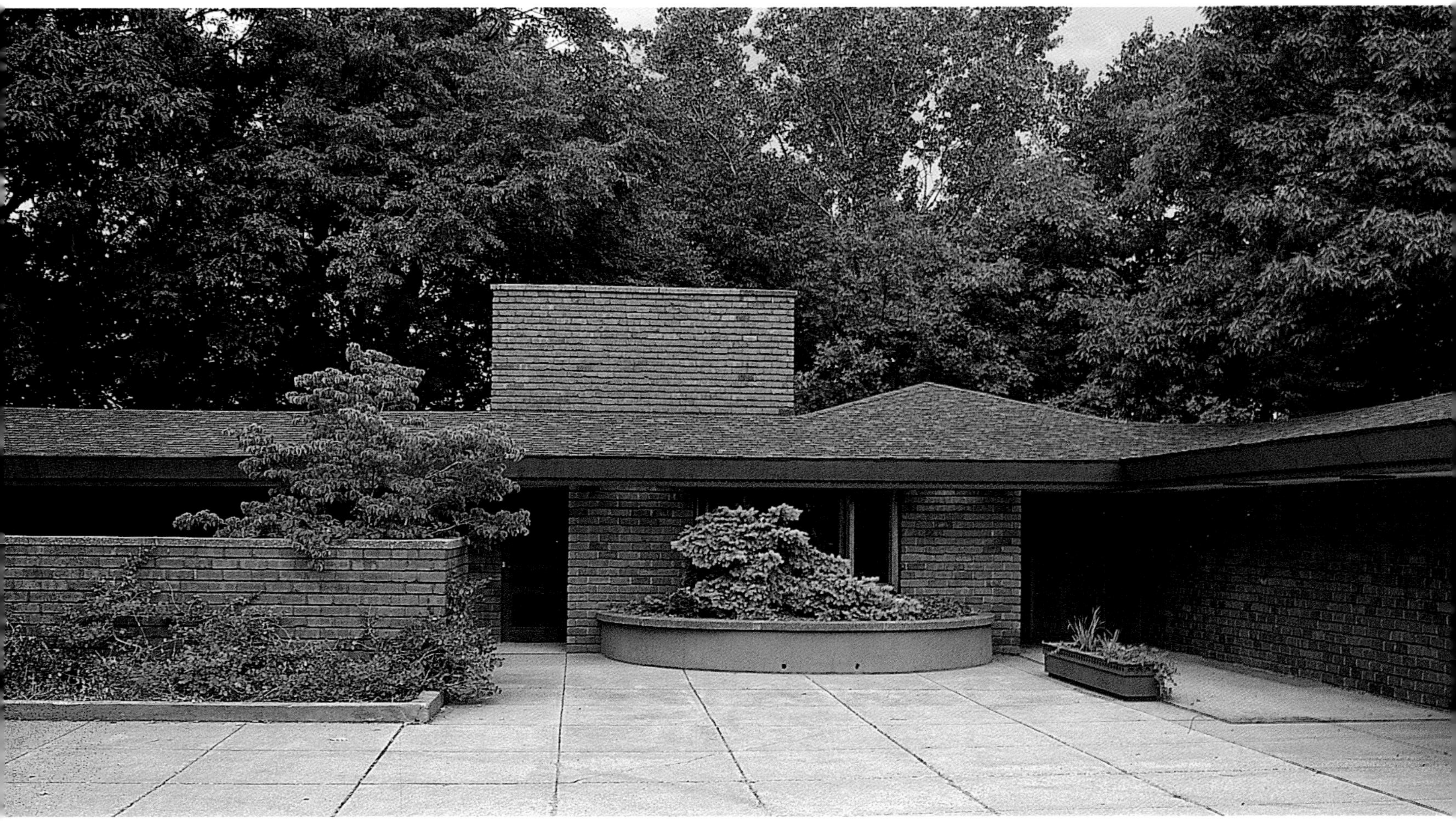

Above: The Seamour Shavin house commands panoramic views of the Tennesse River from the north-facing windows (visible on the left). Unusually for a Wright building, this house does not attempt to blend into the scenery but sits proudly atop the hill.

Shavin, Seamour: House (1950)
This two-bedroom house has a living room which opens onto a northwest-facing patio. It has a "butterfly" roof.

Shaw, Howard Van Doren
A Chicago architect whose style was "establishment." He was apparently on friendly terms with Wright but demonstrated no interest in American architecture for the twentieth century.

Shaw, Richard
The British architect who invented the "Queen Anne" architectural style to reflect the new aestheticism of the late 1800s. Shaw was, by general agreement, the most internationally influential architect of his time, setting styles from the late 1860s until 1914.

Shingle Style
This was an eclectic but quintessentially American mixture of many different elements, united by the use of wooden shingles for walls and roof.

Short, William
Clerk of the works for the **Guggenheim Museum** in the last years of Wright's life.

Shunsho, Katsukawa
One of the finest of the *ukiyo-e* designers and a particular favorite of Wright; he specialized in realistic actor portraits. Shunsho was the master of Hokusai.

Silsbee, Joseph Lyman
A fashionable architect for the *nouveaux riches*, he arrived in Chicago after the great fire of 1871 to exploit the opportunities this presented to his profession. Silsbee was a much sought-after architect of mainly residential buildings in the Norman Shaw **Shingle Style**. Frank

---

"Sixty Years of Living Architecture"
In January 1951 this world-touring exhibition of Wright's work opened in Philadelphia. This showed his original drawings, architectural models, and huge photographs of many of his buildings and decorative objects.

Skidmore, Owings & Merrill
A prominent Chicago architectural firm which was commissioned to build a new academy for the U.S. Air Force in Colorado Springs. Wright was the only other contender for the commission but he withdrew in 1954 when the American Legion threatened to make a public protest if he were chosen. The company was also responsible for the **International Style** Lever Building in **New York**.

skyscrapers
Although Wright had experimented with designing skyscrapers, using his metaphor of a tree with a central trunk and cantilevered slabs for branches, by the 1930s he seemed convinced that the building style was doomed. He felt the "vainglorious skyscraper" should be taxed out of existence. In the early 1950s the success of his **Price Tower**, however, convinced Wright that a case could be made for them after all. Being the man he was, to be persuaded was to become an ardent advocate.

Smith, Frank L: Bank (1905)
First National Bank. This building, with its cut-stone exterior, was renovated in 1970 and is open to the public during banking hours.

Smith, George W.: House (1895-98)
The use of shingles in the construction of this house pre-dates Wright's employment of horizontal board and batten siding which was to become the trademark of his numerous **Prairie** and **Usonian** buildings.

Above far right: The George W. Smith house in Oak Park. The original roofing was of stained red shingles.

Above right and Right: The Frank L. Smith First National Bank. A symmetric stone-clad exterior conceals typical Wrightian treatment of space within.

Lloyd Wright, by now living in Chicago, had an easy introduction to him, as at the time Silsbee was working on a new building for All Souls' Church where his uncle, the Reverend Jenkin **Lloyd Jones**, was pastor. In the spring 1887 Silsbee took on Wright as an apprentice and allowed him to do a little work on the church.

Smith, Melvin Maxwell, House (1946)
Enlarged by **Taliesin Associated Architects** in 1969-70, this is an L-plan **Usonian** brick and batten single-story house. Mel Smith acted as his own contractor because two teachers' salaries (his and his wife Sara's) in the immediate post-war years could not stretch to cover the cost of employing one.

Smith, Richard, House (1950)
This single-story structure, built from limestone, plaster, cypress, and cedar shingles, is noted for its beautiful stonework.

Sondern, Clarence, House (1940)
Originally a standard **Usonian** house, and the first for which John H. **Howe** supervised construction, additional work in 1948 transformed it completely, adding a large living area a quarter-story below the original design.

South Carolina
There are two examples of Wright's architecture in South Carolina. The earliest is dated 1938 — the **Auldbrass Plantation** (see also **Stevens** House) in Yemassee. The site originally contained a private residence, two cottages, a barn with chicken runs, a manager's quarters (destroyed by fire), stables with kennels, and a manager's office (1939). Fire destroyed the barn and chicken runs and natural tannic acid ate through the original copper roofing. Restoration began in the mid-1980s. The other example of Wright's work in South Carolina is the **Austin** House, Broad Margin, in Greenville. Its most obvious characteristic is the huge sheltering roof that seems to extend the hill out over the house. The living spaces of the house extend downhill from the entrance hall nestled in the hillside.

Spaulding, Mr. & Mrs. William
American art collectors from Boston. Wright purchased thousands of prints for them beginning with his 1913 trip to **Japan**. Considered one of the finest collections of Japanese prints in the world, the Spauldings bequeathed their collection to the Museum of Fine Arts, Boston.

Spencer, Dudley, House (1956)
A single-story, stone-built house, with a hemicycle-plan living room facade opening out onto a terrace.

Spencer, George W., House (1902)
One of the five summer residences of the **Delavan**

Left: The George C. Stewart house is the only example of Prairie architecture in California but is a particularly fine building.

Lake Group. It is alleged that Wright disowned this cottage when the boards on the second level were laid vertically instead of horizontally during its construction.

Spencer, Robert C. Jr.
Spencer was one of the number of architects of the **New School of the Midwest**, whom Wright believed were "throwing up sordid little imitations of his work all over the Midwest."

Spring Green, Wisconsin
The village on the north bank of the Wisconsin River where the **Lloyd Jones** family settled (see also **Taliesin**).

Staley, Karl A., House (1950)
A single-story, long I-plan house, built parallel to the Lake Erie shoreline. It is constructed from stone although the facade appears to have been made entirely from glass due to the extensive living room windows. The house was renovated in the 1980s.

Steffens, Oscar, House (designed 1909; since demolished)
Situated near Lake Michigan, the Oscar Steffens House had the typical two-story living room of the **Prairie** style houses.

Steinway Hall
The 11-story office and theater building, designed by Dwight **Perkins**, where Wright and **Corwin** set up their office soon after Wright had left **Adler & Sullivan**. Perkins, Myron **Hunt**, and George W. **Maher** also had offices in this building and the members of the Steinway Hall group are now considered the founders of the **New School of the Midwest** or **Prairie School**.

Stevens, C. Leigh, House (1940)
A brick and cypress construction linked to the other buildings in the **Auldbrass Plantation** complex by esplanades. Restoration of the main house and one of the cottages has been completed and many of the features not finished in the original construction have been correctly included from the original plans.

Stewart, George C., House (1909)
The first of Wright's **California** houses — a lovely drawing of which appeared in the 1910 **Wasmuth Portfolio** of his work — was a Midwestern **Prairie House** on the Pacific Coast. Its design was completed shortly before Wright left for Europe.

Stockman, G. C., House (1908)

This two-story, dark-wood-banded **Prairie House**, Wright's earliest building in Iowa, was moved to its current location in 1989 and restored. It is almost identical to the **Hunt** House. Open to the public for much of the year.

Stohr, Peter C., Arcade Building (built 1909; demolished 1922)

Most of this building was located under the "El" tracks at Wilson Avenue Station. The building incorporated the stairs to the railway as well as ticket booths and rose to three stories where it became free of the tracks.

Stone, Patrick

The judge who sentenced Marcus **Weston** to Sandstone, a prison for political dissenters in **Wisconsin**. When Weston was sentenced, 25 apprentices petitioned the local draft board at Dodgeville, Wisconsin. Judge Patrick Stone accused the apprentices of submitting a document that was seditious. In all there were three **Taliesin** apprentices incarcerated in Sandstone prison for being **conscientious objectors**.

Stonorov, Oskar

A German-born architect who became director of the Philadelphia Housing Association, Stonorov was also a noted town planner. He was a good friend of Wright and, as he had studied sculpture and was a clever portraitist, he suggested that he sculpted Wright's head. The work was begun but never finished. Stonorov was the man who organized the exhibition **"Sixty years of Living Architecture."**

Storer, John, House (1923)

A most lavish example of a **textile block** house using a split-level plan with wings to each side (bedrooms west, service east). In this house, Wright, as usual, designed all of the furniture and fittings. Construction was supervised by the architect himself.

Strauss, Nathan

A journalist and public official, Strauss headed the **U.S. Housing Authority** from 1937 to 1942. the Strauss family owned Macy's department store in **New York** City. Wright distrusted Strauss's motives and is quoted thus: "Out of the slums of today, you are making the slums of tomorrow."

Stromquist, Don M., House (1958)

Completed by the **Taliesin Associated Architects**, this **exposed concrete block** structure is built on a

The G.C. Stockman house is another refinement of the "Fireproof House for $5,000" concept and as such is a square-plan building. Interesting features are the broad cantilevered roof and the dark wood banding at the corners of the house. Moved in 1989 to avoid demolition, the house benefited from restoration during 1991 and 1992. In common with other square-plan houses, the Stockman residence has a central fireplace (**below**) which separates the living and dining areas.

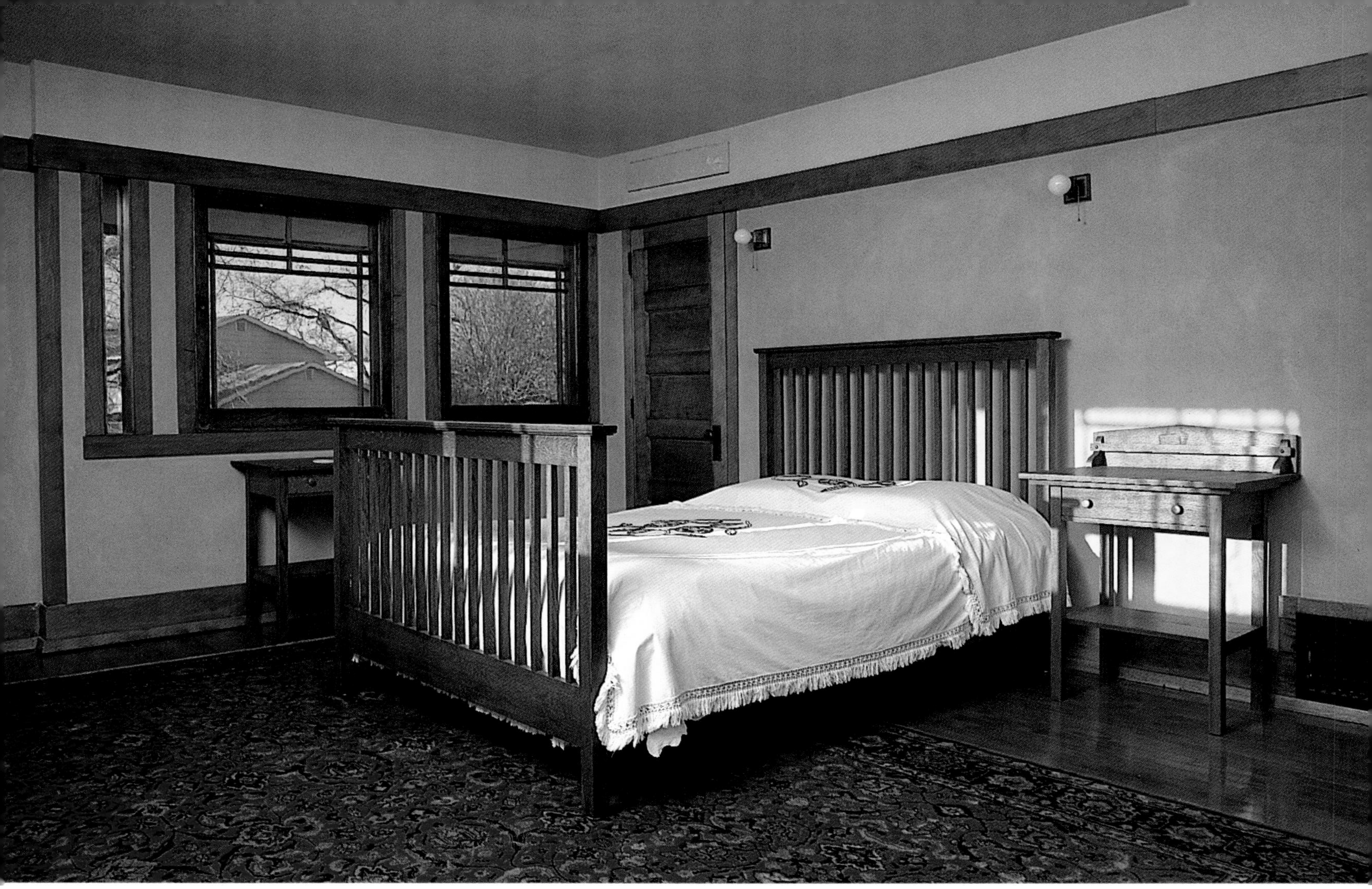

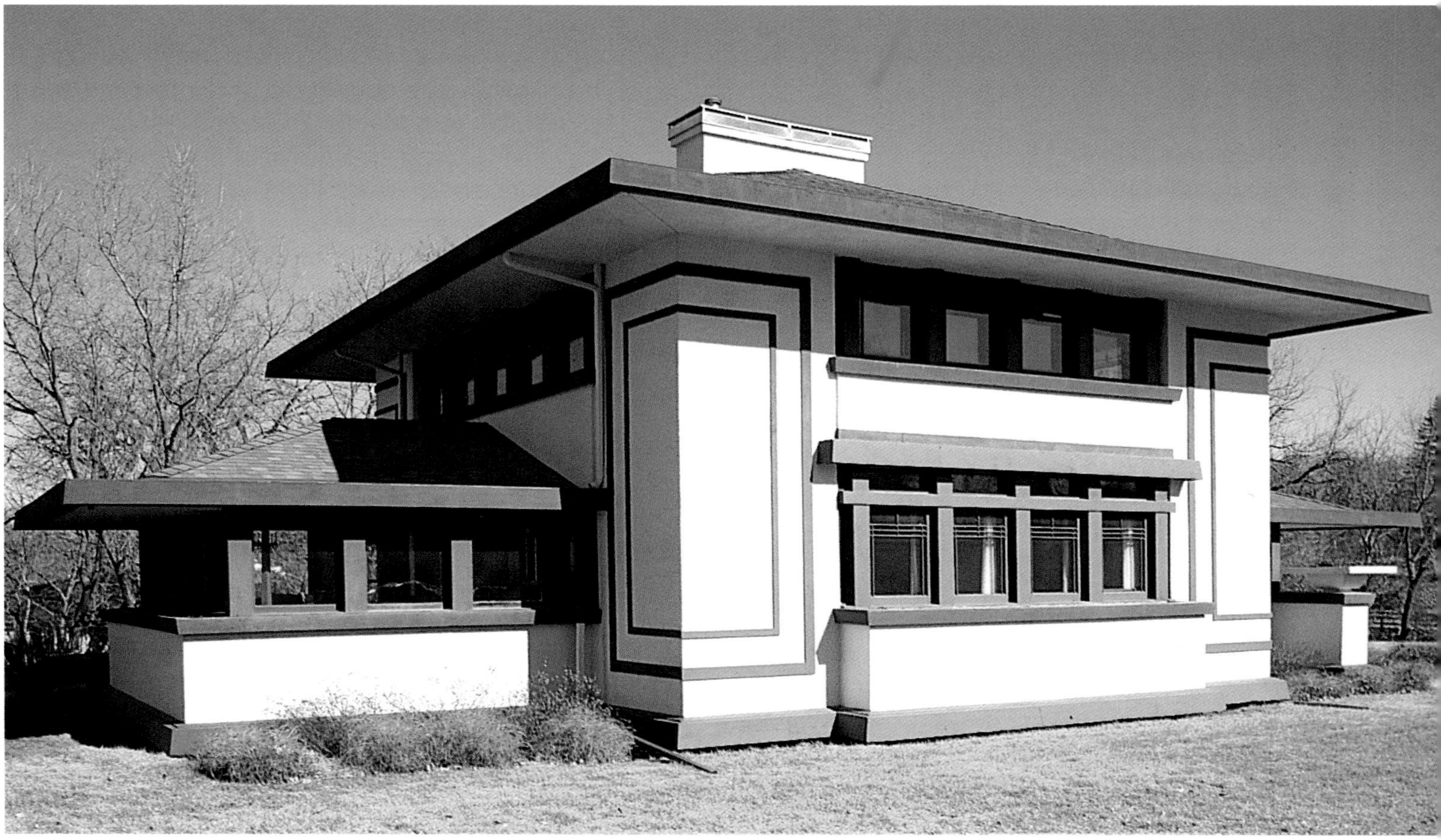

triangular module. The triangular master bedroom and living room feature, respectively, a balcony and a terrace. Because of deterioration under the second owner, restoration work has been completed.

Strong, Gordon
The Chicago millionaire who bought **Sugarloaf Mountain** and the 3,000 acres surrounding it with a plan to maintain it as a nature park. Strong never decided whether he preferred Wright's concept for the park or one of the four ideas he had commissioned from other architects.

Studio, Magazine
The magazine which first brought the ideas of the **Arts and Crafts Movement** to a wide audience.

Sturges, George D. House (1939)
Alarmingly cantilevered out from a hillside, this house is constructed from brick with wood siding. The whole east side of the house opens out onto a balcony.

Sugarloaf Mountain. Frederick County, Maryland
Wright was commissioned by Gordon **Strong** in 1924 to design observation platforms, restaurants, gift shops, movie theater, planetarium, and so on for his grand plans for a 3,000-acre nature park built on Sugarloaf Mountain. Wright rose to the challenge and prepared hundreds of drawings but the project was never realized (see Gordon **Strong**).

Sullivan, Albert, House (designed 1892, demolished 1970)
Louis **Sullivan** lived in the house for four years before his brother occupied the premises. Wright designed it in the style of his "Lieber Meister" (Dear Master) while working for Sullivan.

Sullivan, Louis Henri
The American architect Louis Sullivan was one of the partners of **Adler & Sullivan**, the company Wright joined in 1887. He was one of the founders of the Chicago school of architecture and a key figure in the development of American architecture. His brilliant early designs for steel-frame **skyscraper** construction led to the emergence of the skyscraper as the distinctive American building type. As the design partner of the firm he formed in 1881 with Dankmar **Adler**, Sullivan produced several buildings internationally recognized for their functional form, extravagant ornamentation, and significance in the evolution of the skyscraper. Sullivan strove in his architectural designs to reconcile the romantic world of nature with the mechanistic world of science and technology. While his urban buildings were functional in character, the rich organic ornamentation endows each of the structures with an individual identity. Sullivan was an articulate and poetic spokesman for what came to be called **organic architecture**. This successful integration of architectural and decorative elements profoundly impressed a whole generation of American and European architects. His most famous pupil was Frank Lloyd Wright, who acknowledged Sullivan as his master — Wright called him "Lieber Meister" (dear master) — and he had a profound influence on Wright's work.

Sullivan, Louis, Summer House and Stables (designed 1890; additions 1970; stables demolished 1942)
The original T-plan was altered by the addition of a new dining room. The high-pitched roof is characteristic of Wright's early work and the woodwork in the rooms remains in good condition despite the many alterations made during restoration in the 1930s.

Sunday, Robert T., House (1955)
Designed by Wright as an L-plan **Usonian** house with a substantial living room, it had an addition in 1970, making it a T-plan. One of the last brick Usonian homes, construction was undertaken after Wright's death by John H. **Howe** who also designed the later addition.

Suntop Homes. (1938)
Wright's idea was a radically different way of producing concentrated living space rather than the time-honored approach with vertically-stacked single-floor apartments. His plan was to produce "quadrants" of four dwellings, with two stories per dwelling and was based on his **Broadacre City** models. Built of brick and horizontal lapped wood siding for the Ton Company, the sole building is divided into four quarters, each with two stories, basement, and sunroof. It was intended to have four of these units built in Ardmore but in the end only one was constructed. Local protests stopped the construction of more and a further attempt to try out the idea in 1942 in Pittsfield came to nothing. Damage led to reconstruction which did not follow Wright's original plans.

Sutton, Harvey P. House (1905)
This **Prairie** style house is Wright's only work in **Nebraska**. It is the usual plaster-surfaced wood-trimmed construction.

Sweeney, James Johnson
Sweeney replaced Hilla **Rebay** as future director of the **Guggenheim Museum**. Wright and Sweeney were in

constant conflict over the nature of the proposed museum and found it almost impossible to agree about anything.

◆ Sweeton, J. A., House (1950)

The house is built to a T-plan using a four-foot-square module. It is constructed with a red concrete-slab floor and interior redwood plywood board and batten. The red roof, originally laid out in overlapping boards, is now covered with asbestos shingles. It also has a cantilevered fireplace and carport.

Right: Louis Henri Sullivan. Wright's mentor and a highly influential architect in his own right.

Below: The George D. Sturges house.

Tafel, Edgar
One of the founding group of apprentices of the **Taliesin Fellowship**. He was one of Wright's principal assistants, acting as supervisor for the construction of some major projects, including **Fallingwater** and the **Johnson Wax** buildings.

Taliesin
When Wright returned from Europe in 1911 with Mamah Borthwick **Cheney** it was impossible to return to Chicago because of the scandal. Wright's mother gave him a tract of family land in **Spring Green,** WI. The land, although very hilly and rocky, was ideal for a rural estate and Wright christened it Taliesin, the Welsh for "shining brow." At Taliesin the architect was able to develop fully and display his ideas of using natural materials and elements combined in a setting of harmony and sympathy with the overall environment. Wright desired that Taliesin should be "of the hill, not on the hill." His first house was inspired by the **Villa Medici** in Tuscany, **Italy** and he relished the challenge of designing a house that would express everything he

thought and believed. The complex of buildings was developed over a period of 45 years and was continuously remodeled and rebuilt. It incorporated a farm and other functional buildings stretching across the hill. Eventually, Taliesin acquired 3,000 acres.

Fire of 1925
In April, 1925, an electrical storm short-circuited a new telephone system that Wright had installed in the house and set off a fire. Fanned by the high winds that accompanied the storm, the fire was soon out of control. The living quarters were lost but a dramatic change of wind direction and heavy rain saved the studio and workrooms. Wright lost a number of priceless art treasures but the insured building could be reconstructed. Taliesin had grown piecemeal as the need to expand had arisen and now Wright had the opportunity to design to a new and orderly, unified plan.

Pages 302/303, Above, and Right: Various views of Taliesin in Spring Green, WI.

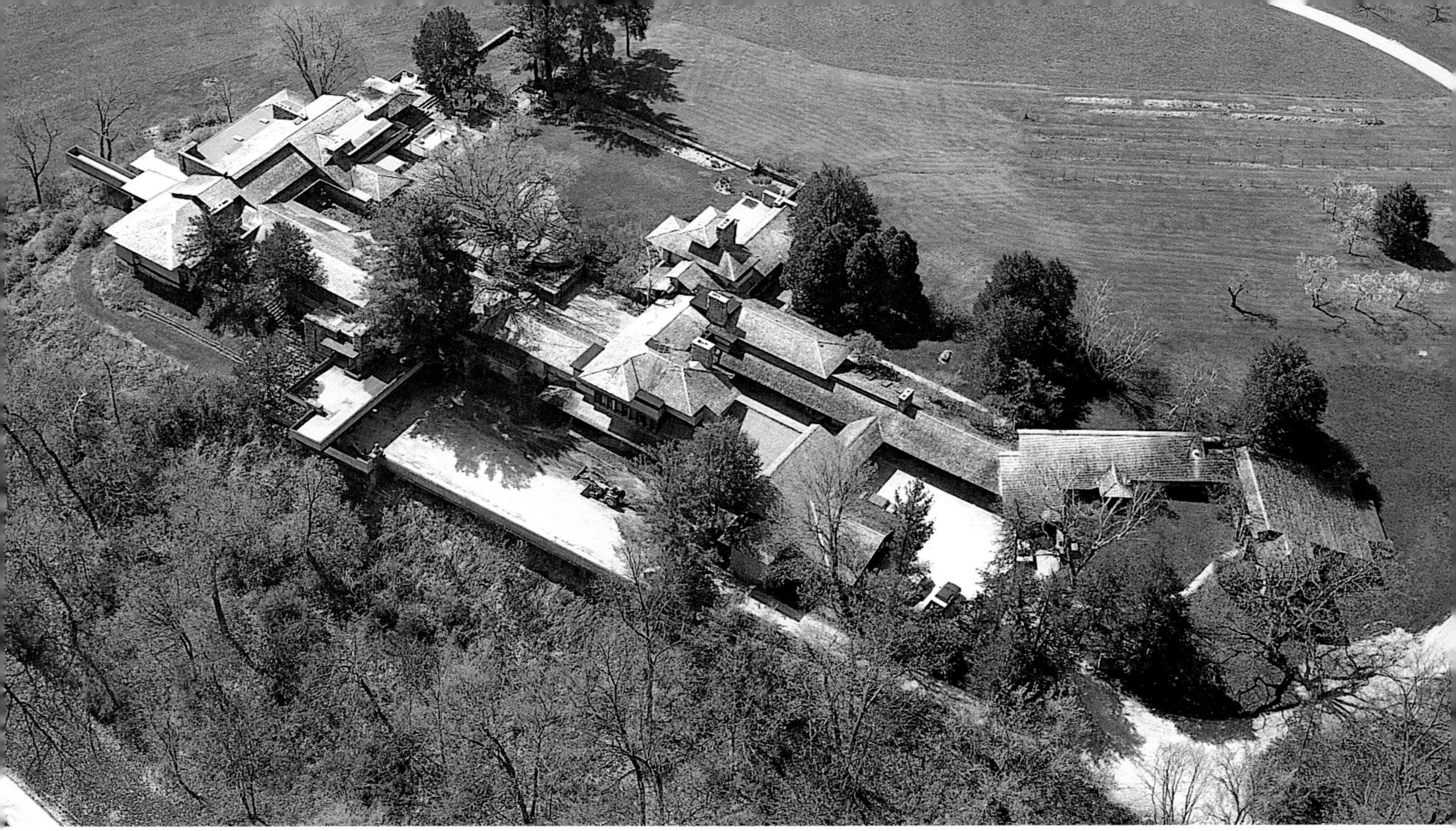

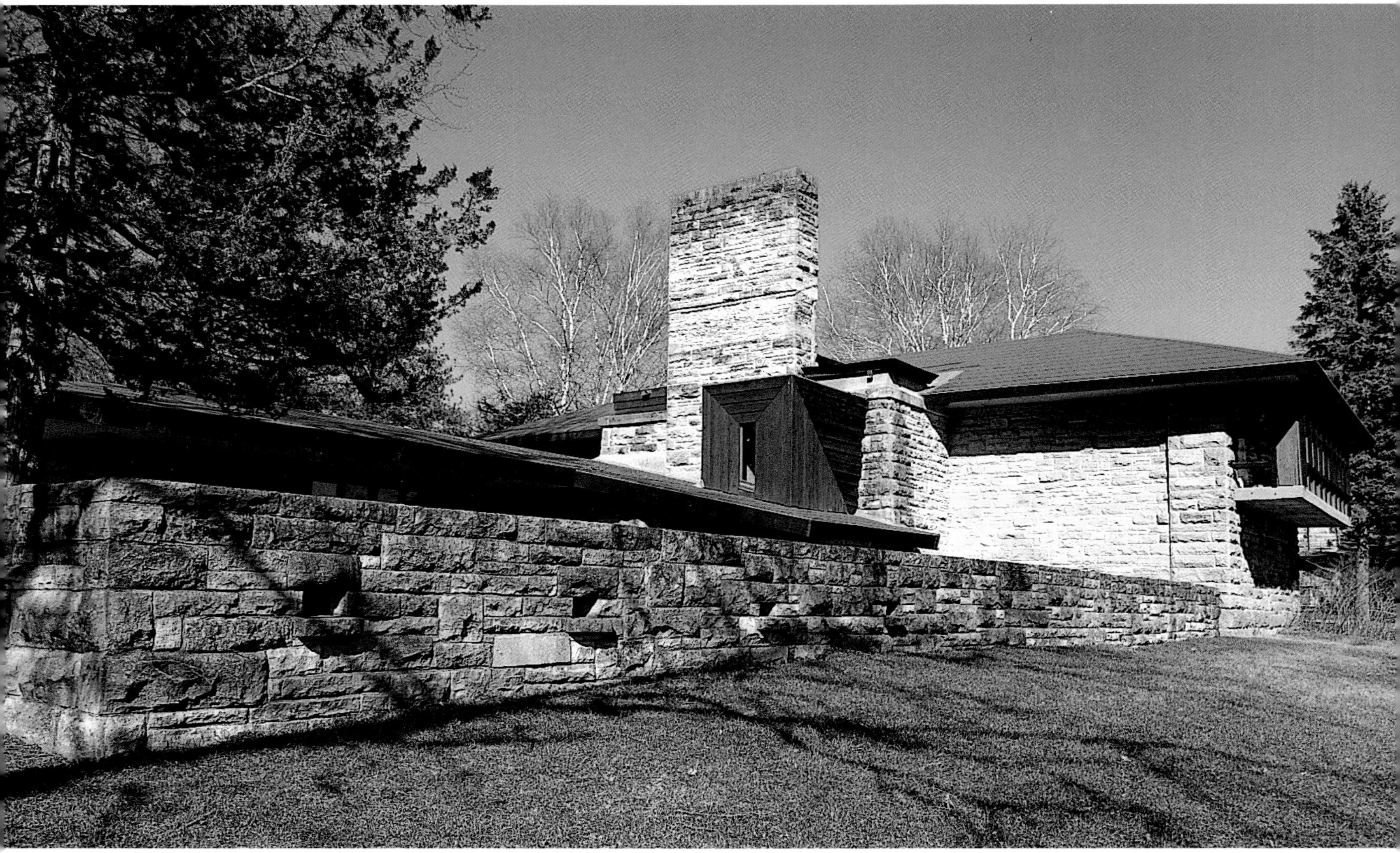

Fire of 1927

There was another fire at Taliesin in February, 1927, again caused by faulty wiring. This was a minor fire but it was fortuitous for Wright as it delayed foreclosure on the property while the bank totalled up its losses and made a new appraisal.

Early restorations and additions

After the **Taliesin murders** in 1914, the living quarters were destroyed but the studio remained and Wright began to restore Taliesin with no expense spared. The building complex was extensive: an enlarged studio, with new living quarters for several draftsmen, newly erected farm buildings, stables, guest quarters, servant's quarters, and a handsome residence for Wright himself. After the 1925 fire Wright made 40 sheets of pencil studies in pursuit of his latest vision for Taliesin reborn, but rebuilding it for a third time proved a tremendous drain on his financial resources.

Taliesin I (designed 1911; living quarters destroyed by fire in 1914).

This was the original building before the 1914 fire.

Taliesin clings to the side of the hill in its idyllic setting. The building materials are primarily native limestone, wood, and plaster surfacing, and the complex has seen many alterations over the years to accomodate the changing requirements of the Wright family and the Fellowship.

Taliesin II and III

Taliesin II had its living quarters destroyed by fire in 1925; Taliesin III — much of which was part of Taliesin I and II — is the major Wrightian site in the U.S. Originally used to indicate Wright's house, the name Taliesin has come to identify the whole valley, situated just off the Wisconsin River, in a valley opposite the "Welsh Hills" of Bryn Maur, Bryn Carol, and Bryn Bach. Here Wright rebuilt his life after the trauma of the 1909-11 period. Returning from Europe with Mamah **Cheney** he designed and built the first Taliesin and would go on to modify and build all over the area. Now preserved and run by the Frank Lloyd Wright Foundation, the Taliesin Preservation Commission oversees the buildings which encompass the complex:

1. **Romeo and Juliet Windmill** (1896)

2. Andrew **Porter** House (1907)

3. **Taliesin** (I 1911, II 1914, III 1925)

4. **Taliesin Fellowship** Complex

5. Taliesin Visitors' Center

6. **River View Terrace Restaurant**

Founded as a school for architects, one of the first apprentices was John H. **Howe.** Various buildings were created or remodeled for the Fellowship, including the Drafting Studio (1922), Playhouse (1933 and rebuilt after the fire in 1952 as the Theater), the Midway Barns (1938), and Dairy and Machine Sheds (1947), all of which helped house, feed, and nurture the community. Fellows at the Taliesin Complex ate food provided by the

Above, Right, and Pages 310/311: Further views of Taliesin. The buildings are a perfect complement to the beautiful natural landscape of the Spring Green. The Visitor Center provides guided tours throughout most of the year.

rich **Wisconsin** soil at the working agricultural estate. Later, the barns and the dairy sheds provided accommodation for the expanding architectural community of Taliesin. One of the 17 buildings designated to be retained by the **A.I.A.**, the current Taliesin was built in 1925 after fire destroyed much of Taliesin I (1914) and II (1925). The house was constructed mainly from native limestone, wood, and plaster surfacing. It has been continually altered over the years. In 1945 dams created a small lake which is used to irrigate the land as well as for recreational purposes. The garden design was Wright's last sketch. Tours are available from April to December.

Taliesin the Third or Taliesin East

Wright remodeled an apartment in the **Hotel Plaza** to use as temporary accommodation while working on the **Guggenheim Museum** and his other projects in **New York** and Connecticut. It was known to some as Taliesin the Third or Taliesin East.

Taliesin. The Legend

A Welsh bard of mythical stature, a characteristic hero figure of Celtic myth. His symbolic name means "shining-brow" and Wright used this as an explanation for choosing it to adorn the house he had built on the side of a hill. The legend of Taliesin tells of a supernatural being who is destined to die and be reborn.

Taliesin Associated Architects (T.A.A.)

Wright's designs are still being built today by the Taliesin Associated Architects (T.A.A.). For example, the design

and construction of the futuristic **Marin County Civic Center** in San Rafael, Wright's only work for the U.S. Government, was underway when Wright died in 1959 and was finished under the aegis of Aaron **Green**, William Wesley **Peters**, and the Taliesin Associated Architects.

Taliesin Fellowship

With the encouragement that he received, and the general revival of interest following the publication of his An Autobiography, Wright established the Taliesin Fellowship at **Spring Green, Wisconsin**. It was started in 1932, at the worst point of the **Great Depression** and was conceived along the lines of a utopian community of worker-apprentices who paid a fee to come and work and live with the great architect. The community grew as apprentices arrived, and much of their attitude was fostered by Olgivanna **Wright** who created an almost mystical reverence for Frank Lloyd Wright. Despite paying for the honor, part of the apprentices' daily routine was to do chores around the house and grounds between working on their assigned design projects. They assisted Wright on many of his projects with drawings and model-making and some of them later went to work for the architect on **Taliesin West**. Construction of Taliesin West started in 1934 as a winter home for Wright, and by 1938 it was largely complete, having been extended to include offices and studios to become the new home of the Taliesin Fellowship.

Taliesin murders

On Saturday, August 15, 1914, two Taliesin draftsmen,

Brodelle and **Fritz**, foreman **Brunker**, Billy **Weston**, his son Ernest, and David **Lindblom**, the gardener, were all having lunch in the main dining room. Mamah Borthwick **Cheney** and her children were sitting elsewhere when **Carlton** attacked them with an axe. He then set fire to the house and as the occupants attempted to flee he also attacked them. Mamah Borthwick, her children John and Martha, Emil Brodelle and Thomas Brunker were killed at the scene, Ernest Weston and David Lindblom died from burns later. Of the nine who had sat down to lunch that Saturday, only two, Herbert Fritz and Billy Weston survived.

Taliesin Square-Papers

The Taliesin Square-Papers, 17 of which were published from January 1941 to February 1953, served as a vehicle for Wright to voice his views.

Taliesin West (1937–59)

Frank Lloyd Wright's winter home for the **Taliesin Fellowship** is a complex of buildings which includes a theater, music pavilion, and sun cottage and offered a new challenge in building materials. He first started work on the site in 1938 with apprentices from Taliesin North. For the first two years of construction they all lived on the desert in tents or temporary wood and canvas shelters. Life was primitive with no water, electricity, heating or plumbing. Every winter for the next 22 years, he and his students would continue the work, revising and enlarging the complex. It was built using what Wright described as **"desert rubblestone"** construction, which involves large stones set in concrete, to produce a

Taliesin West is a treasury of Wrightian design. When creating his own homes the architect was free to express his vision to the fullest extent and the completed buildings are testament to his genius. Note how well the complex becomes part of the natural landscape — the manifestation of Wright's organic philosophy.

more colorful and natural effect than pure concrete. Influenced by the wooden structure erected for the **Ocatillo Desert Camp**, Wright built much of Taliesin West from linen canvas on redwood frames, which diffused the harsh desert sun; today fibreglass and steel have replaced much of this. Taliesin West has been designated by the **A.I.A.** as one of 17 examples of Wright's architectural contribution to American culture that must be kept unspoiled. It is open to the public and tours are available. Taliesin West now houses the Taliesin Fellowship for much of the year.

Tallmadge, Thomas Eddy
After serving as a draftsman for Daniel **Burnham**, Tallmadge opened his own practice in the Chicago area. His **Prairie** style work was characterized by historical reference, which increasingly moved towards out and out medievalism.

Tallmadge & Watson

A firm of architects, part of the **New School of the Midwest**, who Wright believed were "throwing up sordid little imitations of his work all over the Midwest."

Tanyderi (also seen as Tan-y-Deri; designed 1907) The cottage beside **Hillside School** that Wright designed for his sister Jane and her husband Andrew in 1907. Those who had been burned fighting the fire on the day of the **Taliesin murders** were brought over to Tanyderi and laid on improvised beds on the porch. The name means "under the oaks" in Welsh.

Teater, Archie Boyd, Studio Residence (1952) Built from a parallelogram module, this spacious studio residence has plate glass opening it to the sunlight. Its construction is of quartzite stone and oak and it has a concrete slab floor. It was substantially renovated in the 1980s.

Tenbrink, Howard A **Taliesin Fellow** who, sharing Wright's pacifist views, was sent to a C.O. camp during the Second World War.

Tennessee A hilltop house in Chatanooga is Wright's only work in Tennessee. It is a straightforward in-line **Usonian** house built mainly of native Tennessee limestone.

Texas The four examples of Wright's work in Texas are all from the 1950s and two stand out as being special. The first is the massive single-story John **Gillin** House, which has floor-to-ceiling glass along its east-facing living room and grass terrace. The other notable building is the **Dallas Theater Center** or, as it is known locally, the Kalita Humphreys Theater, which seats 440 people in 11 rows. Building was finished after Wright died by the **Taliesin Associated Architects**, as was the Sterling **Kinney** House. The other Wright building in Texas, the **Thaxton** House, fell into disrepair and was close to demolition until a sympathetic purchaser arrived in 1991 and restoration began.

textile block From 1917 to 1924 Frank Lloyd Wright spent much of his time in **California** where he designed a number of important houses using a new building process which he called his textile block system. This technique involved the use of precast **exposed concrete blocks**, decorated on both sides, which were bound together at the building site with steel tie rods and poured concrete.

Thaxton, William L., House (1954) This triangular-moduled house is built to an L-plan which encloses a swimming pool. It has **exposed concrete block** walls.

Thayer, Sally Casey An art collector for whom Wright bought Japanese art to supplement his income while working in Tokyo on the **Imperial Hotel** project. Sally Thayer's collection eventually went to the Spencer Museum at the University of Kansas.

Thomas, Frank Wright, House (1901) The first of Wright's **Prairie** style houses to be built in **Oak Park**. It was nicknamed the "Harem."

Thompson, Jim Along with Herbert **Fritz** on the cello, Svetlana **Peters** on the violin, and Blaine **Drake** on the viola, Jim Thompson played the recorder in what Wright called the **"Farmer-Labor Quartet."** They entertained the Wrights and their guests after dinner at **Taliesin**.

Thurber Art Gallery (designed 1909; since demolished) As with **Pebbles & Balch Shop** and **Browne's Bookstore**, Wright took great care over the interior spaces. Two long panels of leaded glass lit the gallery on sunny days concealing the otherwise indirect lighting.

Timothy, David The stonemason who built the **Unity Chapel** and the **Hillside School**. He came from the same area of Wales as the **Lloyd Jones** family.

Tobin, Arthur Colson Youngest brother of Catherine, Wright's first wife.

Tobin, Catherine Lee (See Catherine Lee Tobin **Wright**)

Tobin, Charlie Twin of Robert, brother of Catherine, Wright's first wife.

These perforated blocks could be used to allow light into the house and were sometimes inset with glass.

Right: The Frank Wright Thomas residence is the first example of Prairie architecture in Oak Park.

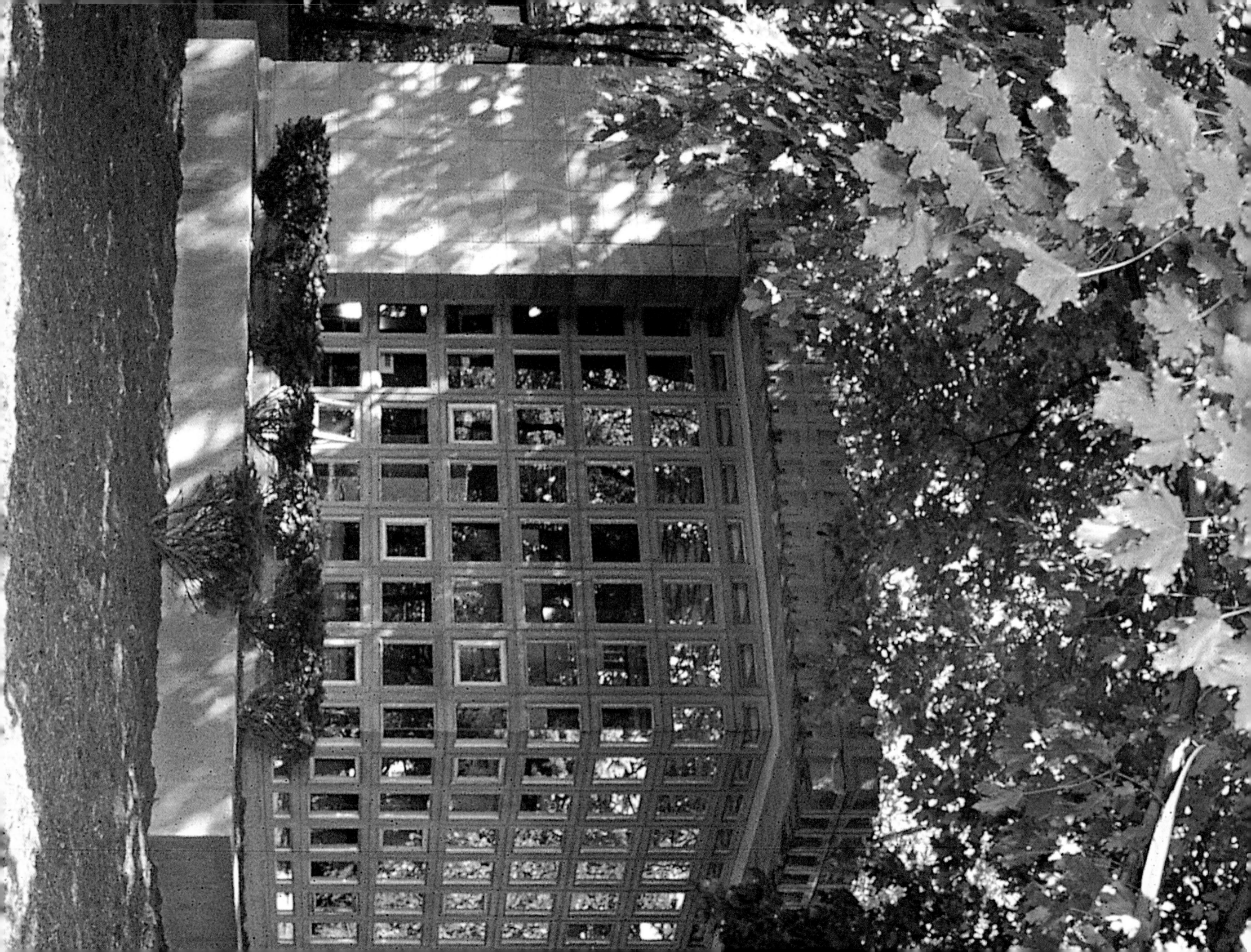

Above: The Tomek house. The cantilevered roof extension is particularly daring.

Pages 316/317 and Right: The Dorothy H. Turkel house is the only two-story Usonian automatic house to be built.

Below: The Tracy residence is an excellent example of the Usonian project and features several different type of block throughout its construction.

Tobin, Flora Parish
Flora was the mother of Catherine, Wright's first wife. She was a brilliant teacher and the first woman principal in the Chicago public school system. She was called "Blue Gramma" by Wright's children because his son Lloyd was color blind and he thought that her red hair was blue.

Tobin, Robert
Twin of Charlie, brother of Catherine, Wright's first wife.

Tobin, Samuel Clark
Samuel was the father of Catherine, Wright's first wife. He was a wholesale salesman and the Tobins were a prosperous and socially respectable family of Unitarians living on Chicago's fashionable South Side.

Tomek, F. F., House (1904)
This house was built to an L-plan. It is a **Prairie** style house with a small second-story built over the large main floor. The terrace roof supports now apparent are a later addition. This was the prototype for the **Robie** House.

Tonkens, Gerald B., House (1954)
This L-plan building, with a second L incorporating a cantilevered carport, represents a classic example of a **Usonian automatic** house. It is constructed on a two-foot module with the standard wall block surface two feet by one foot. The wood paneling is of Philippine mahogany. The clerestory admits light through pierced blocks to the kitchen space.

Tracy, W. B., House (1955)
A **Usonian automatic** house. It employs different blocks for its inside and outside corners, walls, and roof.

Trier, Paul J., House (1956)
A late design, this is a single-story wood-trimmed building with later additions taking place in 1960.

Turkel, Dorothy H., House (1955)
An L-plan **Usonian automatic** construction with a two-story living room. There are no windows; light is admitted through floor-to-ceiling pierced blocks.

Twyman, Joseph
The English architect who coined the phrase "in the nature of materials." He was a follower of William **Morris** and one of the early advocates of his ideas in Chicago.

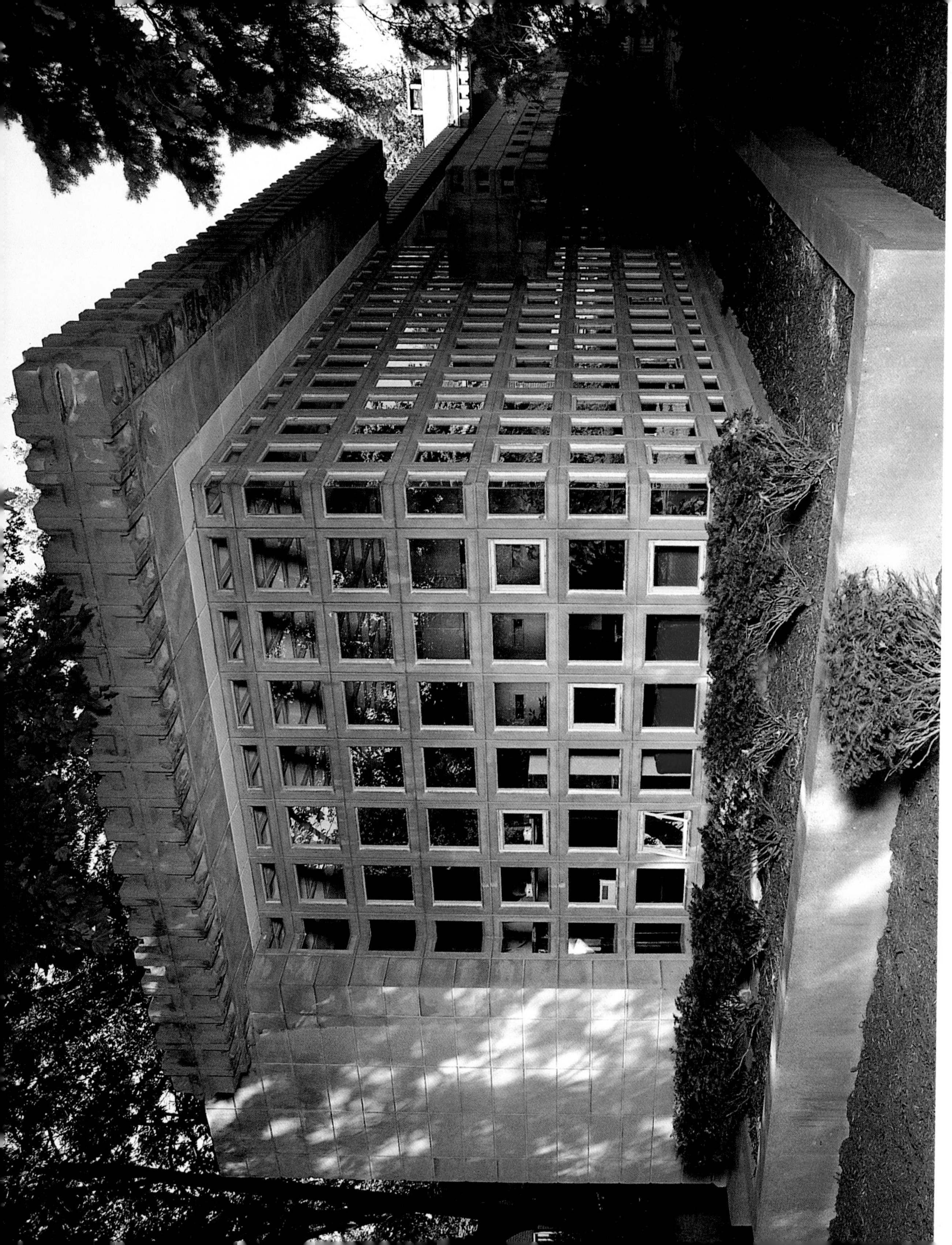

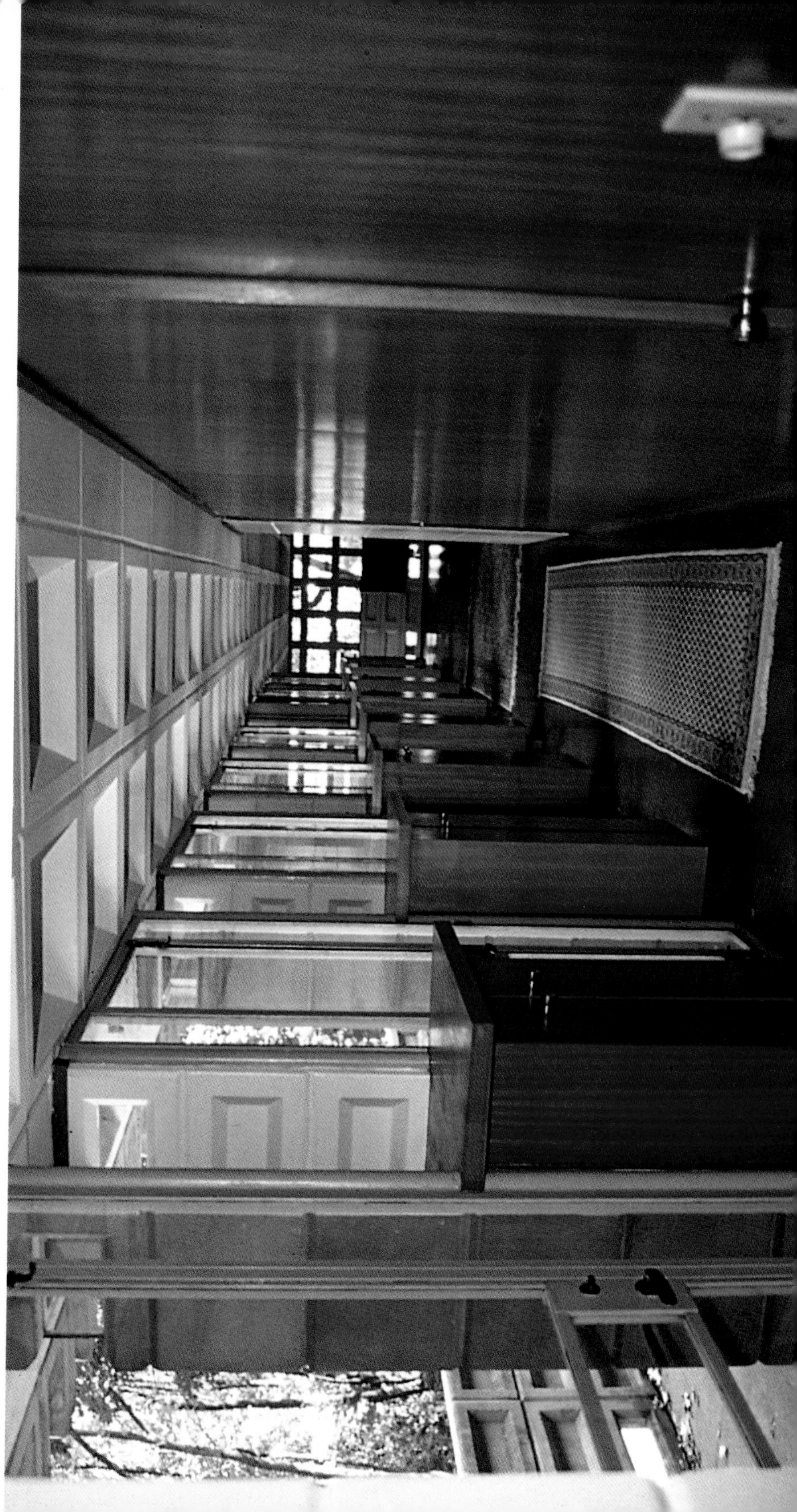

Unitarian Meeting House (1947)

One of the 17 buildings designated to be retained by **A.I.A.** The main construction materials of the church are limestone and oak. The rising green copper roof is said to symbolize hands closed in prayer. An additional wing was later added by the **Taliesin Associated Architects.** Guided tours available during summer.

Among the early members of the Unitarian society were Wright's parents and the architect participated in the organization's events as a boy.

Unity Chapel, Spring Green, Wisconsin

In 1885, the young Frank Lloyd Wright was allowed to oversee the construction of the **Silsbee** designed chapel. If it is true that the ceiling, designed in squares, was Wright's invention, then this would have been his first architectural undertaking. The chapel was opened in the summer of 1886.

Unity Chapel Inc.

A Wright family corporation established to restore the chapel and tend the burial grounds.

Unity Temple, Oak Park (designed 1904; dedicated 1907; opened 1908)

The Unity Temple was one of the first buildings in the world to be constructed of exposed concrete of a fine pebble aggregate. Wright's interest in reinforced concrete had been developing for a number of years, but this was the first opportunity that he was offered to use it on the large scale demanded by church design. The simple exterior forms were embellished with cast-concrete decorative details and the church itself contains a number of innovative features, including highly sophisticated practical amenities such as hot air integrated circulation within the structure.

Unity Temple, Spring Green, Wisconsin

At the time of Wright's death he had been working on plans for a new chapel which would serve as his

Pages 320/321, Above, and Right: The Unitarian Meeting House. Wright was active in the fund-raising for this church as were the Taliesin Fellowship and a great many parishioners who helped to haul the limestone — the main construction material — from a quarry 30 miles away.

Van Veen, Felicia
Former executive director of the **American Academy of Arts and Letters** who awarded Wright the gold medal for architecture in 1949.

Vaudremer, Émile
A leading figure of the **École des Beaux-Arts** in Paris under whom Louis **Sullivan** studied.

Villa Medici, Fiesole, Italy
The Villa Medici, one of the great country houses of **Italy**, is situated on a hillside with commanding views of the Tuscany countryside. This house was the inspiration for Wright's design of the first **Taliesin**. Wright loved the villa and placed his own **Wisconsin** country house in the same position and emphasised the importance of this choice forever afterward. His plans for Taliesin expressed everything he thought and believed in and the maze of courtyards, terraces, and flower beds called to mind the hill gardens around **Fiesole**.

Viollet-le-Duc, Eugène
A French contributor to the **Arts and Crafts** Movement who stressed the principles of design. Wright studied his works *The Grammar of Ornament, Les Discours,* and *Dictionnaire raisonné.*

Virginia
There are three examples of Wright's work in Virginia, all attractive **Usonian** houses. The **Pope-Leighey** House

is notable for having moved location from Falls Church to Mount Vernon where it was unsympathetically sited in its new location. Ownership and restoration are now entrusted to the National Trust for Historic Preservation. The **Marden** House at McClean is a hemicycle on a steep slope with views of the Potomac; finally, the **Cooke** House is an interesting combination of a hemicycle and a parallelogram wing. It is made from imported clay from West Virginia to blend with the sand of the adjacent Crystal Lake and is topped with a copper roof.

Vogelsang, John
The Chicago restaurateur who had the contract for the **Midway Gardens.**

von Holst, Hermann
The young architect whom Wright entrusted with closing down his studio when he went to Berlin in 1909 to prepare the **Wasmuth Portfolios.**

Vosburgh, Ernest, Summer House (1916)
This **Prairie House** is the only one of the three that Wright designed in Grand Beach that remains much as built. It has a two-story living room and looks out toward Lake Michigan.

Voysey, C. F. A.
An influential British **Arts and Crafts** architect who also designed furniture that could be seen as having inspired specific designs by Wright.

Walker, Mrs. Clinton, House (1948)
A **Usonian** stone house rising from a rocky promontory on the beach front, looking out over Monterey Bay. The metal living room roof is cantilevered away from the masonry core so that no weight rests on the corbelling bands of glass. The landscape architect was Thomas D. Church.

Walker, Ralph
A **New York** City architect of large industrial plants, office **skyscrapers** and housing projects, and the president of the **American Institute of Architects** who introduced Wright when he received his gold medal from the American Academy of Arts and Letters in 1949.

Wall, Carlton D., House (1941) Snowflake
Called Snowflake by Wright because of its hexagonal grid, the house is constructed from brick and cypress. The living room, with its cantilevered roof, opens out onto a walled, east-facing, terrace, and there is also an enclosed patio.

Walker, Edward C.
Wright was commissioned by Waller to design the other jobs convinced Wright of the necessity of opening a Chicago office to be nearer the majority of his clients and contractors.

Midway Gardens pleasure palace in Chicago. This and

Waller, Edward C., House Remodeling (designed 1899; since demolished)
The remodeling of this large house in Auvergne Place included the dining room and other interior work. The separate stables were also demolished.

Waller apartments (designed 1895; since demolished)
Five blocks of apartments. One of which has been destroyed by fire; the others are due to be restored.

Pages 328/329: The Lowell Walter residence.

Above and Above right: The Clinton Walker house.

Right: The Waller apartments.

Wallis, Henry, Summer House (1900) and Boathouse (1897)
Part of the **Delavan Lake Group**, the Wallis Cottage features horizontal board and batten siding which has been extensively replaced.

Walser, J., House (1903)
Typical **Prairie** style house of wood with plaster surface.

Walter, Lowell, House (1945) and River Pavilion (1948)
The main house, which Wright called his "Opus 497" — what he roughly thought to be the number of designs he had produced by 1945 — is a **Usonian** I-plan brick and steel construction with the garden/living room turned to give better views of the Wapsipinicon River. The pavilion, sited further down the hill on the river, is a brick boathouse with a sun terrace and room above. It was restored in 1991. The house is open to the public during the summer months.

Walton, Robert G., House (1957)
A T-plan **Usonian exposed concrete block** house with wood fascia and trim.

Washington
All three of Washington State's Frank Lloyd Wright buildings have concrete as their main building material. The **Usonian automatic Tracy** House, uses perforated blocks with glass inlays between living room and terrace and also in the clerestory, while the Ray **Brandes** House in Issaquah, is made from **exposed concrete blocks**. The Chauncey and Johanna **Griggs** House is the oldest of the three designs. Unlike the other two, this was designed to be built from stone but had to be built from concrete because of the cost of rarer materials in the immediate post-war years.
Although there are only three examples of Wright's work in Washington, his influence was felt strongly in the state as architects from colleges in **Illinois**, who knew his work, moved into the area. Wright himself visited the region in 1931 and his impact continued as a later generation of the **Taliesin Fellowship** made their homes there.

Above right: The Henry Wallis summer house on Lake Delavan, Wisconsin is one of five seasonal homes in the vicinity. The siding is horizontal board and batten.

Right and Far right: The Lowell Walter house is derivative of the "glass house," which appeared in the *Ladies' Home Journal*. The house was given to the people of Iowa when Walker died and is now known as Cedar Rock Park.

Pages 334/335: The Walter house and River Pavilion (main photo).

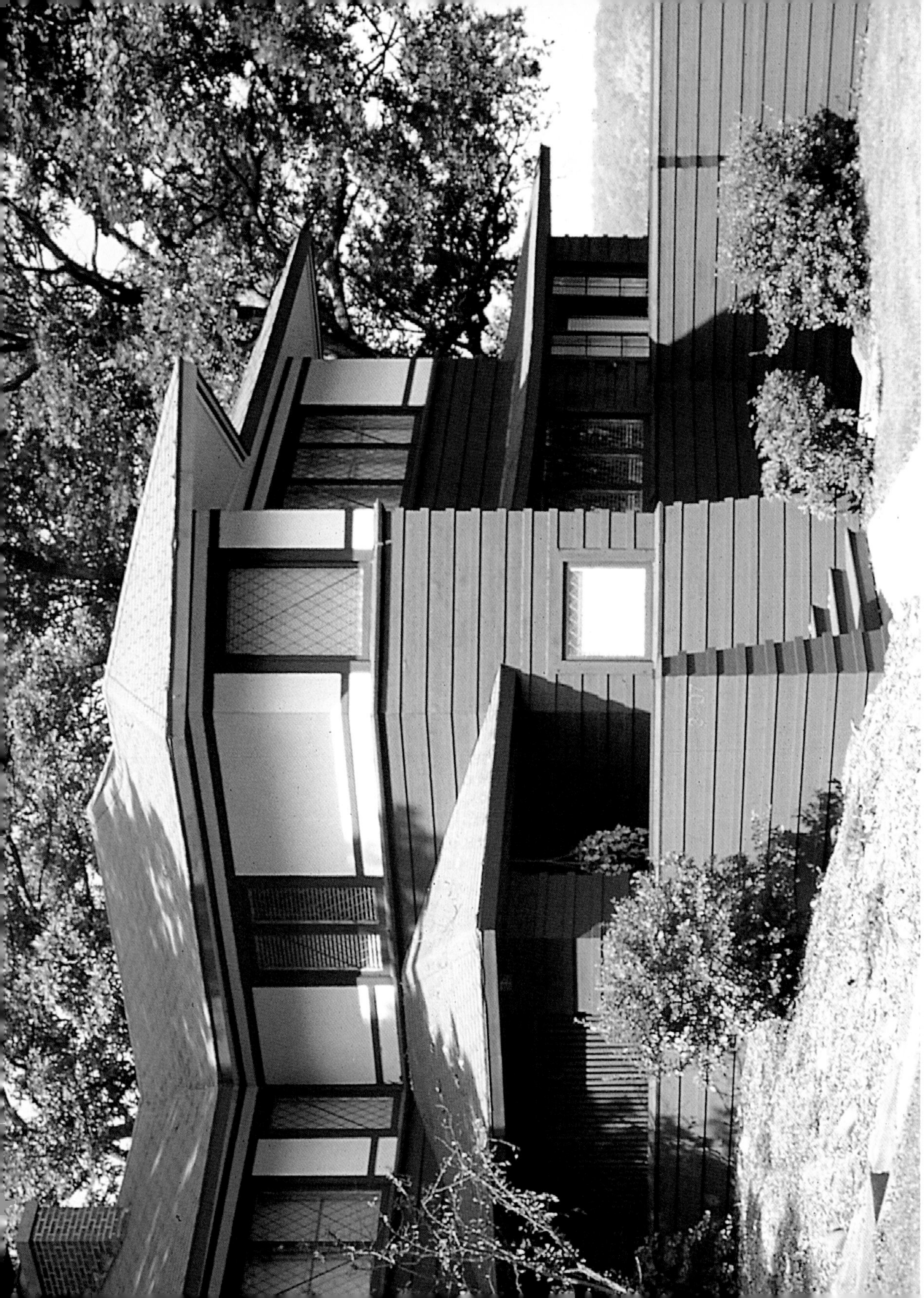

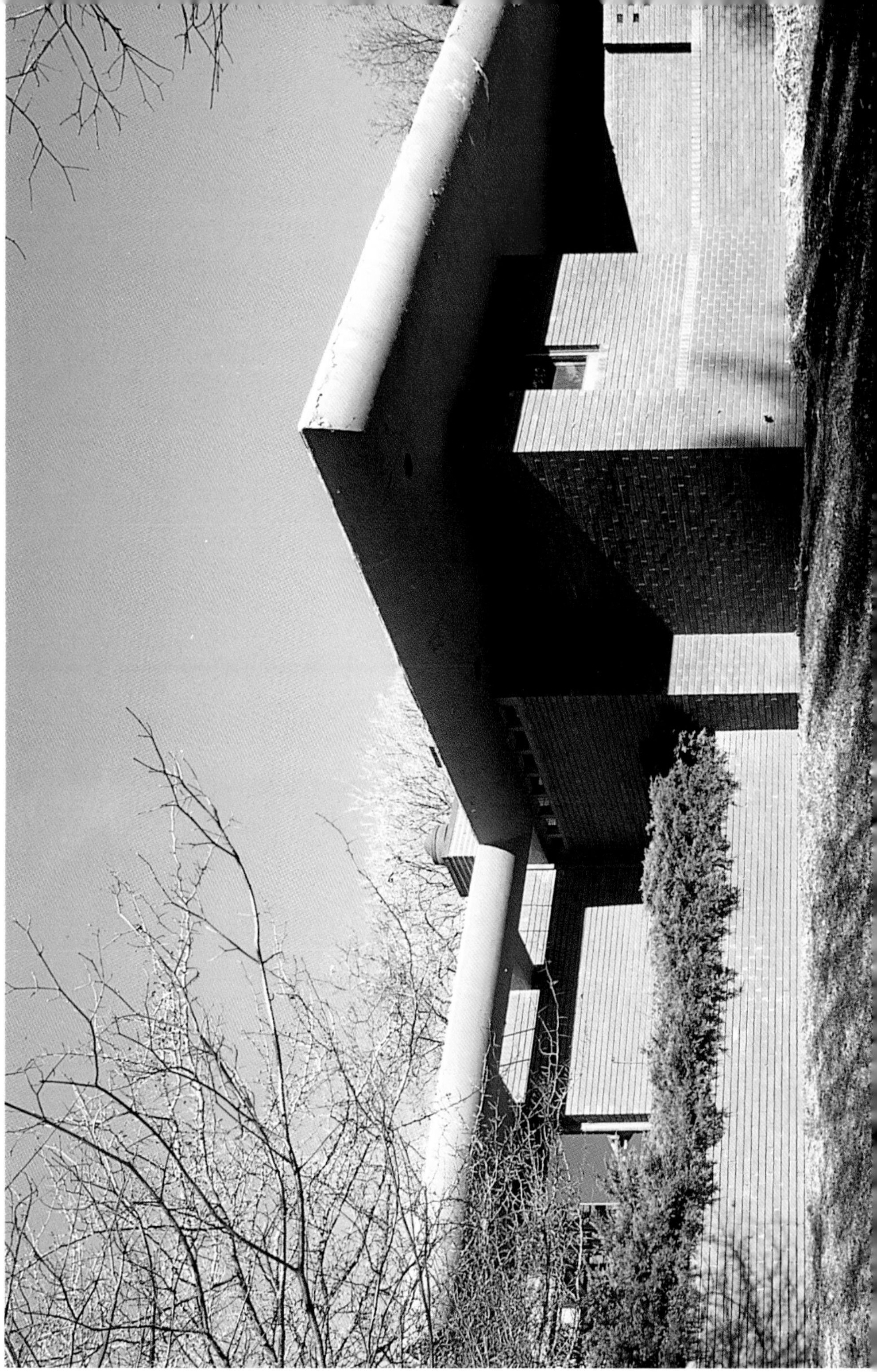

Wasmuth, Ernst
Wasmuth, a German publisher, published a complete monograph of Wright's architectural work to date. The publication of the two portfolios in 1910-1911 and the exhibition of 1911, in Berlin, established Frank Lloyd Wright as an international architect whose qualities were increasingly appreciated in Europe.

Wasmuth Portfolios
The complete folio of Wright's work to that date, a handsome edition known as the *Ausgeführte Bauten und Entwürfe* became a collector's item. Wright worked out a complex business arrangement with **Wasmuth** by which he would buy the American rights. The Wasmuth Portfolio, published in 1910 and 1911 received far more attention and acclaim in Europe than in America.

Waterston, Henning
A **Taliesin** apprentice who bought Uncle John's (**Lloyd Jones**) old farmhouse which had for many years served as the official post office for the town of Hillside. Wright encouraged his apprentices to buy land and settle in **The Valley.**

Webb, Philip
The English architect who designed William **Morris**'s own home, the **"Red House"** which was considered the prototype for the **Arts and Crafts** concept of the smaller, or artistic, house.

Weisblat, David I., House (1948)
One of the **Galesberg Country Homes**, this house was enlarged by the **Taliesin Associated Architects** in 1960. The first of the four Galesberg homes, it is built to a T-plan, employing Wright's **textile block** and wood construction. The living room roof is cantilevered, to maximize living room window space.

Weltzheimer, Charles E., House (1948)
An L-plan **Usonian** structure using more masonry than the norm. The house has been much changed since Wright's original plan, with many alterations and restoration taking place. Guided tours are available through the Allen Memorial Art Museum.

Westcott, Burton J., House (1904)
A large square-plan **Prairie House**, built from wood with plaster surface.

Weston, Ernst
The 13 year-old son of Billy **Weston** who was killed in the **Taliesin murders** of 1914.

Weston, Marcus Earl
A **Taliesin** apprentice, son of William, who, following Wright's pacifist inclinations, refused to appear for induction into the army during the Second World War and was imprisoned.

Weston, William ("Billy")
One of Wright's craftsmen — a master carpenter — Weston had helped to build **Taliesin**. Billy Weston and Herbert **Fritz** were the only two of the nine people who sat down to dinner that day to survive the **Taliesin murders**. Billy lost his son, Ernst, that day but remained a loyal servant to Wright for many years after that August day in 1914.

White, Charles E. Jr.
A young and ambitious architect from the hills of Vermont who joined Wright's studio in 1903. He went on to join the architects who became the **New School of the Midwest.**

White, William Allen
Editor of the *Emporia Gazette*, published in **Kansas**. A Dutch architect, founder and editor of an architectural magazine called *Wendingen*, who in the 1920s planned to publish a book about Wright's life. In 1932, Wright asked Wijdeveld to run his proposed school at **Taliesin** but the Dutchman declined.

Wijdeveld, H. Th.
about whom Wright wrote a warm and touching tribute in 1944. Wright obviously had great affection for William and his widow Sally.

Willey, Malcolm E., House (1933)
A single-story house which represents a major link between Wright's **Prairie** style houses and his later **Usonian** house plan as the kitchen directly adjoins the living room. It is constructed from dark red sand and paving brick, with cypress wood-trim.

Williams, Chauncey I. (1895)
A client of Wright who in 1895 joined forces with another client, William **Winslow**, to found a small publishing firm. Williams was a publisher by profession and Wright joined the firm, called the **Auvergne Press,** as chief designer.

Williams, Chauncey I., House (1895)
A two-story building with a steeply pitched roof. The house features Roman brick beneath the sill line, which is colorfully offset by the plaster between the eaves.

Above and Below: The Chauncey Williams house is the first of Wright's designs to reveal an oriental influence. The steep roof and the Japanese garden style boulders are offset by the Roman brick to create a colorful impression.

Williams-Ellis, Clough
The Welsh architect who designed Portmeirion. He accompanied Wright on part of his one and only visit to Wales in 1956.

Willis, George
One of the talented young draftsmen who helped Wright in his first year of independence after leaving **Adler & Sullivan**. He quickly followed Myron **Hunt** to **Los Angeles**.

Willits, Mr. and Mrs. Ward W.
Two wealthy clients in Highland Park with whom Wright and his wife struck up a friendship and joined in a visit to **Japan** in 1905 at which time Wright took the opportunity to buy a considerable quantity of **Japanese art.**

Willits, Ward, House (1901)
One of the 17 listed Wright buildings. It is an important building because it shows the culmination of all Wright's feelings about residential architecture. A classic **Prairie House** constructed from wood and steel with exterior plaster work and wood trim, the living quarters are all raised above ground level by a chunky stylobate. Each wing of the house comes off a central core in a pinwheel

Above and Below: The Ward Willits house which Willits occupied until his death at the age of 92. The building marks a significant point in Wright's career and represents the maturity of many of his ideas in residential architecture.

Above and Below: The William H. Winslow house, Wright's first independent commission for which he earned $20,000. A feature of the building, and a rarity in the architect's work, is the use of double hung windows.

configuration. The end wall of the living room is floor-to-ceiling glass. The core of the house is a substantial central fireplace. Wright also designed a gardener's cottage and stables behind the house. These are in the wood and plaster structure of the Prairie fashion. Wright also designed furniture for the stylish interior.

Wilson, Abraham, House (1954) additions (1970)
This house has a two-story living room with bedrooms over the kitchen. It is constructed from **exposed concrete blocks** with wood trim.

Winn, Robert, House (1950)
The only two-story house in **Parkwyn Village,** the Winn House has a breathtaking curved, cantilevered, enclosed, skylighted balcony attached to its living room. It is built with Wright **textile blocks** and wood.

Winslow, William H.
William Winslow's house in **River Forest** was Wright's first commission after he left **Adler & Sullivan.** In 1895, Winslow joined forces with another client, Chauncey **Williams,** to found a small publishing firm called the **Auvergne Press.** Winslow was an amateur and probably the chief financial backer of the press which Wright soon joined as chief designer.

Winslow, William H., House (1894)
The house features the architect's early octagonal geometry using the basic materials of Roman brick, stone and plaster. This two-story building was Wright's first independent commission.

Wisconsin
Wright was born in Wisconsin but it was to be 48 years before a design of his was erected there. The only work in his town of birth is the **German** warehouse, an imposing cube of brick and cast-in-place concrete which now houses the **Richland Museum.** The full scope of Wright's designs are well illustrated in Wisconsin: from waterside cottages on **Lake Delvan,** examples of both No. I and No. 2 **Erdman** Company prefabs, through to two of his finest religious buildings, the **Unitarian Meeting House** at Shorewood Hills and the **Annunciation Greek Orthodox Church** in Wauwatosa. Two of his residential masterpieces are also situated in this state; the last — and Wright thought the best — of the **Prairie Houses,** Herbert **Johnson's Wingspread,** and the first of the **Usonians** (the Herbert **Jacobs** First House) as well as his great commercial triumph, the **Johnson Administration Building** and **Research Tower.** Along with **Taliesin**

Above: Frank Lloyd Wright.

ings, explaining and illuminating his ideas so that his thoughts, at least, are not lost to posterity.

Frank Lloyd Wright was born to his father's second wife, Anna Lloyd Carey **Wright**, on June 8, 1867, in **Richland Center, Wisconsin**. His mother championed her son's cause to the detriment of everyone else, especially her husband William Carey **Wright**, and even her two subsequent daughters Jane and Maginel (**Barney**). Frank's mother drilled into him her Unitarian values of faith in the family and a general liberal philosophy towards life.

In 1876, an important, possibly life changing, influence was experienced by the young Frank Lloyd Wright. His mother went to the Centennial Exhibition in Philadelphia. Here she was enthused with the ideas of the great **German** educationalist, Friedrich W. A. **Froebel** who had developed the kindergarten system for very young children and, more pertinently for Frank and his mother, had also devised a system of games which involved putting together simple, primary color, geometric shapes to make imaginative constructions. They were in essence building blocks. In his autobiography, Wright claimed that these simple "toys" (as Froebel called them) were deeply influential to his architectural work.

Despite his mother's intensive educational ideas and prompting, Wright failed to graduate high school and in 1885 became apprenticed to the only builder in **Madison**, Allan D. **Conover**. As luck would have it

Conover was also dean of engineering at the **University of Wisconsin** and he allowed his young apprentice to attend classes in the department of engineering. When Wright entered the University of Wisconsin in 1884, his interest in architecture had already declared itself. Here Wright received the only strict training, of any sort, that he was to receive — in draftsmanship. However, at the same time he was also receiving practical building experience in the office and by working part-time on a construction project at the university. The two years of classes which he attended before dropping out showed that the young Frank Lloyd Wright had a remarkable ability in draftsmanship.

After leaving university, Wright moved to Chicago. He was now 20 years old and living in one of the most exciting cities in the United States. Devastated in 1871 by a great fire, it was only now recovering and rebuilding fully. Architects and designers from all over America, especially the eastern seaboard, were arriving to take up the golden architectural opportunity this presented. Notable among these men was Joseph Lyman **Silsbee**, a much sought-after architect of mainly residential buildings. In the spring of 1887, Wright had an easy introduction to him as, at the time, Silsbee was working on a new building for the church where Wright's uncle, the Reverend Jenkin **Lloyd Jones**, was pastor. Silsbee took Wright on as an apprentice but he soon became bored with the "safe" architecture of Silsbee's practice and in the autumn of 1887 he moved on to work for the firm of **Adler & Sullivan**.

The progressive style of Adler & Sullivan was much more to Wright's taste. One of the partners of this company, the American architect Louis **Sullivan**, had a profound influence on Wright's work and his epigram, "form follows function," came also to be at the heart of Wright's work. Wright quickly settled into the firm and, in 1889, signed a five-year contract. By this time he was given the majority of the domestic commissions that came to the firm while the principals worked on their larger, public commissions. The following year he took sole responsibility for all domestic work handled by the firm. In 1892, Wright gained a degree of recognition with one of his domestic commissions, the **Charnley** House; furthermore his own house at **Oak Park** became greatly admired. Now, although he was only a draftsman, clients, many of them wealthy suburban businessmen and Oak Park neighbors, started coming to him personally to design and build their homes.

These **"bootlegged houses,"** as Wright called them, soon revealed an independent talent quite distinct from that of Sullivan. Such work also proved a great financial boon as Wright's five children were cripplingly expensive to feed and clothe. Inevitably Sullivan found out about the "bootlegged" projects and was not impressed. They parted company after a furious row and were not reconciled for 20 years. Together with several other young architects, Frank set up his own practice in Steinway Hall, Chicago. The work flowed in and he was able to build up a successful, if unremarkable, business doing "period" homes for local clients, again many of them his **Oak Park** neighbors. In 1894, Wright wrote *The Architect and the Machine*, the first of many papers and writings in which he would expound his theories. In his radically original designs as well as in his prolific writings he championed the virtues of what he termed **"organic architecture,"** a building style based on natural forms.

By 1900, Wright's architectural style had matured and he built the **Bradley** House and **Hickox** House in Kankakee, **Illinois.** He was now into his **Prairie House** period in which he built 33 houses in roughly ten years — from 1900 onwards. By 1908 he had originated most of the principles that are today the fundamental concepts of modern architecture. Exhausted by the traumas of building the **Larkin** Company administration headquarters in Buffalo, Wright decided to recover with a visit to **Japan** in 1905, a country whose culture and traditions — particularly artworks — had been of considerable interest to him for some time.

During the 20 years that followed he became one of the best-known and, because of a tempestuous personal life, one of the most notorious architects in the United States. From a distance it seems that Wright spent much of his life embroiled in controversy: from the quarrels within his own family between his parents, the emotional conflicts he brought upon himself by abandoning Catherine, his first wife and mother of his six children, for a married woman — Mamah **Cheney** — his noisy pacifism during the Second World War which brought him many new enemies, not to mention his anti-establishment stance towards fellow architects, other people's architecture, planning regulations, and bureaucracy and society in general. Always arrogant and obdurate, Frank Lloyd Wright, while able to make enemies with ease, also made strong friendships and inspired tremendous loyalty from his followers.

Throughout his career, architects who were more conventional than Wright opposed his unorthodox methods and, beset with personal difficulties and professional antagonisms, he passed a year of self-imposed exile (1909-10) in Europe. Two editions of his work brought out in 1910 and 1911 by the Berlin publisher **Wasmuth**, along with a parallel exhibition that traveled throughout Europe, boosted Wright's fame in European

architectural circles and influenced such key figures in contemporary architecture as Ludwig **Mies van der Rohe** and **Le Corbusier.**

Upon his return, and with his reputation assured on both sides of the Atlantic, Wright established **Taliesin,** (near **Spring Green**, WI, and named after a sixth century Welsh bard,) the home and school that he built for himself and his followers. Wright established a studio-workshop for apprentices who assisted him on his projects and also founded the **Taliesin Fellowship** to support such efforts. He embarked on a career of ever-widening achievements and began to reinforce the philosophical underpinnings of his innovative "organic" building style with its bold claim that the structural principles found in natural forms should guide modern American architecture. Wright's view of architecture was essentially romantic; although he often paid lip service to the rational systems called for by mass-produced building, his efforts in those directions seemed half-hearted at best.

Frank Lloyd Wright's winter home for the **Taliesin Fellowship** was **Taliesin West**, a complex of buildings which included a theater, music pavilion, and sun cottage, and which offered a new challenge in building materials. He first started work on the site in 1938 with apprentices from Taliesin North, and every winter for the next 22 years he and his students would continue the work of revising and enlarging the complex. Wright returned to Taliesin West in 1959 after the taxing **Guggenheim Museum** project had taken its toll on his health. Now aged 91, he was operated on in Phoenix to remove an

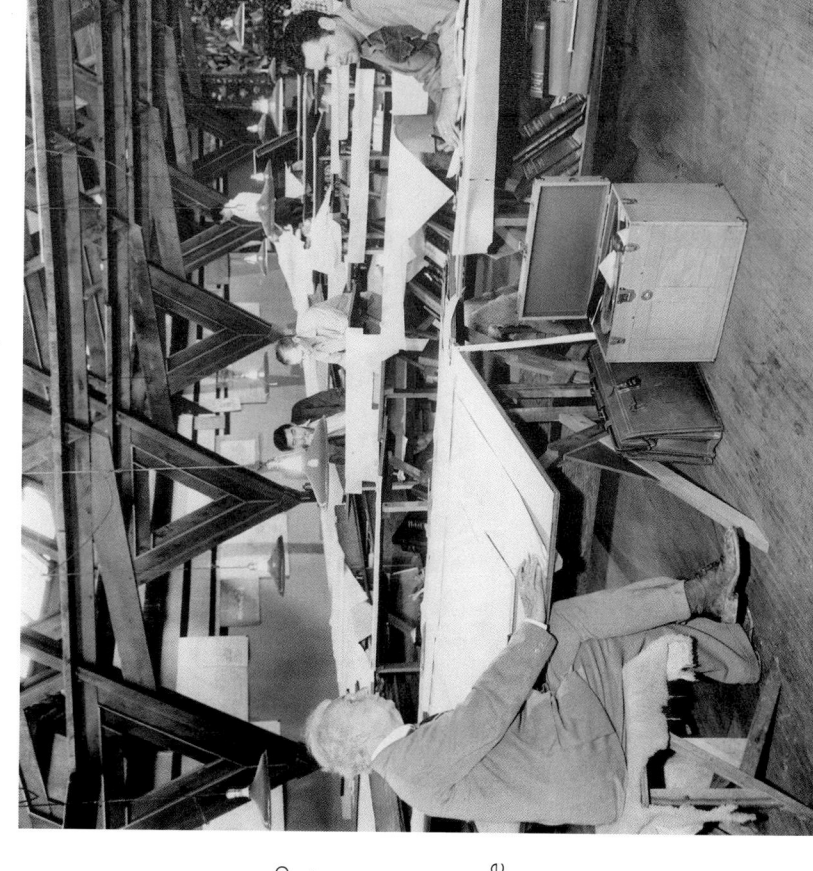

Below: Frank Lloyd Wright with William Wesley Peters.

intestinal obstruction and despite his frailty, he appeared to come through the operation successfully. Five days later, on April 9, 1959, Wright died. His body was taken back to his old home in Spring Green, Wisconsin, where it was placed in the family burial ground a few hundred yards from Taliesin, next to his mother and Manah Cheney. Frank Lloyd Wright left behind a rich heritage of completed buildings of almost uniform splendor. However, few of his adherents could match the special genius reflected in his works. Wright was essentially an idiosyncratic architect whose influence was immense but whose pupils were few.

Wright, Frank Lloyd, Home and Studio (1889-1911) Wright's home and studio have been much renovated since the 1970s and preservation is now the responsibility of the Frank Lloyd Wright Home and Studio Foundation. These buildings are listed for preservation by the **A.I.A.** The Foundation's **Oak Park** Visitor's Center is at 154 North Forest Avenue. Open to the public, tours are available.

Wright, Frank Lloyd Jnr: Born on March 31, 1890. The eldest son of Frank and his first wife, Catherine, was always called Lloyd. He began his working life as a landscape draftsman in the Boston offices of **Olmsted** & Olmsted (1910-11), and later moved out to the West Coast to join the offices of Irving J. **Gill** where he worked as a draftsman and delineator before establishing himself in independent practice in 1915. A year later he became head of the design department at Paramount Studios and would also work closely with his father on many Californian projects including the construction and landscaping for **Hollyhock House** and **Olive Hill**.

Wright, George Irving The second child of Frank's father William by his first marriage to Permelia. George went on to study law and eventually became a judge. When the **Lloyd Jones** brothers of Anna, persuaded William to leave her, there was a complete loss of contact between the two sides of Frank Lloyd Wright's family.

Wright, Iovanna Lazovich Born December 2, 1925. The daughter of Frank Lloyd Wright and his then mistress, Olgivanna Lazovich. She was the only child by Olgivanna and was Wright's seventh and last child.

Wright, Jennie (see **Porter**, Mary Jane Wright)

Above and Right: Exterior and interior of Frank Lloyd Wright's home and studio in Oak Park. As with his later homes the architect was able to fully express his vision and the building is a monument to form, structure and ornamentation.

Pages 346/347: An aerial view of the Wright home and studio.

Wright, John The second son of Frank and his first wife Catherine, born in 1892. He worked for his father and oversaw the work at **Midway Gardens**. He accompanied his father from Chicago to **Spring Green** following the **Taliesin murders**. John was also one of the supervisors overseeing the construction of the **Imperial Hotel** during Wright's absences.

Wright, Kira Markham The actress wife of Lloyd Wright, Frank's eldest son.

Wright, Maginel (see **Barney**, Maginel Wright)

Wright, Maude Miriam Noel She was born in a suburb of Memphis, **Tennessee**, on May 9, 1869, and was descended from a distinguished family of Southerners whose origins went back to the 1700s in colonial **Virginia**. In a letter of condolence sent

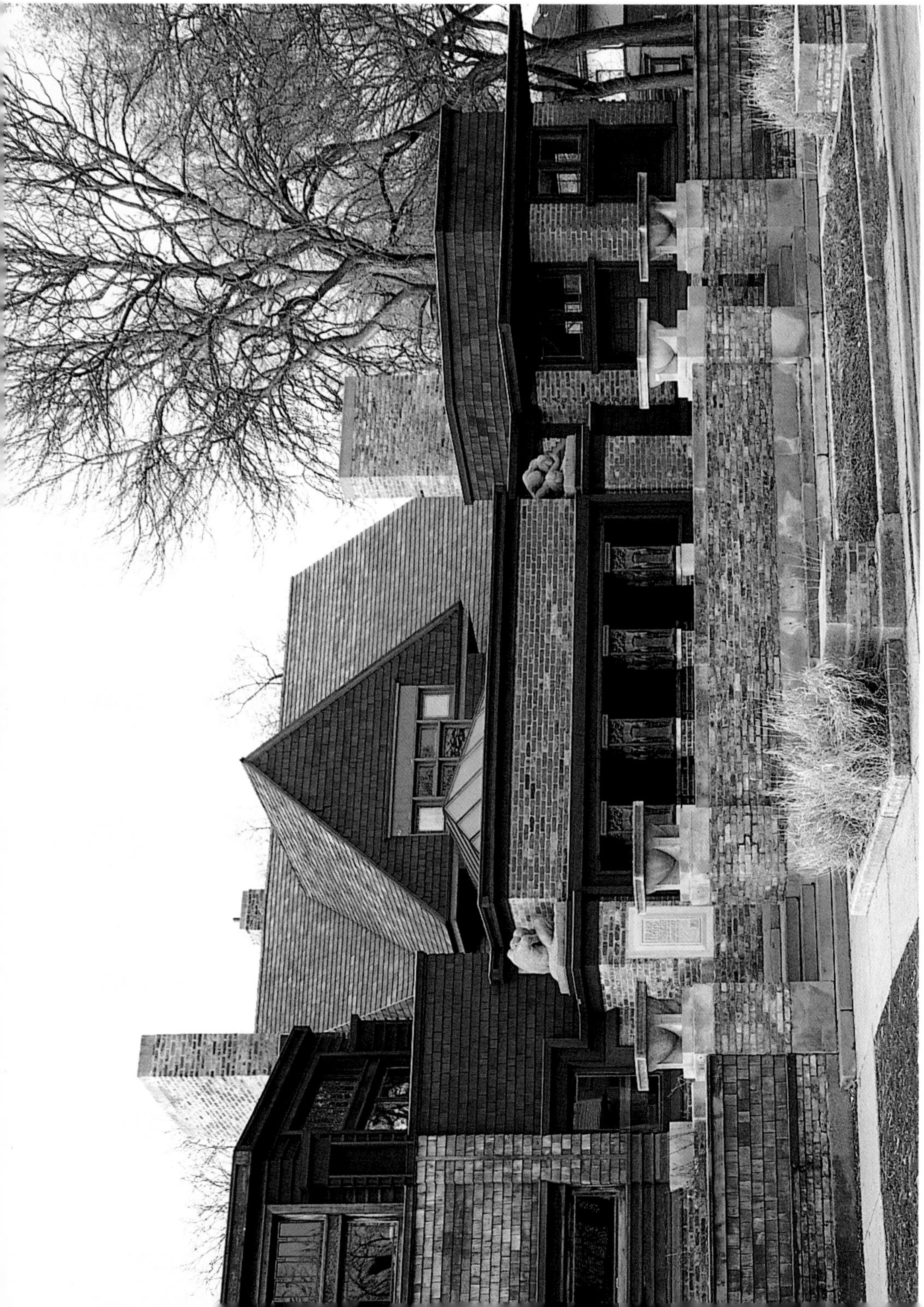

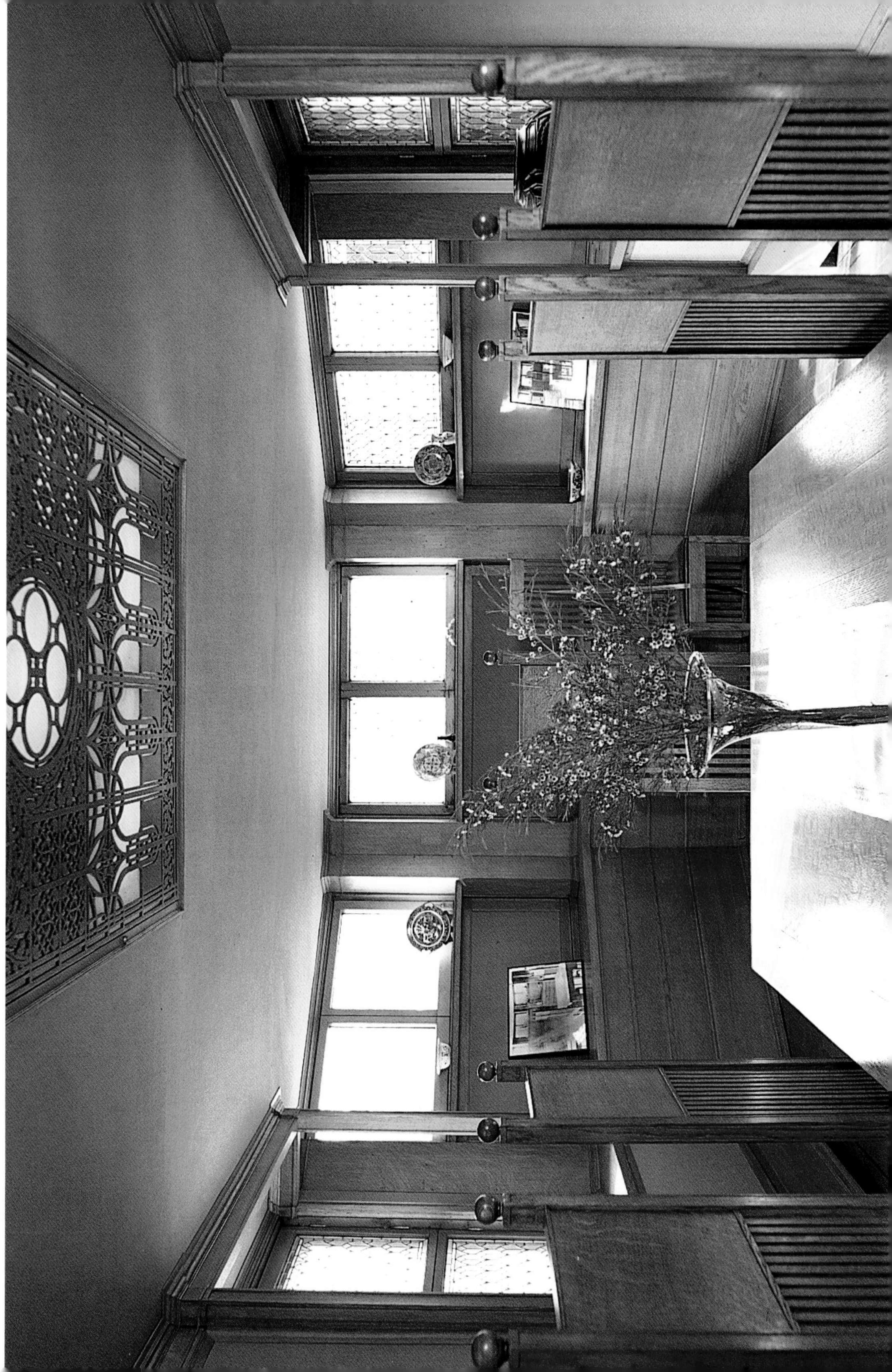

Interior and exterior views of Wright's home and studio in Oak Park. The house is richly appointed with oak (one of Wright's favorite woods). While the house is highly original and gives an indication of the future, it is not as radical as the buildings that were to come and develops contemporary trends rather than breaking away from them. However, it is an innovative example of his early work and was a showroom for prospective clients as much as a home for his family.

to Wright after the **Taliesin murders** Miriam Noel, whom the architect had never met, expressed such empathy that he agreed to her request to meet him. So started a self-destructive relationship that lasted the better part of ten years. Miriam was artistic but unbalanced, her emotional state aggravated by her morphine addiction. In December 1916, Wright and Miriam sailed for Tokyo together where they lived while the architect worked on the **Imperial Hotel** project. When Wright returned full time to the United States in 1922 his first wife, Catherine, at last agreed to grant him a divorce on the grounds of 12 years' desertion. Wright hoped that by marrying Miriam he would be able to give her the emotional security she so badly needed and this would improve their relationship but, after six intolerable months, they separated. When Wright met and moved in with Olgivanna Lazovich, Miriam conducted a bitter and acrimonious divorce campaign against him. The decree was eventually granted in Madison on August 26, 1927. Miriam died on 3 January, 1930.

Wright. Olgivanna Ivanovna Lazovich
Born in Cetinje, Montenegro, on December 27, 1898, Olgivanna was the ninth and last child of highly unusual parents. A dancer who had been educated in Tsarist Russia, she met Wright in 1924, during his troubled second marriage. Wright was immediately attracted to Olgivanna Lazovich and within three months she moved into **Taliesin** with Svetlana (see **Peters**), her daughter from her first marriage to Vlademar **Hinzenberg**. Late the following yea, she produced Iovanna, a daughter for Wright. The financial demands of his second wife and the

Left: Olgivanna Ivanovna Lazovich Wright (center) with the architect and their daughter Iovanna.

virulent press attacks forced Wright to go into hiding with Olgivanna. They quietly withdrew from **Wisconsin** and moved to a cottage in Minneapolis where they lived for a time under assumed names. In 1927, Wright was again divorced and finally, in August, 1928, in **Rancho Santa Fe**, Frank married Olgivanna with whom he lived for the rest of his life. When Olgivanna died on March 1, 1985, Wright's remains were disinterred from **Spring Green**, cremated, and taken to **Taliesin West** in **Arizona**, where their ashes were mingled together and buried in a new grave.

Wright. Permelia Holcomb
The first wife of Frank Lloyd Wright's father William Carey. It is known that Permelia and Frank's mother, Anna, had relatives in common. The **Lloyd Jones** were near neighbors of a family named Thomas, and Anna was related to them through her mother; Permelia was also related to the same family through her mother. When Permelia died in childbirth her children were put in care of their maternal grandmother and this is probably how William came to meet Anna.

Wright. Robert Llewellyn
Born in the autumn of 1903, the sixth and last child of Frank and his first wife Catherine. Always known simply as Llewellyn, he became a Washington attorney.

Wright. Robert Llewellyn, House (1953)
This two-story **exposed concrete block** hemicycle was built for Wright's sixth child, Robert Llewellyn Wright. With a stunning second-story balcony coming off the master bedroom and a cantilevered porch, it perches over a ravine, with a southwest-facing terrace and pool.

Wright. William Carey
Frank's father, William, was a New Englander from a family of non-conformists who had emigrated from England early on in the seventeenth century. He earned his living as a music teacher and traveling Baptist minister until he finally settled his wife and three children at Lone Rock, WI. After being widowed he married Anna **Lloyd Jones**, mother of Frank. William left home when Frank was 18 and eventually divorced Anna. Under the influence of his mother Frank became increasingly estranged from his father, even to the extent that the architect was not present at his funeral.

Wright Memorial Foundation

A non-profit, Wisconsin educational corporation to which Wright transferred all of his personal property during a threatened foreclosure in 1939.

Wrigley, William Jr.

The chewing-gum magnate who bought out the stockholders of the **Arizona Biltmore Hotel** project after the stock market crash of 1929. He continued to develop the property and the hotel reopened in November 1929. It survived the **Great Depression** and is today one of America's most famous hotels.

Writings by Frank Lloyd Wright

Books

Ausgeführte Bauten und Entwürfe von Frank Lloyd Wright [Building Plans and Designs of Frank Lloyd Wright]; Ernst Wasmuth, Berlin, 1910.

Frank Lloyd Wright: Ausgeführte Bauten [Frank Lloyd Wright: Building Plans]; Ernst Wasmuth A.G., Berlin, 1911.

The Japanese Print: An Interpretation; The Ralph Fletcher Seymour Co., 1912 and revised and enlarged edition, Horizon Press, 1967.

Modern Architecture; Being the Kahn Lectures for 1930 Princeton University Press, 1931.

An Autobiography (1932; rev. ed. 1943) First published in 1932 by Longmans, Green and Company. Revised and enlarged editions: Faber and Faber, 1945; Horizon Press, 1977. This work, although shamelessly biased and self-promoting, stimulated new interest in Wright and his work and young architects started to consider him as a sage but eccentric elder statesman.

The Disappearing City; William Fraquhar Payson, 1932.

Architecture and Modern Life (with Baker Brownell); Harper and Brothers, 1937.

An Organic Architecture: The Architecture of Democracy (transcript of four lectures given at the Royal Institute of British Architects in London); Lund Humphries and Co., 1939.

When Democracy Builds; University of Chicago Press, 1945.

Genius and the Mobocracy; Duell, Sloan and Pearce, 1929. Enlarged edition, Secker and Warburg, 1972. Wright's biography of and tribute to his old mentor Louis **Sullivan** who had died in obscurity and poverty in Chicago in 1924. As regards Sullivan's, and indeed Wright's, own belief in the principle of **organic architecture** he insisted that "A building can only be functional when integral with environment and so formed in the nature of materials according to purpose and method as to be a living entity".

The Future of Architecture; Horizon Press, 1953.

In this, the most complex of all the Wrightian definitions can be found that most crucial of the elements of architecture — that of "space." Wright defined space as "the continual becoming, invisible fountain from which all rhythms flow to which they must pass. Beyond time or infinity. The new reality which organic architecture serves to employ in building. The breath of a work of art."

The Natural House; Horizon Press, 1954.

The Story of the Tower: The Tree That Escaped The Crowded Forest; Horizon Press, 1956.

A Testament; Horizon Press, 1957.

The Living City; Horizon Press, 1958.

Drawings for a Living Architecture; Horizon Press, 1959.

Catalogues and Pamphlets

Hiroshige: An Exhibition of Color Prints from the Collection of Frank Lloyd Wright; The Art Institute of Chicago, 1906.

Antique Color Prints from the Collection of Frank Lloyd Wright; The Arts Club of Chicago Exhibition, 1917.

Experimenting with Human Lives; The Ralph Fletcher Seymour Co., 1923

The Frank Lloyd Wright Collection of Japanese Antique Prints (Auction catalogue); The Anderson Galleries, New York, 1927.

Articles

"The Architect and the Machine" (1894)

Wright's first essay on architecture which he read to the University Guild at Evanston, IL.

"A Home in a Prairie Town," **Ladies' Home Journal** 18, No. 3, February 1901.

First of two articles Wright was commissioned to write for the **Ladies' Home Journal** which brought him to more than just parochial architectural attention. His project was to develop a comfortable home for about $7,000. He presented a revolutionary approach to flexible, open-plan living and in time, this innovative concept became to be considered his earliest major contribution to modern architecture.

"The Art and Craft of the Machine," **Brush and Pencil** 8, No. 2, May 1901.

An early essay by Wright which was both a defence of the **Arts and Craft Movement** in Britain and its principles, and a critique of those exhibiting an out-and-out hostility to machine production.

"A Small House with Lots of Room in It," **Ladies' Home Journal** 18, No. 8, July 1901.

"In The Cause of Architecture," Architectural Record 23, No. 3, March 1908.

"In The Cause of Architecture: Second Paper," Architectural Record 35, No. 5, May 1914.

"In The Cause of Architecture: In the Wake of the Quake: Concerning the Imperial Hotel, Tokyo: I," *Western Architect* 32, No. 11, November 1923: Part II: *Western Architect* 33, No. 2, February 1924.

"Why the Japanese Earthquake Did Not Destroy the Imperial Hotel," *Liberty* 4, December 3, 1927.

"In the Cause of Architecture: The Third Dimension" (1925) — published in the Dutch *Wendingen*.

"In the Cause of Architecture: I. The Logic of the Plan," *Architectural Record* 63, No. 1, January 1928.

"In The Cause of Architecture: II. What 'Styles' Mean to the Architect," *Architectural Record* 63, No. 2, February 1928.

"In The Cause of Architecture: III. The Meaning of Materials — Stone," *Architectural Record* 63, No. 4, April 1928.

"Broadacre City: A New Community Plan," *Architectural Record* 77, No. 4, April 1935.

"Frank Lloyd Wright," *Architectural Forum* 68, No. 1, January 1938.

"Wake up America!" (November 1940) An essay published in *Christian Century* in which Wright aired his pacifist views urging America not to enter the Second World War. His stance gathered Wright many enemies as did his sympathy for the Japanese, even after Pearl Harbor. As a consequence he fell out with many of his friends and even his cousin **Richard Lloyd Jones.**

"Life Presents" in Collaboration with the Architectural Forum Eight Houses For Modern Living Especially Designed by Famous American Architects for Four Representative Families Earning $2,000 to $10,000 a Year," *Life* 5, September 26, 1938.

"Frank Lloyd Wright," *Architectural Forum* 88, No. 1, January 1948.

Collections of *Wright's drawings, writings* and *talks*

Drexler, Arthur, ed.: *The Drawings of Frank Lloyd Wright*; Horizon Press, 1962.

Gutheim, Frederick, ed.: *Frank Lloyd Wright on Architecture: Selected Writings, 1894-1940*; Duell, Sloan and Pearce, 1941.

Gutheim, Frederick, ed.: *In The Cause of Architecture: Frank Lloyd Wright, Architectural Record* and McGraw Hill, 1975.

Kaufmann, Edgar, ed.: *An American Architecture: Frank Lloyd Wright*; Horizon Press, 1955.

Kaufmann, Edgar, and Raeburn, Ben, eds.: *Frank Lloyd Wright: Writings and Buildings*; Horizon Press, 1960.

Pfeiffer, Bruce Brooks, ed.: *Frank Lloyd Wright Collected Writings 1894-1930*; Introduction by Kenneth Frampton, Rizzoli, in association with the Frank Lloyd Wright Foundation, 1992.

Wyoming

Wright's only design in the state is the Quintin **Blair** House (1952) in Cody. A stone and wood house with an upward tilting living room ceiling built on the Wyoming plains east of the Yellowstone National Park. As with many of Wright's houses the porch has now been enclosed.

Wyoming Valley Grammar School (1956)

This building is actually a two-room school with central loggia. It is constructed from **exposed concrete block** and redwood with a shingled roof and has skylighted rooms. It is the only public elementary schoolhouse built from a Wright design.

Right: Frank Lloyd Wright, architect, 1867-1959

Below: Wright with the poet Carl Sandburg (left). The two men were great friends and Wright adopted a similar style to Sandburg's for his autobiography.

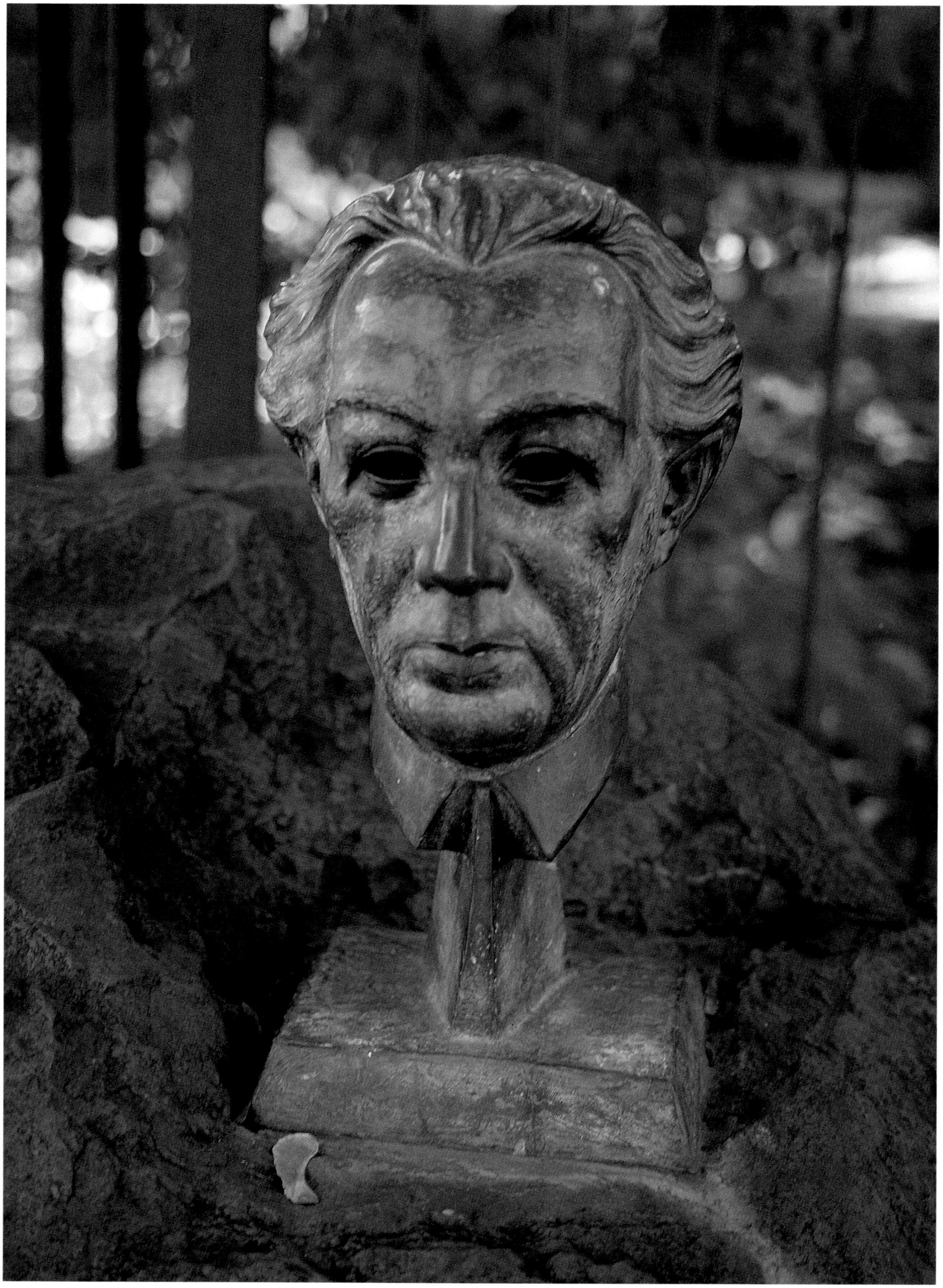

University Avenue Power House

Frank Lloyd Wright House

Romeo and Juliet Windmill Tower

Robie House

1917

Aline Barnsdall House (Hollyhock House)

Ennis House 1923

CHRONOLOGY

Jacobs House

Johnson House

S.C. Johnson Wax Company Research Tower

Anderton Court Center

Grady Gammage Memorial Auditorium

Feldman House
(built after Wright's death)

↔ = illustrated
bold text = houses built
plain text = plans or projects

TYPE   PAGE   BUILDING

200   **Lamp Cottage** (demolished)
Lake Mendota, Madison, Wisconsin

Library and Museum (competition project)
Milwaukee, Wisconsin

340   **Woolley House**
1030 Superior Street, Oak Park, Illinois

1894

36   **Bagley House**
121 County Line Road, Hinsdale, Illinois

42   **Bassett House** (remodeling, demolished)
Oak Park, Illinois

Concrete Monolithic Bank

Orrin Goan House
LaGrange, Illinois

McAfee House
Chicago, Illinois

280   ↔ **Roloson Rowhouses**
3213-3219 Calumet, Chicago, Illinois

339   ↔ **Winslow House**
515 Auvergne Place, River Forest , Illinois

1895

Amusement Park
Wolf Lake, Illinois

Baldwin House
Oak Park, Illinois

112   **Francis Apartments**
Chicago, Illinois

112   ↔ **Francisco Terrace Apartments** (demolished)
Chicago, Illinois

Lexington Terrace Apartment Building
Chicago, Illinois

BUILDING	PAGE	TYPE
Luxfer Prism Company Skyscraper *Chicago, Illinois*		
Moore House (rebuilt after fire: 1923) ↔ *333 Forest Avenue, Oak Park, Illinois*	232	
Waller Apartments (demolished) *2840–2858 West Walnut Street, Chicago, Illinois*	330	
Williams House *530 Edgewood Place, River Forest, Illinois*	336	
Frank Lloyd Wright House (playroom addition) *951 Chicago Avenue, Oak Park, Illinois*	344	
Young House (additions and remodeling) *334 North Kenilworth Avenue, Oak Park, Illinois*	356	
1896		
Devin House *Chicago, Illinois*		
Goodrich House ↔ *534 North East Avenue, Oak Park, Illinois*	126	
Heller House *5132 Woodlawn Avenue, Chicago, Illinois*	144	
Perkins Apartment *Chicago, Illinois*		
Roberts House (remodeling) *317 and 321 North Euclid Avenue, Oak Park, Illinois*	276	
Roberts Houses (four houses) *Ridgeland, Illinois*		
Romeo and Juliet Windmill Tower ↔ *Hillside Home School, Spring Green, Wisconsin*	280	
1897		
All Souls Building *Abraham Lincoln Center, Chicago*		
Chicago Screw Company Factory Building *Chicago, Illinois*		

↔ = illustrated
bold text = houses built
plain text = plans or projects

TYPE	PAGE	BUILDING
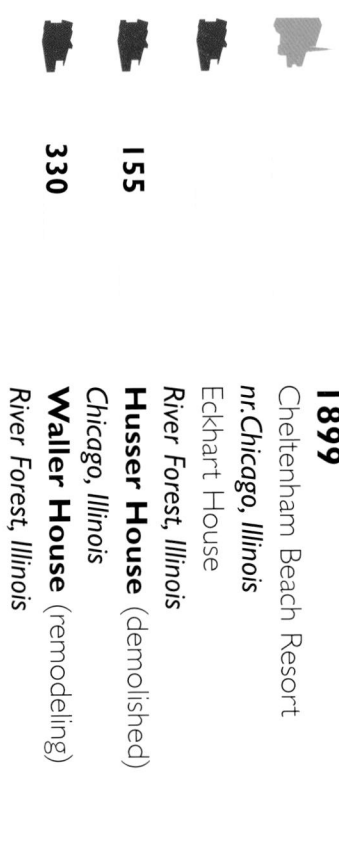	116	**George Furbeck House** *223 North Euclid Avenue, Oak Park, Illinois*
	116	↔ **Rollin Furbeck House** *515 Fair Oaks Avenue, Oak Park, Illinois*
	120	**Thomas H. Gale** (Summer House) *5318 South Shore Drive, Whitehall, Michigan*
	116	**Wallis Boathouse** *Lake Delavan, Illinois*
	344	**Frank Lloyd Wright House** (studio addition) *Oak Park, Illinois*

1898

TYPE	PAGE	BUILDING
	332	Mozart Gardens restaurant remodeling *Chicago, Illinois*
	294	↔ **Smith House** *404 Home Avenue, Oak Park, Illinois*
	276	**River Forest Golf Club** (additions: 1901) *River Forest, Illinois*
		Eckhart House *River Forest, Illinois*

1899

TYPE	PAGE	BUILDING
		Cheltenham Beach Resort *nr.Chicago, Illinois*
	330	**Husser House** (demolished) *Chicago, Illinois*
	155	**Waller House** (remodeling) *River Forest, Illinois*

1900

TYPE	PAGE	BUILDING
		Abraham Lincoln Center *Chicago, Illinois*
	18	**Jessie Adams House** *9326 South Pleasant Avenue, Chicago, Illinois*

BUILDING	PAGE	TYPE
Bradley House *701 South Harrison Avenue, Kankakee, Illinois*	56	
Foster House *12147 Harvard Avenue, Chicago, Illinois*	112	
Goodsmith House *Lake Delavan, Wisconsin*	148	
Hickox House *687 South Harrison Avenue, Kankakee, Illinois*	148	
Jones House *3335 South Shore Drive, Lake Delavan, Wisconsin*	186	
Francis W. Little House I *Peoria, Illinois*		
Motion Picture Theater *Los Angeles, California*		
Pitkin Lodge *Desbarats, Ontario, Canada*	258	
School *Crosbytown, Texas*		
Wallis House (gatehouse remodeled: 1901) *3407 South Shore Drive, Lake Delavan, Wisconsin*	332	
1901		
Buffalo Exposition Pavilion (demolished) *Buffalo, New York*	60	
Davenport House ‹+› *559 Ashland Avenue, River Forest, Illinois*	86	
Fricke House ‹+› *540 Fair Oaks Avenue, Oak Park, Illinois*	114	
Henderson House *301 South Kenilworth Avenue, Elmhurst, Illinois*	146	
Thomas House ‹+› *210 Forest Avenue, Oak Park, Illinois*	314	
Willits House *1445 Sheridan Road, Highland Park, Illinois*	338	

↔ = illustrated
bold *text* = houses built
plain *text* = plans or projects

TYPE	PAGE	BUILDING

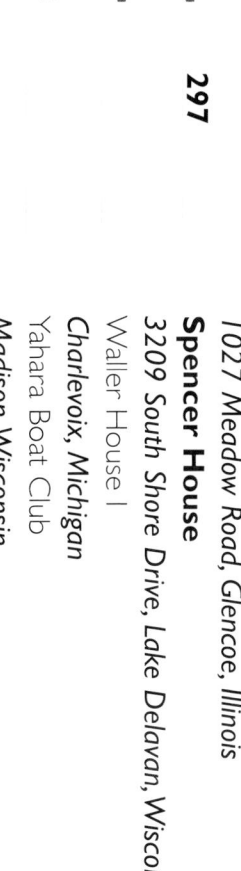

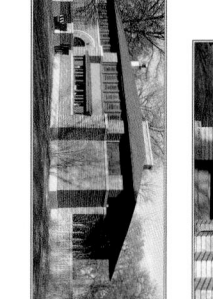

TYPE	PAGE	BUILDING
	42	**Barton House**
		118 Summit Avenue, Buffalo, New York
	70	**Cheney House**
		520 North East Avenue, Oak Park, Illinois
		Chicago and Northwestern Railway (stations for Chicago suburbs)
		Chicago, Illinois
	114	**Freeman House**
		Hillsdale, Illinois
	204	**Lamp House**
		Madison, Wisconsin
	204	**Larkin Company Administration Building**
		Buffalo, New York
		Roberts Quadruple Block Plan (24 houses)
		Oak Park, Illinois
	292	**Scoville Park Fountain** (demolished)
		Replica in Oak Park, Illinois
		Waller House II
		Charlevoix, Michigan
	332	**Walser House**
		42 North Central Avenue, Chicago, Illinois
		Frank Lloyd Wright Studio-House
		Oak Park, Illinois

1904

TYPE	PAGE	BUILDING
		Baldwin House I
		Kenilworth, Illinois
		Bank Building I
		Dwight, Illinois
		Clarke House
		Peoria, Illinois
	120	**Mrs. Thomas H. Gale House**
		6 Elizabeth Court, Oak Park, Illinois

↔ = illustrated
bold *text* = houses built
plain *text* = plans or projects

BUILDING	PAGE	TYPE
Fox River Country Club (remodeling) *Geneva, Illinois*	112	
Hunt House ←→ *345 South Seventh Avenue, LaGrange, Illinois*	154	
Larkin Company Pavilion for Jamestown Exposition (demolished) *Virginia*		
McCormick House *Lake Forest, Illinois*		
Municipal Art Gallery *Chicago, Illinois*		
Pebbles and Balch Shop *Oak Park, Illinois*	256	
Andrew Porter House *Spring Green, Wisconsin*	260	

1908

BUILDING	PAGE	TYPE
Bitter Root Inn (destroyed) *Stevensville, Montana*	49	
Boynton House *Rochester, New York*	56	
Browne's Bookstore *Chicago, Illinois*	60	
Davidson House *57 Tillinghast Place, Buffalo, New York*	88	
Evans House *9914 Longwood Drive, Chicago, Illinois*	100	
Gilmore House ←→ *120 Ely Place, Madison, Wisconsin*	125	
Guthrie House *Sewanee, Tennessee*		

CHRONOLOGY

↔ = illustrated
bold text = houses built
plain text = plans or projects

TYPE	PAGE	BUILDING

1911

Adams House I
Oak Park, Illinois

American System Ready-Cut Houses (prototypes) for Richards Company — 274
Milwaukee, Wisconsin

Angster House (demolished) — 24
Lake Bluff, Illinois

↔ **Balch House** — 36
611 North Kenilworth Avenue, Oak Park, Illinois

Christian Catholic Church
Zion, Illinois

Coonley House, greenhouse and kindergarten
Riverside, Illinois

Cutten House

Downer's Grove, Illinois

Ebenshade House

Milwaukee, Wisconsin

Heath House, garage and stables
Buffalo, New York

Lake Geneva Inn — 124
Lake Geneva, Wisconsin

Madison Hotel
Madison, Wisconsin

North Shore Electric Tram, waiting stations for the Chicago suburbs

Chicago, Illinois
Pavilion
Banff National Park, Alberta, Canada

Porter House III

Spring Green, Wisconsin

Schroeder House
Milwaukee, Wisconsin

BUILDING	PAGE	TYPE
Taliesin I (living quarters destroyed by fire in 1914) *Spring Green, Wisconsin*	**306**	
1912		
Avery Coonley Playhouse *Riverside, Illinois*	**77**	
Dress Shop *Oak Park, Illinois*		
Florida House *Palm Beach, Florida*		
Francis Little House II (demolished) *Deephaven, Minnesota*	**208**	
Greene House ↔ *1300 Garfield Avenue, Aurora, Illinois*	**129**	
Kehl Dance Academy House and Shops *Madison, Wisconsin*		
San Francisco Call newspaper building *San Francisco, California*		
Schoolhouse *LaGrange, Illinois*		
Taliesin Cottages (two buildings) *Spring Green, Wisconsin*		
1913		
Adams House II ↔ *710 Augusta Avenue, Oak Park, Illinois*	**18**	
Block of City Row Houses *Chicago, Illinois*		
Carnegie Library *Ottowa, Ontario, Canada*		
Hilly House *Brookfield, Illinois*		
Kellog House *Milwaukee, Wisconsin*		

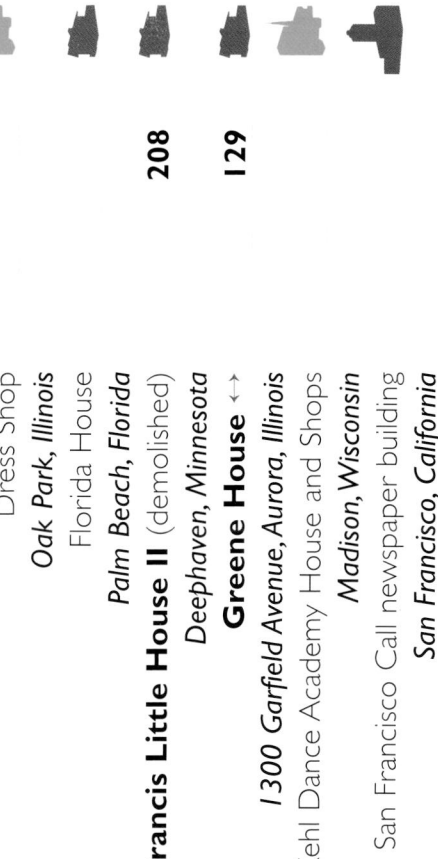

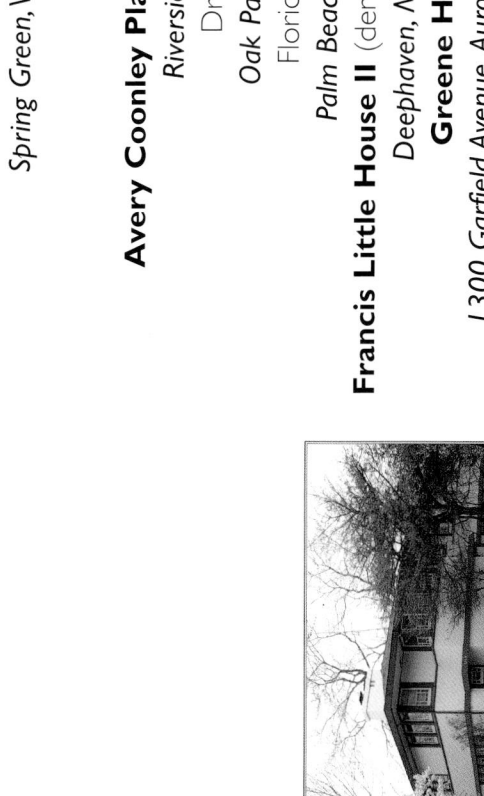

↔ = illustrated
bold text = houses built
plain text = plans or projects

| TYPE | PAGE | BUILDING |

BUILDING	PAGE	TYPE
Charles Perry House	256	🏠
Glencoe, Illinois		
Ravine Bluffs Housing Development	270	🏠
Glencoe, Illinois		
Arthur L. Richards Bungalow	274	🏠
1835 South Layton Street, Milwaukee, Wisconsin		
Arthur L. Richards Small House	274	🏠
2714 West Burnham Street, Milwaukee, Wisconsin		
Root House ↔	280	🏠
1030 Meadow Road, Glencoe, Illinois		
Ross House		🏠
Glencoe, Illinois		
Wood House		🏠
Decateur, Illinois		

1916

BUILDING	PAGE	TYPE
Allen House	23	🏠
255 North Roosevelt Boulevard, Wichita, Kansas		
Bagley House	36	🏠
47017 Lakeview, Grand Beach, Michigan		
Behn House		🏠
Grand Beach, Michigan		
Bogk House ↔	54	🏠
2420 North Terrace Avenue, Milwaukee, Wisconsin		
W. S. Carr House	68	🏠
46039 Lakeview, Grand Beach, Michigan		
Converse House		🏠
Palisades Park, Michigan		
Arthur Munkwitz Duplex Apartments (demolished)	235	🏠
Milwaukee, Wisconsin		
Arthur L. Richards Duplex Apartments ↔	274	🏠
2720-2734 West Burnham Street, Milwaukee, Wisconsin		
Vosburgh House	327	🏠
46208 Crescent Road, Grand Beach, Michigan		

↔ = illustrated
bold text = houses built
plain text = plans or projects

TYPE   PAGE   BUILDING

1917

↔ Aline Barnsdall House (Hollyhock House)
4808 Hollywood Boulevard, Los Angeles

152   Hayashi House
Tokyo, Japan

154   Hunt House
1165 Algoma Boulevard, Oshkosh, Wisconsin

Odawara Hotel
Nagoya, Japan

Powell House
Wichita, Kansas

1918

Fukuhara House
Hakone, Japan

115   Count Immu House
Tokyo, Japan

Viscount Inouge House
Tokyo, Japan

Motion picture theater
Tokyo, Japan

356   Yamamura House
Ashiya, Japan

1919

Japanese Print Gallery for the Spaulding Collection
Boston, Massachusetts

Monolith Homes
Racine, Wisconsin

1920

Apartments, theater, and shops
Olive Hills, Los Angeles, California

140   Barnsdall House A and B
Los Angeles, California

TYPE

PAGE

BUILDING

Cantilevered Steel Skyscraper

1921

Block House
Los Angeles, California
Doheney Ranch Development
nr. Los Angeles, California
Jiyu Gakuen School of the Free Spirit
Tokyo, Japan
Glass and Copper Skyscraper
Baron Goto House
Tokyo, Japan

1922

Barnsdall Kindergarten
Los Angeles, California
Desert Springs House
Mojave Desert, California
Johnson Desert Compound and Shrine
Death Valley, California
Merchandising Building
Los Angeles, California
Tahoe Summer Colony
Lake Tahoe, California

1923

Ennis House ←→
96
2655 Glendower Avenue, Los Angeles, California
Freeman House
114
1962 Glencoe Way, Hollywood, California

C H R O N O L O G Y

↔ = illustrated
bold *text* = houses built
plain *text* = plans or projects

TYPE   PAGE   BUILDING

1930

Automobile with cantilevered top
Cabins for desert or woods
YMCA, Chicago, Illinois
Chicago, Illinois
Grouped apartment towers
Noble Apartment House
Los Angeles, California

1931

The Capital Journal Newspaper Building
Salem, Oregon
House on the Mesa
Denver, Colorado
Three schemes for "A Century of Progress"
World's Fair, Chicago, Illinois

1932

Automobile and airplane filling and service station
Highway overpass
Movie House and shops
Michigan City, Indiana
New theater
Overhead filling station
Pre-fabricated sheet steel farm units
Pre-fabricated sheet steel and glass roadside markets
Willey House I
Minneapolis, Minnesota

1933

308   ↔ **Taliesin Fellowship complex** (additions to existing
Hillside Home School. Partly built theater destroyed by fire
in 1952) *Spring Green, Wisconsin*

BUILDING	PAGE	TYPE
Willey House	336	
255 Bedford Street S.E., Minneapolis		
1934		
Broadacre City model and exhibition plans		
Helicopter project		
Road machine project		
Train project		
Willey House II		
Zoned House Number I		
1935		
Hoult House	194	
Wichita, Kansas		
Kaufmann House (Fallingwater) ←→		
Mill Run, State Highway 381, Pennsylvania		
Lusk House		
Huron, South Dakota		
Marcus House		
Dallas, Texas		
Zoned City House		
Zoned Country House		
Zoned Suburban House		
1936		
Hanna House ←→	138	
737 Frenchman's Road, Stanford, California		
Jacobs House ←→	170	
441 Toepfer Street, Madison, Wisconsin		
S.C. Johnson Wax Company Administration Building	184	
1525 Howe Street, Racine, Wisconsin		
Little San Marcos in the Desert Resort Inn		
Chandler, Arizona		

↔ = illustrated
bold *text* = houses built
plain *text* = plans or projects

TYPE	PAGE	BUILDING

276 **Abby Roberts House**
County Highway 492, Marquette, Michigan

1937

100 All Steel Houses
Los Angeles, California

Borglum Studio
Black Hills, South Dakota

Bramson Dress Shop
Oak Park, Illinois

178 ↔ **Johnson House**
33 East 4 Mile Road, Wind Point, Wisconsin

194 **Edgar J. Kaufmann Sr. Office**
Pittsburgh, Pennsylvania

"Memorial to the Soil" chapel
Southern Wisconsin

Garage for Parker House
Janesville, Wisconsin

272 **Rebhuhn House**
9a Myrtle Avenue, Great Neck Estates, New York

312 ↔ **Taliesin West** (Wright's winter headquarters)
Scottsdale, Arizona

1938

Auldbrass Plantation/Stevens House
7 River Road, Yemassee, Austin, South Carolina

43 **Bazett House**
101 Reservoir Road, Hillsborough, California

108 ↔ **Florida Southern College (construction through 1959)**
South Johnson Avenue at Lake Hollingworth Drive, Lakeland, Florida

32/297 Jargensen House
Evanston, Illinois

TYPE	PAGE	BUILDING
		Jester All-Plywood Houses (design constructed by Bruce Brooks Pfeiffer, Director of Archives at the Frank Lloyd Wright Foundation, in the grounds of Taliesin West, Scottsdale, Arizona, 1971)
		Johnson Gatehouse and Farm Group
		Wind Point, Wisconsin
	220	**Manson House**
		1224 Highland Park Boulevard, Wausau, Wisconsin
		McCallum House
		Northampton, Massachusetts
	304	**Midway Farm Buildings**
		Spring Green, Wisconsin
		Monona Terrace (building commenced in 1994 based on revised plans from 1959.) ↔
		Madison Civic Center, Wisconsin
	258	**Pew House**
		3650 Lake Mendota Drive, Shorewood Hills, Wisconsin
	300	**Suntop Homes** (quadruple house)
		152-158 Sutton Road, Ardmore, Pennsylvania
		Smith House
		Piedmont Pines, California
		1939
	26	**Armstrong House**
		Cedar Trail at The Ledge, Ogden Dunes, Indiana
		Bell House (project built in 1974 as Feldman House in *Berkeley, California*)
		Los Angeles, California
		Carlson House
		Superior, Wisconsin
		Crystal Heights Hotel, Shops, and Theaters
		Washington D.C.
	100	**Euchtman House**
		6807 Cross Country Boulevard, Baltimore, Maryland

↔ = illustrated
bold text = houses built
plain text = plans or projects

TYPE   PAGE   BUILDING

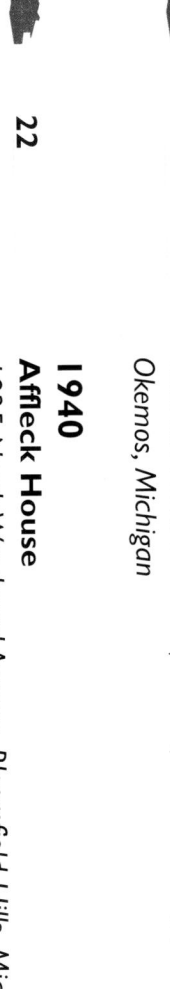

BUILDING	PAGE	TYPE
Methodist Church		
Spring Green, Wisconsin		
Model House (exhibition project)		
Museum of Modern Art, New York		
Nesbitt House		
Carmel Bay, California		
Oboler Gatehouse ←→	**246**	
32436 West Mulholland Highway, Malibu, California		
Pence House		
Hilo, Hawaii		
Rentz House		
Madison, Wisconsin		
Richardson House ←→	**274**	
63 Chestnut Hill Place, Glen Ridge, New Jersey		
Sondern House	**297**	
3600 Bellview Avenue, Kansas City, Missouri		
Watkins Studio		
Barnegate City, New Jersey		
1941		
Barton House		
Pine Bluff, Wisconsin		
Dayer Music Studio		
Detroit, Michigan		
Ellinwood House		
Deerfield, Illinois		
Field House		
Peru, Illinois		
Guenther House, Mountain Lakes		
East Caldwell, New Jersey		
Oboler Retreat ←→	**246**	
Los Angeles, California		

↔ = illustrated
bold *text* = houses built
plain *text* = plans or projects

TYPE	PAGE	BUILDING

Peterson House
West Racine, Wisconsin
Schevill House
Tucson, Arizona
Sigma Chi Fraternity House
Hanover, Indiana
Sundt House
Madison, Wisconsin

Wall House 330
12305 Beck Road, Plymouth, Michigan
Waterstreet Studio
nr. Spring Green, Wisconsin

1942
Burlingham House (two versions of the planned house were built in the 1980s: one in **Santa Fe, New Mexico**, the second in *Phoenix, Arizona*.)
El Paso, Texas
Circle Pines Center
Cloverdale, Wisconsin
Cloverleaf Quadruple Housing
Pittsfield, Massachusetts
Co-operative Homesteads: Housing for Detroit Auto Workers
Michigan
Jacobs House
Middleton, Wisconsin

1943
Hein House
Chippewa Falls, Wisconsin
McDonald House
Washington, D.C.

BUILDING	PAGE	TYPE
Richardson Restaurant and Service Station *Spring Green, Wisconsin*		
1944		
Harlan House *Omaha, Nebraska*		
Jacobs House II ↔ *7033 Old Sauk Road, Middleton, Wisconsin*	170	
S.C. Johnson Wax Company Research Tower ↔ *1525 Howe Street, Racine, Wisconsin*	184	
Loeb House, Pergola House *Redding, Connecticut*		
Wells House *Minneapolis, Minnesota*		
1945		
Adelman Laundry *Milwaukee, Wisconsin*		
Berdan House *Ludington, Michigan*		
Elizabeth Arden Desert Spa *Phoenix, Arizona*		
Friedman House *"The Fir Tree," Pecos, New Mexico*	114	
"Glass House" project for *Ladies' Home Journal*		
Haldorn House, The Wave *Carmel, California*		
Slater House *Rhode Island*		
Stamm House *Lake Delavan, Wisconsin*		
Taliesin Dams ↔ *Spring Green, Wisconsin*	308	

↔ = illustrated
bold text = houses built
plain text = plans or projects

322 | ↔ **Walter House** (River Pavilion: 1948)
2611 Quasqueton Diag. Boulevard, Quasqueton, Iowa

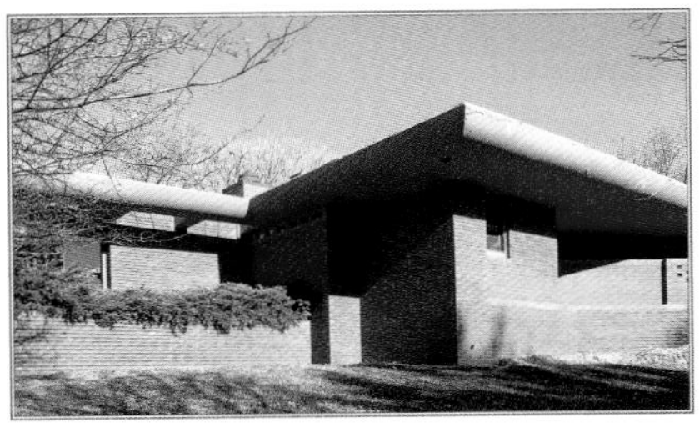

1946

Dayer House and Music pavilion
Bloomfield Hills, Michigan

Garrison House
Lansing, Michigan

128 **Grant House**
3400 Adel Drive S.E., Cedar Rapids, Iowa

130 **Griggs House**
7800 John Dower S.W., Tacoma, Washington

Hause House
Lansing, Michigan

Housing for State Teacher's College
Lansing, Michigan

230 **Miller House**
1107 Court Street, Charles City, Iowa

Morris House I
San Francisco, California

Munroe House
Knox County, Ohio

Newman House
Lansing, Michigan

Oboler Studio
Los Angeles, California

Panshin House
State Teacher's College, Lansing, Michigan

Pinderton House
Cambridge, Massachusetts

Pinkerton House
Fairfax County, Virginia

President's House
Olivet College, Michigan

BUILDING	PAGE	TYPE
Rogers Lacy Hotel		
Dallas, Texas		
Sarabhi Administration Building and Store		
Ahmedabad, India		
Smith House	297	
5045 Pon Valley Road, Bloomfield Hills, Michigan		
Van Dusen House		
Lansing, Michigan		
1947		
Alpauch House	23	
71 North Peterson Park Road, Northport, Michigan		
Bell House		
East St. Louis, Illinois		
Black House		
Rochester, Minnesota		
Boomer House		
Phoenix, Arizona		
Bulbulian House	60	
1229 Skyline Drive S.W., Rochester, Minnesota		
Butterfly Bridge over the Wisconsin River		
Spring Green, Wisconsin		
Cottage Group Resort Hotel		
Los Angeles, California		
Daphne Funeral Chapels		
San Francisco, California		
First Unitarian Society Meeting House ↩	322	
900 University Bay Drive, Shorewood Hills, Wisconsin		
Hamilton House		
Brookline, Vermont		
Hartford House		
Hollywood, California		
Houston House		
Schuyler County, Illinois		

TYPE PAGE BUILDING

←→ = illustrated
bold *text* = houses built
plain *text* = plans or projects

BUILDING	PAGE	TYPE
Brauner House ←→	58	
2527 Arrow Head Road, Okemos, Michigan		
Buehler House	60	
6 Great Oak Circle, Orinda, California		
Crater Resort		
Meteor Crater, Arizona		
Daphne House		
San Francisco, California		
Ellison House		
Bridgewater Township, New Jersey		
Eppstein House	100	
11098 Hawthorne Drive, Galesberg, Michigan		
Feenberg House		
Fox Point, Wisconsin		
Sol Friedman House	114	
11 Orchard Brook Drive, Pleasantville, New York		
Hageman House		
Peoria, Illinois		
Hughes House	154	
306 Glenway Drive, Jackson, Mississippi		
Lamberson House	200	
511 North Park Avenue, Oskaloosa, Iowa		
Levin House	206	
2816 Taliesin Drive, Kalamazoo, Michigan		
Margolis House		
Kalamazoo, Michigan		
Master plans for Galesburg Village Dwellings and Parkwyn Village Dwellings Kalamazoo, Michigan and	120/254	
Usonia Homes, Pleasantville, New York		
McCord House		
North Arlington, New Jersey		
Meyer House ←→	228	
11108 Hawthorne Drive, Galesberg, Michigan		

↔ = illustrated
bold text = houses built
plain *text* = plans or projects

	234	Miller House, *Pleasantville, New York*
		Mossberg House, *1404 Ridgedale Road, South Bend, Indiana*
		Muehlberger House, *East Lansing, Michigan*
↔	266	**Pratt House**, *11036 Hawthorne Drive, Galesberg, Michigan*
		Scully House, *Woodbridge, Connecticut*
↔	234	**V.C. Morris Gift Shop**, *140 Maiden Lane, San Francisco, California*
		Valley National Bank and Shopping Center, *Sunnyslope, Arizona*
↔	330	**Walker House**, *Carmel, California*
	332	**Walter River Pavilion**, *Quasqueton, Iowa*
	336	**Weisblatt House**, *11185 Hawthorne Drive, Galesberg, Michigan*
	336	**Weltzheimer House**, *127 Woodhaven Drive, Oberlin, Ohio*

1949

	26	**Anthony House**, *1150 Miami Road, Benton Harbor, Michigan*
		Bloomfield House, *Tucson, Arizona*
↔	60	**Eric Brown House**, *2806 Taliesin Drive, Kalamazoo, Michigan*
	312	**Cabaret-Theater**, *Taliesin West, Scottsdale, Arizona*
		Dabney House, *Chicago, Illinois*

BUILDING	PAGE	TYPE
Drummond House		
Santa Fe, New Mexico		
Edwards House	**94**	
2504 Arrow Head Road, Okemos, Michigan		
Goetsch-Winkler House II		
Okemos, Michigan		
John House		
Oconomowoc, Wisconsin		
Kauffman Self Service Garage		
Pittsburgh		
Laurent House ↔	**204**	
Spring Brook Road, Rockford, Illinois		
Lea House		
Ashville, North Carolina		
McCartney House	**228**	
2662 Taliesin Drive, Kalamazoo, Michigan		
Neils House	**238**	
2801 Burnham Boulevard, Minneapolis, Minnesota		
Publicker House		
Haverford, Pennsylvania		
San Francisco Bay Bridge: Southern Crossing		
Serlin House	**292**	
12 Laurel Hill Drive, Pleasantville, New York		
Theater for the New Theater Corp.		
Hartford, Connecticut		
Windforhr House		
Fort Worth, Texas		
YMCA Building		
Racine, Wisconsin		

1950

Achuff House		
Wauwatosa, Wisconsin		

C H R O N O L O G Y

↔ = illustrated
bold text = houses built
plain text = plans or projects

TYPE	PAGE	BUILDING

↔ = illustrated
bold text = houses built
plain text = plans or projects

TYPE	PAGE	BUILDING

BUILDING	PAGE	TYPE
Reisley House 44 Usonia Road, Pleasantville, New York	273	
Rubin House 518 44th Street N.W., Canton, Ohio	284	
Schevill Studio Tucson, Arizona		
1952		
Affleck House II Bloomfield Hills, Michigan	24	
Anderton Court Center ↔ 332 North Rodeo Drive, Beverly Hills, California		
Balleres House Acapulco, Mexico		
Blair House Greybull Highway, Cody, Wyoming	49	
Brandes House 212th Avenue at 24th Street, Issaquah, Washington	58	
Clifton House Oakland, New Jersey		
Cooke House Virginia Beach, Virginia		
Hillside Playhouse (redesign and rebuilding) Spring Green, Wisconsin	308	
Hillside Theater Spring Green, Wisconsin	308	
Leesburg Floating Gardens Florida		
George Lewis House 3117 Okeeheepkee Road, Tallahassee, Florida	206	
Lindholm House Route 33 at Stanley Avenue, Cloquet, Minnesota	207	
Marden House 600 Chainbridge Road, McLean, Virginia	220	

C H R O N O L O G Y

↔ = illustrated
bold text = houses built
plain text = plans or projects

TYPE   PAGE   BUILDING

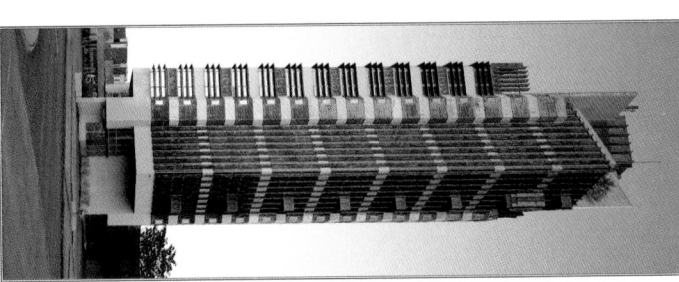

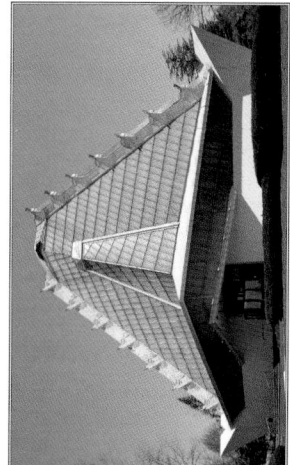

TYPE   PAGE   BUILDING

↔ = illustrated
bold *text* = houses built
plain *text* = plans or projects

↔ = illustrated
bold text = houses built
plain *text* = plans or projects

TYPE	PAGE	BUILDING

PAGE	TYPE	BUILDING
56		**Bott House**
		3640 North Briarcliff Road, Kansas City, Missouri
		Bramlett Hotel
		Memphis, Tennessee
68		**Cass House**
		Bunington Hills, Illinois
114		**Allen Friedman House**
		200 Thornapple, Bannockburn, Illinois
		Golden Beacon skyscraper
		Chicago, Illinois
		Gross House
		Hackensack, New Jersey
132		**Solomon R. Guggenheim Museum** ↔
		Fifth Avenue, New York City
		Hunt House
		Scottsdale, Arizona
228		**Kenneth L. Meyers Medical Clinic**
		5441 Far Hills Avenue, Dayton, Ohio
		Mile High Skyscraper
		Chicago, Illinois
		Morris House, Quietwater
		Stinson Beach, California
312		**Music Pavilion**
		Taliesin West, Scottsdale, Arizona
344		**Lloyd Wright Studio remodeling**
		Oak Park, Illinois
		O'Keefe House
		Santa Barbara, California
		Pre-Fab I for Marshall Erdman Associates ↔
		Madison, Wisconsin
		Roberts House
		Seattle, Washington
		Schuck House
		South Hadley, Massachusetts

↔ = illustrated
bold *text* = houses built
plain *text* = plans or projects

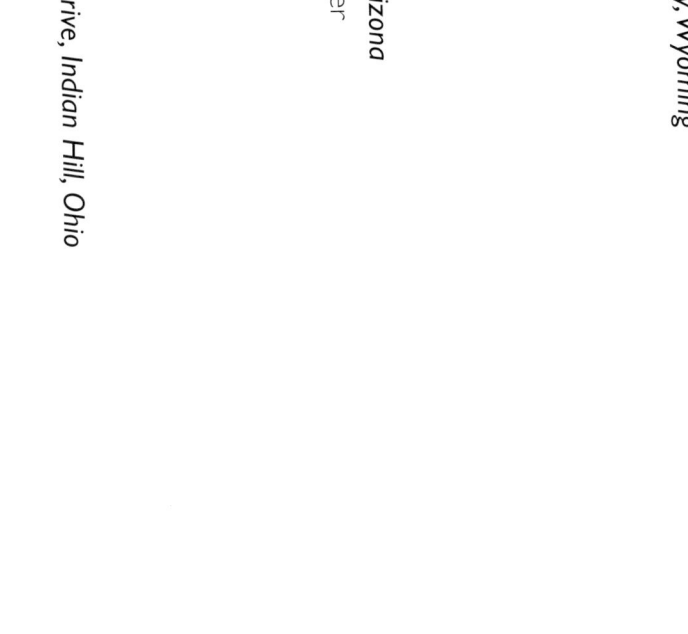

TYPE	PAGE	BUILDING
		Gate Lodge for Fallingwater *Bear Run, Pennsylvania*
	104	**Fasbender Clinic** ←→ *State Highway 55 at Pine Street, Hastings, Minnesota*
		Fisher Housing Project *Whiteville, North Carolina*
	128	**Gordon House** *303 S.W. Gordon Lane, Wilsonville, Oregon*
		Hartman House *Lansing, Michigan*
		Hennesy Houses (two projects) *Smoke Rise, New Jersey*
		Herberger House *Maricopa County, Arizona*
		Highway Motel *Madison, Wisconsin*
		Hoyer House *Maricopa County, Arizona*
	158	**Frank Iber House** *Springville Drive at U.S.5, Stevens Point, Wisconsin*
	170	**Jackson House** *7655 Indian Hills Trail, Beaver Dam, Wisconsin*
		Juvenile Cultural Study Center Building A ←→ *University of Wichita, Kansas*
		Juvenile Study Center Building B *University of Wichita, Kansas*
	196	**Sterling Kinney House** *Amarillo, Texas*
	207	**Lindholm Service Station** *Route 45 at Route 33, Cloquet, Minnesota*
	218	**Macbean House** *1532 Woodland Drive S.W., Rochester, Minnesota*
	224	**Marin County Civic Center** ←→ *North San Pedro Road at U.S. 101, San Rafael, California*

↔ = illustrated
bold text = houses built
plain text = plans or projects

TYPE	PAGE	BUILDING

BUILDING	PAGE	TYPE
Wedding Chapel for the Claremont Hotel		
Berkeley, California		
Wilson House		
Morgantown, North Carolina		
Duey Wright House	341	
904 Grand Avenue, Wausau, Wisconsin		
Zieger House		
Grosse Isalnd, Michigan		
1958		
Ablin House ↔	18	
4260 Country Club Drive, Bakersfield, California		
Colgrove House		
Hamilton, Ohio		
Crosby-Lambert House		
Colbert County, Alabama		
Franklin House		
Louisville, Kentucky		
Guttierez House		
Albuquerque, New Mexico		
Hanley Airplane Hangar		
Benton Harbor, Michigan		
Jones Chapel (Trinity Chapel)		
University of Oklahoma, Norman, Oklahoma		
Lagomarsino House		
San Jose, California		
Leuchauer Clinic		
Fresno, California		
Libbey House		
Grand Rapids, Michigan		
Lockridge, McIntyre and Whalen Clinic	210	
Whitefish, Montana		
Lovness Cottages		
Stillwater, Minnesota		

↔ = illustrated
bold text = houses built
plain text = plans or projects

TYPE	PAGE	BUILDING

Mike Todd Universal Theater
Los Angeles, California

Mollica House
1001 West Jonathan Lane, Bayside, Wisconsin

232 **Olfelt House**
226 Parkland Lane, Saint Louis Park, Minnesota

↔ **250** **Peterson Cottage**
Hastings Road off Ferndell Road, Lake Delton, Wisconsin

↔ **256** **Pilgrim Congregational Church** (partly built)
2850 Foothill Boulevard, Redding, California

258 Pre-Fab III and Pre-Fab IV for Marshall Erdman Associates
Madison, Wisconsin

Spring Green Auditorium
Spring Green, Wisconsin

298 **Stromquist House**
1151 East North Canyon Road, Bountiful, Utah

Unity Chapel
Taliesin Valley, Spring Green, Wisconsin

1959

Art Gallery
Arizona State University, Tempe, Arizona

Donohoe House
Phoenix, Arizona

120 Furgatch House
San Diego, California

↔ **Grady Gammage Memorial Auditorium**
Arizona State University, Apache Boulevard at Mill Avenue,
Tempe

Mann House
Putnam County, New York

212 **Norman Lykes House**
6836 North 36th Street, Phoenix

BUILDING	PAGE	TYPE
Penfield House II *Willoughby, Ohio*		▪
Daniel Wieland House *Hagerstown, Maryland*		▪
Gilbert Wieland House *Hagerstown, Maryland*		▪
1960		
Lafond House (built after Wright's death) *Saint Joseph, Minnesota*	104	▪
1961		
Zaferiou House (built after Wright's death) *Blanvert, New York*		▪
1974		
Feldman House (built after Wright's death) *13 Mosswood Road, Berkeley, California*		▪

BIBLIOGRAPHY

Abernathy, Ann, and Thorpe, John; **The Oak Park Home and Studio of Frank Lloyd Wright**; Frank Lloyd Wright Home and Studio Foundation, 1988.

Blake, Peter; Frank Lloyd Wright: **Architecture and Space**; Penguin, 1964.

Brooks, H. Allen; **The Prairie School: Frank Lloyd Wright and His Midwest Contemporaries**; University of Toronto Press, 1972.

Connors, Joseph; **The Robie House of Frank Lloyd Wright**; University of Chicago Press, 1984.

Costantino, Maria; **Frank Lloyd Wright**; Crescent Books, 1991.

Costantino, Maria; **Frank Lloyd Wright Design**; Brompton Books, 1995.

Gebhard, David, and Zimmerman, Scott (photographs); Romanza: **The California Architecture of Frank Lloyd Wright**; Thames and Hudson, 1989.

Gill, Brendan; **Many Masks: A Life of Frank Lloyd Wright**; Heinemann, 1988.

Greene, Aaron G.; **An Architecture for Democracy**; The Marin County Civic Center; Grendon Publishing, 1990.

Hanks, David A.; **The Decorative Designs of Frank Lloyd Wright**; Dutton, 1979.

Hanks, David A.; **Frank Lloyd Wright: Preserving and Architectural Heritage; Decorative Designs from The Domino's Pizza Collection**, Studio Vista, 1989.

Hanna, Paul R. and Jean S.; **Frank Lloyd Wright's Hanna House**; Southern Illinois University Press, 1987.

Hitchcock, Henry-Russell; **In the Nature of Materials: The Buildings of Frank Lloyd Wright 1887-1941**; Da Capo Press, 1973.

Hoffman, Donald; **Frank Lloyd Wright's Fallingwater: The House and Its History**; Dover, 1978.

Hoffman, Donald; **Frank Lloyd Wright: Architecture and Nature**; Dover, 1986.

Hoffman, Donald; **Frank Lloyd Wright's Hollyhock House**; Dover, 1992.

Kaufmann, Edgar Jr.; **Fallingwater: A Frank Lloyd Wright Country House**; The Architectural Press, 1986.

Kaufmann, Edgar Jr.; **9 Commentaries on Frank Lloyd Wright**; MIT Press, 1989.

Lind, Carla; **The Wright Style**; Simon and Schuster, 1992.

Lipman, Jonathan; **Frank Lloyd Wright and the Johnson Wax Buildings**; Rizzoli, 1986.

Manson, Grant Carpenter; **Frank Lloyd Wright to 1910: The First Golden Age**; Reinhold Publishing Corporation, 1958.

Pfeiffer, Bruce Brooks, ed.; **Letters to Clients**: Frank Lloyd Wright; California State University, 1986.

Quinan, Jack; **Frank Lloyd Wright's Larkin Building: Myth and Fact**; MIT Press, 1987.

Sanderson, Arlene, ed.; Wright Sites: **A Guide to Frank Lloyd Wright Public Places**; Princeton Architectural Press, 1995.

Secrest, Meryle; **Frank Lloyd Wright**, Chatto & Windus Ltd, 1992.

Scully, Vincent Jr.; "Frank Lloyd Wright"; **Masters of World Architecture Series**, George Braziller, 1960.

Pages 412/413 and right: Herbert Johnson's Wingspread.

Sergeant, John; **Frank Lloyd Wright's Usonian Houses: The Case for Organic Architecture**; Whitney Library of Design, 1984.

Smith, Kathryn; Frank Lloyd Wright: **Hollyhock House and Olive Hill**; Rizzoli, 1992.

Storrer, William; **The Architecture of Frank Lloyd Wright: A Complete Catalog**; MIT Press, 1979.

Storrer, William; **The Frank Lloyd Wright Companion**; University of Chicago Press, 1993.

Sweeny, Robert L.; **Wright in Hollywood: Visions of a New Architecture**; MIT Press, 1994.

Wright, Olgivanna; **Frank Lloyd Wright: His Life, His Work, His Words**; Horizon Press, 1961.